The Life of Jesus

David Holdaway

Sovereign World

Sovereign World Ltd
PO Box 777
Tonbridge
Kent TN11 0ZS
England

ISBN 1 85240 247 4

Typeset by CRB Associates, Reepham, Norfolk
Printed in England by Clays Ltd, St Ives plc.

'This is the book I have waited a lifetime to see.'

Professor David Short
Emeritus Professor of Medicine
University of Aberdeen
Former Physician to the Queen in Scotland

'David Holdaway's harmony of the Gospel narratives will help new readers to get a broad understanding of the career and teaching of Jesus and prepare them for going on to study the Gospels individually. His easy style of writing makes for a very readable account of the significance of Jesus that will challenge people to answer the question, "Who do you say that I am?"'

Rev. Professor I. Howard Marshall
Head of Department of Divinity with Religious Studies,
Aberdeen University

'It is with great pleasure that I commend David Holdaway's book *The Life of Jesus*. Shortly after leaving Elim Bible College, David served with me in the ministry team at the Northampton Elim Church, and I came to appreciate his personal friendship and his outstanding ministry of the Word. His book reflects that keen desire to make the scriptures understood by all, and above all to exalt the name of our Lord Jesus Christ. His attempt to present the life of Christ in a chronological order will greatly assist new Christians to see the overall meaning of the four Gospels. It will also help those more knowledgeable to gain fresh insights into the life of Him who alone is the Way, the Truth and the Life. I pray that God will greatly bless this earnest endeavour to glorify Him.'

Rev. John Lancaster
Teacher and author

'The greatest story ever told has now come into even sharper focus. David Holdaway has married the accuracy of scholarship to cutting-edge relevance in this new harmony of the Gospels. It is the literary equivalent of listening in digital stereo to a much-loved classical masterpiece that had hitherto only been enjoyed in analogue sound. It is as informative as it is inspiring.'

Rev. John Glass
Minister and author

'I pray that God will greatly bless this book.'

Dr David Yonggi Cho
Yoido Full Gospel Church, Seoul, Korea

'An excellent book which will be a great tool for pastors and Bible students and church members alike.'

Rev. Wynne Lewis
General Superintendent Elim Churches

'This book answers a lot of questions as the four Gospels are merged into one.'

Rev. Derek Green
Editor, *Direction* Magazine

'An excellent and easily readable presentation of the life and ministry of Jesus which I warmly recommend to everyone who has a passion to get to know Him more.'

Wesley Campbell
Revival Now!

'A fantastic book to give to new Christians and an excellent introduction for those who don't know Jesus.'

Marilyn Harry
International Evangelist

'David Holdaway brings us a fascinating introduction to the historical Jesus Christ alongside a presentation of the timeless truths of the four gospels in one simple narrative. An inspiring, faith-building book.'

Lyndon Bowring
CARE

Thanks and Acknowledgements

Special thanks to those whose comments have been so helpful and important. To John Lancaster, one of the greatest preachers you will ever hear and with whom I had the privilege of working for three years in Northampton. To John Glass, whose leadership and ministry have been a great help and inspiration not only to me but to countless others. To Professor David Short, a man of great gifting and ability not only in medicine but in theological and church matters. To Professor Howard Marshall, one of the leading Evangelical scholars of our time, whose ministry through writing and teaching is a great blessing to the church. To Wynne Lewis a dynamic leader and preacher who is an inspiration to all.

My great gratitude to the Elim Church which I am privileged to pastor in Aberdeen and to the many there who have made a valued contribution to the writing of this book. To Dr Sue Bailey, the church administrator, who spent many hours reading and helping to edit the manuscript. To Bill Kay for his help and expertise in the preparation and layout of the manuscript and the cover design. To Tom Scrivens for the excellent maps. To my dear wife Jan, whose skill and professional ability as a journalist and editor and most of all as a patient, loving wife have been invaluable.

Dedicated
to
my wonderful wife, Jan,
and
our beautiful daughter, Deborah.

What is a Chronological Harmonisation?

It is simply the four Gospels arranged in order of time and sequence. When two or more events occur of the same instance they are harmonised into one full account.

Did You Know?

1. The visit of the Wisemen to Jesus did not take place when He was a baby but when He was a small child between one and two years of age. They came not to a stable but to a house where He was living with His parents (Matthew 2:11, 16).
2. Between Matthew 4:11, *'Then the devil left him and angels came and attended him,'* and Matthew 4:12 the very next verse, *'When Jesus heard that John had been put in prison, he returned to Galilee,'* there is almost one year's entire ministry that takes place. The same is true between Luke 4:13 and verse 14. This period of ministry, known as Jesus' early Judean ministry, is recorded for us by John in his first four chapters.
3. In Luke 4:16–30, when Jesus read the scroll of Isaiah in the synagogue in Nazareth, He had already been ministering for about a year. This was not His first sermon. Luke says in verse 23 *'Jesus said to them, "Surely you will quote this proverb to me: Physician, heal yourself! Do here in your home town what we heard you did in Capernaum."'* After this rejection Jesus moved His ministry base from Nazareth to the strategic town of Capernaum. Some

think He owned or rented a house there and it may well have been His house that the four friends of the lame man tore the roof off to let their friend down in front of Jesus.

4. The Sermon on the Mount in Matthew 5–7 takes place well into the second year and not at the start of Jesus' ministry.

5. The call of Jesus' first disciples in John 1 was followed up sometime later with another call in Mark 1:14–20 and Matthew 4:18–15, Luke 5:1–11. It seems that they spent some time ministering with Him and then went back to fishing before He called them to leave everything and follow Him.

6. When the twelve disciples reported back to Jesus all that God did through them (Luke 9:10), He had just received news that John the Baptist had been beheaded (Matthew 14:12).

7. The record of the last week of Jesus' ministry is almost seven times longer than that of His first year of ministry.

8. On the night and morning before His crucifixion Jesus had not just one trial, but six, three Jewish and three Roman.

This and so much more becomes clear as you read *The Life of Jesus* in this exciting new presentation.

Contents

Introduction

The Greatest Story Ever Told

What is so special about Christianity that it claims there is only one way to God and that this is through Jesus Christ? What is so special about this Jesus that sets Him above all the other famous religious leaders?

Imagine you were lost, desperately searching for direction, your life and destiny depended on it. It's hopeless; you frantically run around in circles looking for the right way but are getting nowhere. Finally you come across all the great religious leaders in history who claimed to have directions for the way, but there is a problem, they are all dead, all except one. Which one would you ask?

Unlike all other religions, faiths and philosophies, Christianity is not dependent on the teachings of someone who is dead or dying but on the life of one who rose from the grave. I like the story of the scoffer who during the early days of the Church, mocked a young Christian as he enquired, 'What is your carpenter from Nazareth doing now?' The answer was bold, 'Making a coffin for your emperor.'

There are many religions and religious figures in history and in the world today, who have claimed to be divine or whose followers revere as the one who leads the way to God. So what makes Jesus so special? He is the only person who ever chose to be born. He has always existed. He repeatedly stated that He came into this world to do His Father's will. No one else has ever had a choice in whether or not they would be born. He is the only person who chose to die and rise again.

> *'The reason my Father loves me is that I lay down my life only to take it up again.'* (John 10:17)

There are those who may choose how or when to die, but death ultimately is not a choice but a certainty. It was the writer George Bernhard Shaw who said, 'The statistics regarding death are quite impressive, one out of one die.' When in 1865 the British Prime Minister Lord Palmerston was told by his doctor he was dying, he replied, 'Die my dear doctor? That's the last thing I shall do.' For Jesus it was not the last thing. He was crucified and rose on the third day. It's an amazing story recorded in the four Gospels at the start of the New Testament. To put it in the words of a Hollywood film about Jesus, it is 'The Greatest Story Ever Told.'

This book is divided into three sections. The first shows the historicity of Jesus and the trustworthiness of the Gospels. Next is the harmonisation of the Gospels and the third section provides some helpful notes and further detailed information about Jesus' life

The sequence of events concerning Jesus' life is not always recorded in chronological order and neither does just one of the Gospel writers record all that took place. In fact they tell us quite clearly this is only a part of what happened. I have therefore wanted for some time to take the four Gospel narratives to harmonise and put them in chronological sequence. This is not something new in itself, as there are many excellent chronologies and parallel Bible versions available. All I have done is to write out in full what has for a long time been available in lists of Gospel texts.

Doing this has been one of the most rewarding things I have ever done. It has not been easy, even with the help of some excellent chronologies, harmonies and commentaries. This is because there is no absolute agreement when certain events took place and how often some of Jesus' teachings might have been repeated in another place or at another time. It has been correctly pointed out that the style of the

Gospel writers is not always concerned with chronological precision. There are times when they prefer to arrange their material topically, rather than consecutively, a method of composition entirely in keeping with their simplicity of thought and diction.

There are a number of occasions, notably the resurrection accounts, when harmonisation is not easy or straight forward. I do not claim to have answered all the questions or achieved absolute accuracy and harmony. Whereas God's Word cannot be improved, such presentations can.

There are times when I have chosen to repeat some sections of the Gospel narrative, when it has been unclear whether it is the same as mentioned in another Gospel or said on a different occasion. I have also taken out all references to chapters and verses. It was not until AD 1250 that the Bible was divided into chapters by Cardinal Hugo of Santa Clara. The first division into verses was made by the Parisian printer Robert Stephanus centuries after that. Therefore the account is left undivided by chapters and verses. It is however spaced with many headings and an approximate time sequence. I trust that this way it will flow even better as you read it. I have divided the text into fifteen chapters, so by reading just one chapter a day you will be able to read through it completely in only two weeks. Once you start though, I think it unlikely it will take you that long.

I cannot stress strongly enough that the Gospel account as I have presented it, is not and never can be a substitute for reading the four Gospels individually as this is by far the best way to study them.

My desire is that this book will help supplement such reading and not substitute it. This is not a new translation it is the NIV text, neither is it a paraphrase. It is quite simply 'The Greatest Story Ever Told.'

If you enjoy this book and would like to help us to send a copy of it and many other titles to needy pastors in the **Third World**, please write for further information or send your gift to:

Sovereign World Trust
PO Box 777, Tonbridge
Kent TN11 0ZS
United Kingdom

or to the **'Sovereign World'** distributor in your country.

SECTION 1

Historicity of Jesus and the Trustworthiness of the Gospels

Chapter 1

He Will Change Your Life

*'Jesus gives more than a new start in life,
He gives a new life to start with.'*

Jesus Christ has had and continues to have a greater impact on this world than anyone else who has ever lived. Those who acknowledge Him as Lord and Saviour are to be counted not in millions but billions, and if present trends continue it is estimated that by 2025 there will be more than three billion people who call themselves Christian. The record of His life and ministry recorded in the Bible has sold more copies and is more read than any other book. Dr David Barrett, editor of the *World Christian Encyclopaedia*, says, 'The total number of book titles on Jesus in the world's libraries is an amazing 65,571 with 53,094 having Jesus in their title. Last year alone there were 1,500 new titles on Jesus.'

One of the major reasons for this is that reading about Jesus is not only informing but also transforming. It was Karl Marx of all people who said, 'Philosophers have only interpreted the world differently, the point is however to change it.' To that can be added the story of the heckler who was trying to shout down an open-air preacher by boasting that communism was able to take a poor and despairing man and put a new coat on his back. 'What can your Christianity do for him?' he mocked. The preacher responded, 'Christ can take that poor and despairing person and put a new man inside the coat.' Jesus isn't only able to give you a new start in life, He is able to give you a new life to start with. Let me prove this by telling you three amazing true stories, all of which are behind major films.

During World War II a Dutch lady, Corrie ten Boom, was arrested along with her family by the Nazis because they were hiding Jews in their home. She spent many months in concentration camps during which time her beloved sister Betsie, who was sentenced with her, died. Yet she herself was miraculously released due to an administrative error just one week before the order came to kill all the women of her age. After the war she travelled the world with the message that God's grace and power can be known even in the most horrific circumstances.

One of the fascinating accounts she tells was of arriving at Ravensbruck concentration camp in Germany. After being herded like cattle aboard the train and spending several horrendous days travelling deeper and deeper in Germany, she, Betsie and other prisoners arrived at their destination. It was the middle of night when she reached the processing barracks and there to her dismay she saw that each woman had to strip off every scrap of clothing, throw the clothes onto a pile guarded by soldiers, and walk naked past the scrutiny of a dozen guards into the shower room. Coming out of the shower room they were given only a thin regulation dress and a pair of shoes. It was not the humiliation or the scanty clothing that concerned her most, but what would she do with her Bible? How could she take it past so many watchful eyes? She knew that if she were caught trying she would be severely punished. Along with her sister she asked where the toilets were and was told to 'Use the drain holes!' in the shower room. It was empty, waiting for the next batch of 50 naked, shivering women.

A few minutes later she would return here stripped of everything she possessed. Then in a corner she saw a pile of old wooden benches crawling with cockroaches. In an instant she took the little bag that contained her Bible and along with her woollen underwear, hid it behind the benches. Ten minutes later she was herded back into that same room and given her flimsy regulation dress to wear. She took her Bible in its little bag and hung it around her neck. It bulged out obviously beneath her clothes, but she prayed and trusted God. At the exit, guards were searching every prisoner, front, back and sides, so she prayed, 'Oh, Lord, send your angels to surround us.' The woman ahead of her was searched, her sister behind her was searched, but they did not even touch or look at her. Outside the building was the next ordeal, another line of guards was waiting to examine each prisoner again, in case anything had been missed. She slowed down as she reached them, but the captain shoved her roughly by the shoulder without searching her, 'Move along! You're holding up the line.'

It was not long before Corrie and her sister were holding Bible study groups for an ever growing number of believers, and Barracks 28 became known throughout the camp as 'the crazy place where they hope.' Many found Christ as their Saviour, some shortly before they died, either of sickness or punishment. Yet in the midst of this hell they found the Word of God brought them hope, in spite of all human madness and evil. They learned that a stronger power had the final word, even there.

This isn't the only story of God's Word bringing hope and life in the inhuman madness of the concentration camps during the Second World War. In his moving book, *Miracle on the River Kwai*, Ernest Gordon tells his story of life as a Japanese prisoner of war among the men building the infamous Burma Railway. They were treated worse than animals and endured horrific conditions, with what seemed like no hope or purpose to life. Yet even here, God's Word brought about a remarkable transformation.

A few Christians reading their Bibles formed Bible study groups and as they shared and studied with others there came remarkable changes and effects. POWs who had stolen from and cheated one another became men who cared for and even gave their lives for their friends. Those death camps became a place of hope and life because God's Word was at work.

Gordon recounts some of those instances. During one work detail a shovel went missing. As the party was about to be dismissed, the Japanese guard shouted that a shovel was unaccounted for. He insisted that someone had stolen it. Striding up and down before the men he ranted and denounced them for their wickedness and, most unforgivable of all, their ingratitude to the Emperor. As he raved, he worked himself up into a paranoid fury. Screaming in broken English, he demanded that the guilty one step forward to take his punishment. No one moved; the guard's rage reached new heights of violence. 'All die! All die!' he shrieked. To show that he meant what he said, he cocked his rifle, put it to his shoulder and looked down the gun sights, ready to fire at the first man at the end of them. At that moment one of the men stepped forward, stood stiffly to attention, and said calmly, 'I did it.'

The guard unleashed all his whipped up hatred; he kicked the helpless prisoner and beat him with his fists. Seizing his rifle by the barrel, he lifted it high over his head and, with a final howl, brought it down on the soldier's skull, who sank limply to the ground and did not move. The men of the work detail picked up their comrade's body, shouldered their tools and marched back to the camp. When the tools were counted again at the guard house no shovel was missing.

At the end of the war, Gordon went to theological college in Edinburgh and then to Hartford Theological Seminary, Connecticut. He served as assistant minister at Paisley Abbey before returning to America to become Dean of the Chapel of Princeton University.

Let me share one final story with you regarding the transforming power of God's Word. It refers to an event that many may know something about because of the film, *Mutiny on the Bounty*. The real life story behind the picture is much more fascinating than the film. In 1787 Captain Bligh took the ship, the Bounty, on a voyage around the world to collect breadfruit trees. Britain owned a lot of land in the West Indies and most of the food for the slaves then had to be taken all the way from England. This proved to be a most expensive exercise and meant that the price of sugar was very high in England.

The government tried to find something that would grow quickly and easily in the West Indies. They had heard that on the other side of the Pacific, on the island of Tahiti, a tree, which produced pulp like bread, would grow well in the West Indies. So Bligh and his crew were sent to collect samples. When they reached Tahiti they found a veritable paradise. Soon every sailor had a girlfriend and there was a great deal of grumbling when Bligh announced after a few months they were leaving. Not many days out of Tahiti, Bligh woke up to find himself looking down the barrel of a gun. He and 18 other officers were put in a small boat without maps. Fletcher Christian, along with the other mutineers, took the ship back to Tahiti where they convinced twelve of the native girls to go with them. They left and came across another island paradise, it was Pitcairn Island. They took as many of their belongings as possible onto the island and set fire to the ship.

What started as paradise soon turned into ten years of hell. One of the sailors, William McKoy, had once worked in a Scottish whisky distillery and discovered a way of extracting alcohol from the roots of the Ti Tree trees, using the Bounty's copper kettle. They drank the fire water extracted and spent days, even weeks and months on end drunk. Some of the men went mad and became like wild animals, fighting amongst themselves. One jumped off a cliff. Not surprisingly after several years there were only two men left, Edward Young and Alexander Smith, who was old and asthmatic. One night the women seized the guns and barricaded themselves and their 18 children off from the men. Neither the women nor the children would go near them.

One day, Young went to the ship's chest and at the bottom among the papers, he found a book. It was a leather bound, old, mildewed and worm eaten Bible. He had not read it for years and Smith could not read at all so Young taught him from the Bible. The two men, frightened, despairing and utter wrecks, read the Bible together. They started at Genesis and saw from the Old Testament that God was holy and that they were sinful. They did their best to pray.

The little children were the first to come back to the men as they noticed a great change taking place within them. Then the children brought the women who sat and listened to them read. During this time Young died. Then Smith came to the New Testament and something amazing happened to him as he read the story of Jesus. This is what he recorded, 'I had been working like a mole for years, and suddenly it was as if all the doors flew wide open, and I saw the light. I met God in Jesus Christ, and the burden of my sins rolled away, and I found new life in Christ.' He went on to become the island's first Pastor.

Eighteen years after the mutiny on the Bounty, a ship from Boston came across the island of Pitcairn and the captain went ashore. He found a community of people who were gracious and godly. They had a love and peace about them that he had never seen before. On his return to the United States the captain reported that in all his travels he had never seen or met a people who were so good, gracious and loving.

The Word of God and the message of Jesus Christ had changed them. The true story is much better and more exciting than the film.

Chapter 2

The Name of Jesus

'Jesus is the only person to choose His own name before He was born.'

It was a Tuesday afternoon, 21 August, 1860, when one of the largest churches ever built in London opened its doors to hold its first service. The Metropolitan Tabernacle was built because the congregation had grown too large for their previous premises at New Park Street Chapel. Their now famous minister, Charles Haddon Spurgeon, had seen his congregation grow from barely a few hundred to several thousand.

During his 38 years at the Metropolitan Tabernacle Spurgeon was responsible for the swelling of the membership of the church to approximately 14,500. As one biographer put it, 'He was pre-eminently a preacher. His clear voice, his mastery of the English langauge, and his keen sense of humour, allied to a sure grasp of Scripture and a deep love for Christ, produced some of the noblest preaching of any age.'

The major reason for such increase is seen in the first words he spoke during that first service in the Tabernacle, 'I would propose that the subject and ministry of this house, as long as this platform shall stand, and as long as this house shall be frequented by worshippers, shall be the person of Jesus Christ. I am never ashamed to avow myself a Calvinist; I do not hesitate to take the name of Baptist; but if I am asked what is my creed, I reply, "It is Jesus Christ." '

Just ten years previously, prevented by bad weather from

attending his usual place of worship, Spurgeon attended the Primitive Methodist Chapel close to his home. It was a snowy January Sunday morning and because of the conditions the minister of that church was unable to be there. The preacher that day was a shoe maker or tailor or the like, as Spurgeon later described him. He took as his text Isaiah 45:22, *'Look unto me and be saved all the ends of the earth,'* and the few in the congregation about 12–15 were told to look to Christ and Him alone for salvation and forgiveness.

After about ten minutes he looked straight at Spurgeon sitting under the gallery, fixed his eyes on him as if he knew all that was in his heart and said, 'Young man, you look very miserable.' Spurgeon, speaking about this later said he did but he was not accustomed to having remarks made from the pulpit on his personal appearance. 'And you will always be miserable, miserable in life and miserable in death, if you don't obey my text, but if you obey now this moment you will be saved.' Spurgeon added, 'Then lifting up his hands, the man shouted as only a primitive Methodist could, "Young man, look to Jesus Christ, look, look, look, you have nothing to do but to look and live." '

Spurgeon said, 'That morning I passed from darkness into marvellous light, from death to life, simply by looking to Jesus, I was delivered from despair and brought into marvellous joy.' He later said, 'I took one look at Jesus and He took one look at me and we became one forever.' The joy of his life and the theme of his ministry was Jesus. He was a great preacher because he preached a great Christ. It is an interesting and most revealing fact of Church history that the people whom God has used in every renewal and revival have been those who believed the Bible to be the inspired Word of God and Jesus is God in the flesh, whose death and resurrection is all sufficient to forgive sin and the sinner.

When the great German Reformer Martin Luther was asked by his superior, Von Staupitz, what he would put in place of the prayers to the saints, veneration of relics, devotion to Mary and pilgrimages, he replied, 'Christ, man only needs Jesus Christ.'

What's in a Name?

It was William Shakespeare who asked the question, 'What's in a name?' but what is the answer? Names can be very important and significant, just ask any parents of a new-born baby.

Would Sir Cliff Richard be the star he is today if he was still called Harry Webb? What about Frances Gum singing 'Somewhere Over the Rainbow?' Judy Garland sounds much better. Would Cary Grant have been the great American romantic and heart throb as Archibald Leach or John Wayne the all American tough guy as Marion Morrison?

Names can reveal a great deal. The Ford Motor Company paid an advertising agency £50,000 to come up with the name Mondeo for the launch of its new range of cars. The Japanese got it completely wrong when they tried to introduce a car into the American market called the 'Toy O Let.' No one wanted to be seen driving around in a Toy O Let, and who can blame them? The slogan, 'Come Alive with Pepsi,' was a huge success in America, but when the company plastered it on posters all over Germany the translation read, 'Come alive out of the grave with Pepsi.' In Chinese it boldly proclaimed, 'Pepsi brings your ancestors back from the dead.'

Jesus' Name

'Jesus' was a very common name in Bible times. Several other people in the New Testament had the same name, it means 'Jehovah saves.' You could walk down the streets of Jerusalem and say good morning to Jesus the baker, Jesus the tent maker, Jesus the fisherman. Josephus, a Jewish historian, says there were four or possibly five High Priests during Roman rule who bore the name Jesus. This is why when we first read of Jesus in the Gospels He is called, Jesus from Nazareth, Jesus the carpenter, Jesus, Mary and Joseph's son, to clearly identify who was being referred to.

Jesus became a very famous name. As news about Him spread throughout the whole country, rulers and kings heard of Him and wanted to meet Him. His name had become so famous that by the time of the book of Acts the name Jesus was often just used by itself, because everyone knew who was being referred to.

The name Jesus dropped right out of usage towards the end of the first century. It is an amazing fact that this name, so popular and famous, ceased to be used. There are two reasons why it happened. For some His name became a curse and for over 1500 years Jewish teachers never mentioned the name of Jesus. In early Rabbinic literature Jesus is sometimes referred to as 'the man'. During all those years not a line was written by a respectable Jew mentioning the name Jesus. They mentioned Mohammed and Buddha but not Jesus.

The Talmud, a book of Jewish teaching, changed His name from Yeshua, Jehovah Saves, to Yeshu, the letters of a curse, 'Let his name and memory be blotted out.'

Both those in the Roman and Jewish world sought to discredit Him. They suggested that He performed His miracles by means of magic, and scoffed at the belief He was born of a virgin. In Jewish sources a pun was invented on the Greek word for virgin, *'Parthenos,'* for which was substituted Pantheros, which was the name of a Roman soldier, whom they said was the real father of Jesus.

His name became the most hated but also the most loved and Christians wouldn't take such an exalted name and call their children by it. It has been pointed out that this name conquered the Roman Empire, and today we take names of Jesus' followers, many of whom were martyred by the Roman state, and give them to our children, while we take the name of Caesar and give it to our dog.

There are more than 250 names and titles given to Jesus in the Bible, for the simple reason that no one title can fully reveal the extent of His character or the revelation of His person. They can only help us to focus but not express all the fullness of who He is. His name Jesus, by which He is most commonly and easily identified throughout the world, was not given to Him by His earthly parents, but by His Father in heaven. The angel pronounced,

'You shall call his name Jesus for he shall save his people from their sins.'

The Early Church didn't preach a creed or a religion but a name. They simply went everywhere and spoke about Jesus. They healed a lame man in His name, and were warned not to teach and preach or mention that name, to which they replied,

'Salvation is found in no one else for there is no other name under heaven given to men where by we must be saved.'
(Acts 4:12)

They considered it a privilege to suffer for that name. They proclaimed forgiveness through Jesus' name,

'Believe in the Lord Jesus, and you will be saved.'
(Acts 16:31)

They baptised in Jesus' name, raised the dead in His name, cast out demons in His name. That name was to become the most loved and hated, worshipped and despised, in all history. Men and women were willing and still are to die for that name, and down through the ages even to this present day there are those who will kill and murder in an attempt to destroy what that name stands for.

The devil is not impressed by our titles, reputation or status. Demons do not tremble because of what others call us or by what we call ourselves. Imagine saying to the Gadarene demoniac, 'In the name of the Most Rev. Bishop, I command you to leave this man.' Or in the name of a doctor or professor of religion, or in the name of the Elim Church or the Baptist Church or the Church of Scotland, or any other church or denomination. What do you think would have happened? It is when we come under the anointing of the Holy Spirit and minister in the power of the name of Jesus, when we command in Jesus' name, when we pray in Jesus' name, that all hell is shaken and heaven rejoices.

You may have heard of the king who tried to order back the sea, Canute. But why did he try to do this? The answer, amazingly, lies not in Canute's pride and stupidity but in his humility and spirituality. It is an historian by the name Henry of Huntingdon whom we have to thank for recording the details of this event in his *Historia Anglorum*. He records that the king was angered by the flattery of his courtiers who constantly told him he was capable of any achievement, so he arranged the sea-shore experiment, where he commanded the waves to go back and the tide to obey him. After getting his feet wet and failing completely, Canute said, 'Let all men know how empty and worthless is the power of kings, for there is none worthy of the name but He whom earth and sea obey by eternal laws.' Afterwards, according to Henry, Canute never again wore his crown, hanging it instead in Winchester Cathedral.

Centuries later when the Queen was crowned in Westminster Abbey in 1953, there came a moment in the service when the Archbishop of Canterbury, Dr Geoffrey Fisher, extended to her Majesty the royal crown, saying, 'I give thee, O Sovereign Lady, this crown to wear until He who reserves the right to wear it shall return.' The Moderator of the General Assembly of the Church of Scotland handed her a Bible with these words, 'Here is the most valuable thing that this world affords. This is the Royal Law.'

One of the great changes that takes place in a person's life when they become a Christian is how the name of Jesus which they may have used so lightly, even blasphemously, becomes a name that is infinitely precious. They even wince when they hear someone use it in the way they once did. John Newton, the one time slave trader, wrote many famous hymns, the most well known of which is 'Amazing Grace.' The story of Christ's love and forgiveness to him, a ruthless slave trader, has been well recorded by history. He had described himself as the most vile and sinful man on the seas.

Then one day he met with Jesus, terrified by a violent thunder storm on the high seas, God's grace found such a 'wretch as he.' He left the slave trade and supported William Wilberforce all he could to get it abolished. He became a minister and served in Olney, Northamptonshire. Before he gave his life to Christ, the name of Jesus was just a swear word to him. He described himself as the worst of blasphemers, but an amazing change took place in his heart. One day anointed by the Spirit of God, he sat down to write another beautiful hymn, 'How Sweet the Name of Jesus Sounds in a Believer's Ear.'

On his deathbed, 21 December, 1807, he had just learned that the abolition of the slave trade had passed its final readings in Parliament. He had lingered on to hear such news. He joked as he described himself, 'Packed and sealed, waiting for the post.' He was hardly able to speak when a friend, William Jay, leaned over the bed to catch his last words. John Newton whispered, 'My memory is almost gone, but I remember two things. That I am a great sinner,' he paused for breath, 'and that I have a great Saviour.' He had written in that great hymn years before, 'I would Thy boundless love proclaim with every fleeting breath, so shall the music of Thy Name refresh my soul in death.'

Another famous Christian song writer Fanny Crosby, wrote more than 8,000 songs. When she was only six weeks old a minor infection developed in her eyes. The doctor who treated her was careless which caused her to become totally blind. She said she harboured no bitterness against the doctor. One day a friend said to her, 'It's a great pity a lovely Christian like you can't see,' 'Oh,' said Fanny, 'I've got a great advantage over you.' 'What's that?' her friend asked. 'The first thing I'll ever see will be the face of Jesus.'

She went on to write that beautiful hymn, 'Blessed Assurance, Jesus Is Mine!' with the words,

> 'Perfect submission, perfect delight,
> Visions of rapture now burst on my sight,
> Angels descending, bring from above
> Echoes of mercy, whispers of love.'

There are many who believe in God and are very religious, but sadly they have only ever been saved into a creed or a church, they have never been saved into Christ.

When we come to that moment when we look death in the face, creeds and church are not enough. The Apostle Paul testified to God's amazing grace as he prepared for his execution. His crime was that he loved and spoke about the name of Jesus wherever he went. He wrote,

> *'I know in whom I have believed, and I am convinced that he is able, to guard what I have entrusted to him for that day.'*
> (2 Timothy 1:10)

When this life comes to an end and we stand to give account before God, what will be important isn't what we know but who we know. Do you know Jesus personally? Have you accepted Him as Lord and Saviour of your life? Is He is the most wonderful person you know?

Some of the most frightening verses recorded in Scripture are Matthew 7:21–23, Jesus says,

> *'Not everyone who says to me, "Lord, Lord," will enter the kingdom of heaven, but only he who does the will of my Father who is in heaven. Many will say to me on that day, "Lord, Lord, did we not prophesy in your name, and in your name drive out demons and perform many miracles?" Then I will tell them plainly, "I never knew you. Away from me, you evildoers!"'*

Judas went out to heal the sick and cast out demons, but he is the only person mentioned by name in the Bible abandoned to hell.

The most important question you will ever have to answer is not, 'Do you know Jesus' but 'Does Jesus know you?' Yes, He knows all about you, He is God. But He is talking here about relationship not just knowledge. Is Jesus the foundation and focus of your life, or have you merely acknowledged His existence, even prayed in His name, but have kept Him at arm's length out of your life?

Chapter 3

Jesus, a Man of History

'Jesus is not only a man of history,
He is "The man of history."
BC and AD centre on Him.'

I read the story some time ago of Gordon Bailey, an unorthodox evangelist, who was visiting homes on a housing estate, sharing the good news about Jesus Christ. At one house a man opened the door and Gordon spoke to him, asking if he had a few minutes to spare to listen about Jesus. 'I'm not interested in religion,' was the reply. 'But who mentioned anything about religion?' said the evangelist. 'Well, you did.' 'No, I didn't,' countered Gordon. 'Well anyway,' said the man firmly, 'You won't get me to church.' 'Who mentioned anything about church?' 'Well you did,' said the man, 'Didn't you?' There was a moment's silence, and then the evangelist suggested the best thing to do was start the conversation all over again.

So they shut the door, Gordon rang the bell, and the man opened the door a second time. 'Now, listen very carefully. If you've got a few minutes to spare I'd like to talk to you about Jesus.' The man looked at him. 'Well, I'm still not interested.' 'What, not interested in the most famous man who ever lived?' 'Well, I wouldn't quite put it like that.' 'What do you know about him?' asked the evangelist. 'Do you know how He died?' 'Yes, He died on a cross. Crucified.' 'Correct. But do you know that thousands of other people were crucified at about the same time?' 'No, I'd never thought about it.' 'Well don't you think it is strange, that out of all those people who were crucified, you've only heard of one?' The man said, 'Come on in.'

The *Encyclopaedia Britannica* devotes more words to Jesus than to Aristotle, Cicero, Julius Caesar and Napoleon. No life has been so carefully examined, investigated, scrutinised and analysed. No life has reached down so many centuries with so great an impact on so many billions of people.

That Jesus was a man of history is proved beyond any shadow of doubt. Listen to what even those who are not Christians have to say. The famous Indian leader Gandhi said that Jesus was one of the greatest men who ever lived, and H.G. Wells, said, 'I am not a believer but I must confess as a historian that this penniless creature from Galilee is irresistibly the centre of history.' Even the secular historian Lecky said of Christ, 'He was the supreme personality in history who motivated humanity to the best of ethical thinking.'

The church historian Philip Schaff outlined the overwhelming influence which the life of Jesus had on subsequent history and culture of the Western world, in his book, *The Person of Christ*. He says, 'This Jesus of Nazareth without money and arms, conquered more millions than Alexander, Caesar, Mohammed, and Napoleon; without science and learning, He shed more light on things human and divine than all philosophers and scholars combined; without the eloquence of schools, He spoke such words of life as were never spoken before or since, and produced effects which lie beyond the reach of orator or poet; without writing a single line, He set more pens in motion, and furnished themes for more sermons, orations, discussions, learned volumes, works of art, and songs of praise than the whole army of great men of ancient and modern times.'

American Professor Simon Greenleaf was considered to be one of the greatest authorities in the world on the matter of legal evidence. He made a detailed investigation and analysis of the historical evidence for the life and resurrection of Jesus of Nazareth and concluded in his work, *The Testimony of the Evangelists*, that the evidence for Jesus was overwhelming.

It was such evidence that caused Abraham Lincoln at the age of forty to turn from agnosticism (it's impossible to know if there is a God), to embrace Christianity with a genuine faith in Jesus Christ. The change came about after he had read Dr James Smith's brilliant examination called, *The Christian's Defence*, which proved the historical reality of the events of Christ's life. Lincoln said, 'My doubts scattered to the winds and my reason became convinced by the arguments in support of the inspired and infallible authority of the Old and New Testaments.'

In his book *Evidence That Demands a Verdict*, Josh McDowell devotes a whole chapter to ancient historical references proving beyond question the authenticity of Jesus Christ. Jesus' historicity has, however, been repeatedly challenged by those who despite all the evidence ignore and deny His presence in this world. McDowell tells of a debate sponsored by the Associate Students of a midwestern university in America. His opponent was a congressional candidate for the Progressive Labour Party (Marxist) in New York. She said in her opening remarks, 'Historians today have fairly well dismissed Jesus as being historical . . . ' He says that he could not believe his ears, but was thankful she said such a thing because the 2,500 students were soon aware that historical homework was missing in her preparation. He went on to give fully documented evidences to prove conclusively that Jesus is a man of history.

It is not surprising that a Marxist denied the historicity of Jesus. Such belief has its origins in a German theologian way back in 1842, when Bruno Bauer was deprived of his chair of theology on account of his outrageous unorthodox opinions. Karl Marx reacted angrily when he heard of this and concluded that the religious establishment had behaved scandalously and treated Bauer terribly. Bauer's view was that Jesus had never lived, but was a figment of the imagination of the evangelist Mark. Marx never examined Christian origins for himself and was wilfully blind and ignorant of the evidence. There are none so blind as those who will not see.

Historical Evidence

Cornelius Tacitus He was the greatest historian of Imperial Rome and Governor of Asia in AD 112. He was also the son-in-law of Julius Agricola who was Governor of Britain AD 80–84.

He reports in his Annals that when the emperor Nero was suspected of having set Rome on fire, he shifted the blame to the Christians from himself and punished them accordingly. Within some thirty five years of Jesus' death and resurrection, the church was of sufficient size and significance as to provide the emperor of Rome with a scapegoat for his own evil and irresponsible actions.

> 'But not all the relief that could come from man, not all the bounties that the prince could bestow, nor all the atonements which could be presented to the gods, availed to relieve Nero from the infamy of being believed to have ordered the conflagration, the fire of Rome. Hence to suppress the rumour, he falsely charged with the guilt, and punished with the most exquisite tortures, the persons commonly called Christians, who were hated for their enormities. Christus, the founder of the name, was put to death by Pontius Pilate, procurator of Judea in the reign of Tiberius: but the pernicious superstition, repressed for a time, broke out again, not only through Judea, where the mischief originated, but through the city of Rome also.'   (Annals XV.44)

It is clear that Tacitus had no sympathy for Christianity, his evidence is therefore all the more reliable and valuable. His time as Governor in Asia meant he had good opportunity to become well informed about the origins of Christianity, for by AD 112 when he was writing, Christians there were numerous.

Plinius Secundus, Pliny the Younger He was a contemporary of Cornelius Tacitus and from him comes one of the fullest and most intriguing accounts of Christianity from a pagan source. He was sent by the Emperor Trajan to govern the province of Bithynia in Northern Turkey in AD 112. He had a typical bureaucratic mind and wrote letters on every conceivable topic to the Emperor. One of these letters concerns Christianity. He says that everywhere he went in his province, including villages and country districts, he found Christians. Moreover their rapid spread had assumed the proportions of a major social problem. The pagan temples were having to close down for lack of customers, the sacred festivals had been discontinued and all demand for sacrificial animals had ceased.

He explained to the Emperor that he tried to suppress the Christian faith by executing both men and women, boys and girls. There were so many being put to death that he wondered if he should continue killing anyone who was discovered to be a Christian, or if he should kill only certain ones. He confessed that he was perplexed about the nature of their crime. He had discovered from those who recanted through his persecution (he made them bow down to statues of Trajan and also curse Christ, which he says a genuine Christian cannot be induced to do) that no enormities were being practised in the Christian community.

> 'Their whole guilt lay only in this, that they were in the habit of meeting on a certain fixed day (Sunday) before it was light, when they sang in alternate verse a hymn to Christ as to a god, (God) and bound themselves to a solemn oath, not to do any wicked deeds, never to commit any fraud, theft, adultery, never to falsify their word, not to deny a trust when they should be called upon to deliver it up.' (Epistles X.96)

Pliny was perplexed by the apparent harmlessness of all this, hence his letter to the Emperor.

Thallus, the Samaritan Historian He is one of the first Gentile writers to mention Christ, writing in Rome about AD 52. His work is mostly lost, and we only know of it from fragments cited by other writers one of whom is Julius Africanus, a Christian writing about AD 221. One very interesting passage relates to a comment from Thallus, which

Julius refers to when discussing the darkness that fell when Jesus died on the cross.

> 'Thallus, in the third book of his histories, explains away this darkness as an eclipse of the sun, unreasonably, as it seems to me.'

Unreasonably of course because a solar eclipse could not take place at the time of the full moon, and it was at the season of the Paschal full moon that Christ died. It is interesting to note that from this reference, the Gospel account of the darkness that fell upon the land during Christ's crucifixion was well known and was seeking to be explained away by those non-believers who witnessed it.

Justin Martyr   A brilliant apologist for the Christian faith, writing about AD 150, he addresses his Defence of Christianity to the Emperor Antoninus Pius. He referred him to Pilate's report, which Justin supposed must be preserved in the imperial archives. The words, 'They pierced my hands and my feet,' he says, 'are a description of the nails that were fixed in His hands and His feet on the cross; and after He was crucified, those who crucified Him cast lots for His garments, and divided them among themselves; and that these things were so, you may learn from the "Acts" which were recorded under Pontius Pilate.' Later he says, 'That He performed these miracles you may be easily satisfied from the "Acts" of Pontius Pilate' (Apology 1.48).

Flavius Josephus   He is considered to be one of the most important witnesses and historians regarding the period when Christ lived. He was one of the Jewish commanders in the war against Rome, who turned collaborator after the Romans invaded Palestine in AD 67–70. He set out to re-establish the credibility of Judaism in the minds of Roman society in general and the Imperial family in particular. He wrote his *Antiquities of the Jews* (published AD 93) and his *Jewish War* (published AD 75–79) in order to inform the Roman public more accurately about the Jewish faith.

These apologetic works naturally kept to a minimum any material that would irritate their Roman readers. Yet we read in his accounts many of the figures familiar from the New Testament such as Pilate, Annas, Caiaphas, the Herods, Quirinius, Felix, Festus, John the Baptist, James the brother of Jesus, and Christ Himself.

He says in a hotly contested quotation,

> 'Now there was about this time, a wise man, if it be lawful to call him a man, for he was a doer of wonderful works, a teacher of such men as receive the truth with pleasure. He drew over to him both many of the Jews, and many of the Greeks. He was the Messiah, and when Pilate, at the suggestion of the principal men among us, had condemned him to the cross, those that loved him at the first did not forsake him; for he appeared to them alive again on the third day; as the divine prophets had foretold these and ten thousand other wonderful things concerning him. And the tribe of Christians so named from him are not extinct at this day.'
>
> (*Antiquities* 18.63; early second century)

This is of course a most surprising testimony to find in the pages of someone who was not himself a Christian, but all attempts to disprove and undermine its authority have failed. It has as good attestation as anything else written in Josephus for it is included in all the manuscripts.

Evidence from the Rabbinic Sources   The Jewish sources of the first two or three centuries are more hostile toward Jesus and His Church, although they confirm His historical existence and the church's rapid growth. These writings which came to be known as the *Mishna* and the *Talmud*, claim they are quoting rabbis who were (allegedly) active in the first century. Jesus is referred to as a 'certain person,' on the assumption that even to mention His name would be to give Him undue honour. The specific details about this unnamed character and His followers point unmistakably to Jesus. In some passages He is called Ben Stada or Ben Pandira or Ben Panthera, implying that He is the illegitimate son (Ben means 'son of') of a soldier or some other unworthy person. Similarly, His mother is described as disreputable.

Jesus' existence and activity as a teacher and worker of miracles is simply assumed by these writers, they could not deny what was clearly provable and true, so they did everything they could to discredit and ridicule Him. The stories about Jesus are no myth or fantasy, for not only do twenty seven different New Testament documents provide proof, but also the writings of the Early Church Fathers and Jewish, Samaritan and Roman historians.

Evidence in the Dead Sea Scrolls These scrolls are considered to be the most important archaeological manuscript find not only in this century but in the whole of history. They were discovered in 1947 in caves at Qumran on the north-western shore of the Dead Sea. They had been stored there by a strict community of Jews known as the Essenes, which flourished from about 150 BC to AD 70. The scrolls had remained hidden in the caves for almost 2,000 years, until they were discovered by three Arab boys who were looking after sheep and goats. One threw a stone into a cave and heard a 'clank' as the stone hit a jar containing some of the manuscripts. A few days later Muhammed edh-Dhib, the youngest of the three, went back to explore further and found pots containing leather rolls with writing on and made a discovery that startled the world. He didn't realise how valuable the scrolls were and for some weeks they remained in a tent before some of them were sold for £24 and £7!

When the scrolls were first discovered, many Christian scholars naturally wondered if they contained any evidence about Jesus and Christianity. Despite overwhelming interest, the vast majority of scrolls were not translated for publication. For years they remained in the hands of a small group of original scroll scholars who kept control over them. This led to claims by some who had access to the scrolls that they cast doubts upon the origin of the Christian faith. These views were given much publicity at the time even though they were only the considerations of a few.

After forty-five years of research by scroll scholars only 20% of the manuscripts had been translated and published.

Pressure mounted for the scrolls to be made more widely available and after a public relations campaign led by the *Biblical Archaeology Review* magazine, the last of the unpublished scrolls were released to the academic world. To the great joy and excitement of many scholars, the scrolls contain definite references to the New Testament and, most importantly, to Jesus of Nazareth.

One of the most extraordinary of these scrolls released in 1991 actually refers directly to the crucifixion of Jesus. This scroll was translated by Dr Robert Eisenman, professor of Middle East Religions of California State University. He said, 'The text is of the most far reaching significance because it shows that whatever group was responsible for these writings was operating in the same general scriptural and Messianic framework of early Christianity.' This amazing scroll contained information about the death of the Messiah. It referred to 'the Prophet Isaiah' and his Messianic prophecy in chapter 53 of the suffering Messiah who died for the sins of His people.

Archaeological evidence about Jesus Michael Green in his book, *Runaway World*, tells us that one of the most famous early Christian symbols was the fish. It is also frequently used by Christians today. It was commonly used in the Early Church as a mark of identification among Christians expressing what they believed about Jesus. The Greek word for fish is *ichthus*, and each of the five Greek letters stands for a word: *Iesous Christos Theou Huios Soter*; which means, 'Jesus Christ, Son of God, Saviour.' Jesus is an historical person, the Christ the long awaited Jewish Messiah. The Son of God, more than a man but God in the flesh. Saviour, the one who rescues us from sin and death.

Another fascinating discovery was made in 1945 by Israeli Professor Sukenik. In a sealed tomb outside Jerusalem, in a suburb called Talpioth, he found five bone caskets. A coin found in the tomb and the decoration of the caskets confirmed that the tomb was closed in approximately AD 50. On two of the caskets the name of Jesus appears. One reads in Greek, *Iesu Iou* (Jesus help), the other in Aramaic, *Yeshu' Aloth*

(Jesus let him arise). Written barely twenty years after Jesus' death and resurrection they point to believers, who saw Him as the Lord of life, who conquered death. They proclaim that Jesus is the risen Son of God, who will raise the Christian dead from their graves.

Jesus isn't only a man of history, He is 'The Man of History.' In fact He was more than a man, He was God who had come in the flesh. Nicodemus says in John 3:2,

> *'Rabbi, we know you are a teacher who has come from God.'*

This was only partially true. Jesus was God who had come to teach. Now the whole world counts time as Before Christ, BC, and AD, which means Anno Domini, 'In the year of the Lord.'

The Genealogies of Jesus

As you read through the genealogies you will notice that Matthew traces the line of Joseph from Abraham while Luke traces Joseph's line back to Adam. Bible scholars have suggested various explanations for this. The most probable is that Matthew gives Joseph's family line and Luke is tracing the genealogy of Mary.

The cultural background and theological emphases of the two writers is also important, with Matthew, a Jew, writing primarily for Jews and Luke, a Gentile, writing to Gentiles. Therefore Matthew presents Jesus as the Jewish Messiah and traces His line from Abraham through the kings of Judah, while Luke traces the line all the way back to Adam and shows Jesus is the Saviour for the whole world.

Matthew 1:1–17	Luke 3:23–38
A record of the genealogy of Jesus Christ the son of David, the son of Abraham:	Now Jesus himself was about thirty years old when he began his ministry. He was the son, so it was thought, of Joseph,
Abraham was the father of Isaac,	the son of Heli, the son of Matthat,
Isaac the father of Jacob,	
Jacob the father of Judah and his brothers	the son of Levi, the son of Melki,

Matthew 1:1–17

Judah the father of Perez and
Zerah, whose mother was Tamar,
Perez the father of Hezron,
Hezron the father of Ram,
Ram the father of Amminadab,
Amminadab the father of
Nahshon,
Nahshon the father of Salmon,
Salmon the father of Boaz, whose
mother was Rahab,
Boaz the father of Obed, whose
mother was Ruth,
Obed the father of Jesse,
and Jesse the father of King David.

David was the father of Solomon,
whose mother had been Uriah's
wife,
Solomon the father of Rehoboam,
Rehoboam the father of Abijah
Abijah the father of Asa,
Asa the father of Jehoshaphat,
Jehoshaphat the father of Jehoram,
Jehoram the father of Uzziah,
Uzziah the father of Jotham,
Jotham the father of Ahaz,
Ahaz the father of Hezekiah,
Hezekiah the father of Manasseh,
Manasseh the father of Amon,
Amon the father of Josiah,
and Josiah the father of Jeconiah
and his brothers at the time of
the exile to Babylon.

After the exile to Babylon:
Jeconiah was the father of
Shealtiel,
Shealtiel the father of Zerubbabel,
Zerubbabel the father of Abiud,
Abiud the father of Eliakim,
Eliakim the father of Azor,
Azor the father of Zadok,
Zadok the father of Akim,
Akim the father of Eliud,

Luke 3:23–38

the son of Jannai, the son of
Joseph,
the son of Mattathias, the son of
Amos,
the son of Nahum, the son of Esli,
the son of Naggai, the son of
Maath,
the son of Mattathias, the son of
Semein,
the son of Josech, the son of Joda,
the son of Joanan, the son of
Rhesa,
the son of Zerubbabel, the son of
Shealtiel,
the son of Neri, the son of Melki,
the son of Addi, the son of Cosam,
the son of Elmadam, the son of Er,
the son of Joshua, the son of
Eliezer,
the son of Jorim, the son of
Matthat,
the son of Levi, the son of Simeon,
the son of Judah, the son of Joseph,
the son Jonam, the son of Eliakim,
the son of Melea, the son of
Menna,
the son of Mattatha, the son of
Nathan,
the son of David, the son of Jesse,
the son of Obed, the son of Boaz,
the son of Salmon, the son of
Nahshon,
the son of Amminadab, the son of
Ram,
the son of Hezron, the son of
Perez,
the son of Judah, the son of Jacob,
the son of Isaac, the son of
Abraham,
the son of Terah, the son of Nahor,
the son of Serug, the son of Reu,
the son of Peleg, the son of Eber,
the son of Shelah, the son of
Cainan,

Matthew 1:1–17	Luke 3:23–38
Eliud the father of Eleazar, Eleazar the father of Matthan, Matthan the father of Jacob, and Jacob the father of Joseph, the husband of Mary, of whom was born Jesus, who is called Christ. Thus there were fourteen generations in all from Abraham to David, fourteen from David to the exile to Babylon, and fourteen from the exile to the Christ.	the son of Arphaxad, the son of Shem, the son of Noah, the son of Lamech, the son of Methuselah, the son of Enoch, the son of Jared, the son of Mahalalel, the son of Kenan, the son of Enosh, the son of Seth, the son of Adam, the son of God.

Amazing Testimonies

Gilbert West and Lord Lyttleton

Gilbert West and Lord Lyttleton were legal authorities and champions of atheism and rationalism in the eighteenth century. They decided to prove once and for all that Christianity and the Bible were the product of myths and falsehood. West was to prove that the resurrection of Jesus was a legend, whilst Lyttleton sought to prove that the conversion of Paul was a myth.

They believed that by undermining these two key events they would undermine the whole of the New Testament. They took a year to complete their tasks and write their books, then met together to discuss their findings.

'I have written my book,' said Lord Lyttleton, 'And I have a confession to make. When I came to study all the evidence for the story of the conversion of Paul and weighed it up by all the known laws of evidence, I found that Paul was miraculously converted in spite of himself. I am now a Christian and have written my book on that side and not against it.'

Gilbert West replied, 'I have a similar confession to make. I have found the resurrection of Jesus Christ to be a proved fact and I too have become a believer and have written my book on that side.'

The book he wrote was entitled, *Observations on the History and Evidences of the Resurrection of Jesus Christ.* It was printed in 1747 and the motto he wrote on the title page was very significant, 'Blame not before thou hast examined the truth, understanding first and then rebuke.'

Ben Hur

'After six years given to the impartial investigation of Christianity, as to its truth or falsity, I have come to the deliberate conclusion that Jesus Christ is the Messiah of the Jews, the Saviour of the world and my personal Saviour.' These were the words of Lew Wallace who was Governor of Alabama, America, over a century ago. He had started out to write a book against Jesus Christ and in the process was converted to Christianity. He told a friend how it happened.

'I had always been an agnostic and denied Christianity. Robert C. Ingersoll, a famous agnostic, was one of my most intimate friends. After serving my term as Governor I was returning East with Ingersoll. As we neared St Louis, we were in conversation on ordinary things, when we both noticed the forest of church spires. "Isn't it a shame," remarked Ingersoll, "That so many apparently intelligent people continue to believe the foolish doctrines that are being taught under those church spires? When will the time arrive that the teachings of the so-called Bible will be thrown out as foolishness?"

'Suddenly Ingersoll looked at me full in the face and said, "See here, Wallace, you are a learned man and a thinker. Why don't you gather material and write a book to prove the falsity concerning Jesus Christ, that no such man has ever lived, much less the author of the teachings found in the New Testament. Such a book would make you famous. It would be a masterpiece, and a way of putting an end to the foolishness about the so-called Christ and the Saviour of the world."

'The thought made a deep impression on me and we discussed the possibility of such a book. I said I would try to gather material and have it published as the masterpiece of my life and the crowning glory of my work. I went to Indianapolis, my home, and told my wife what I intended. She was a member of the Methodist Church and naturally did not like my plan. But I decided to do it and began to collect material in libraries here, and in the old world. I gathered everything over that period in which Jesus Christ, according to saying, should have lived. Several years were spent in this work. I had written nearly four chapters when it became clear to me that Jesus Christ was just as real a personality as Socrates, Plato, Caesar and other ancient men. The conviction became a certainty. I knew that Jesus Christ had lived on earth because of the facts connected with the period in which he lived.

'I was in an uncomfortable position. I had begun to write a book to prove that no such person as Jesus Christ had ever lived on earth. Now I was face to face with the fact that He was just as historic a personage as Julius Caesar, Mark Anthony, Virgil, Dante and a host of other men who had lived in olden days. I asked myself candidly, "If He was a real person (and there was no doubt), was He not then also the Son of God and the Saviour of the world?" Gradually the consciousness grew that, since Jesus Christ was a real person, He probably was the one He claimed to be.

'The conviction became so strong that one night it grew into certainty. I fell on my knees to pray for the first time in my life, and I asked God to reveal Himself to me, forgive my sins and help me to become a follower of Christ. Towards morning the light broke into my soul. I went into my bedroom, woke my wife and told her that I had received Jesus Christ as my Lord and Saviour. "O Lew," she said, "I have prayed for this ever since you told me of your purpose to write this book, that you would find Him while you wrote it!"'

Lew Wallace did write a very famous book, it was a masterpiece and the crowning glory of his life's work. He changed the book he was originally writing and used all his research to write another book he called, *Ben Hur*. Now every time I watch that epic film and see Charlton Heston racing those four magnificent white horses in that amazing chariot race, I think to myself, there is a greater book behind this one. I wonder how many who have seen the film, with its moving references to Jesus, know it was written by a man who wanted to disprove that Jesus ever existed and instead became convinced that He was the greatest man who ever lived!

Chapter 4

The World in Which Jesus Lived

*'Men must either choose to be governed by
God or they condemn themselves
to be ruled by tyrants.'*
(*William Penn*, who gave his name to Pennsylvania)

Jesus was a Jew who ministered to people in real life situations in first century Palestine. The first Christians were Jews and Christianity's birthplace was the capital of the nation. Therefore it is important to understand the political, social, cultural and religious world in which Jesus lived if we are to grasp and understand the full implications of what took place and is recorded in the four Gospels about Him.

The Religious World

The last of the Old Testament prophets lived more than 400 years before John the Baptist appeared. This time between the last book of the Old Testament, Malachi, and Matthew, the first book of the New Testament, is known as the intertestamental period, during which God appears to be silent as there is nothing recorded in the Scriptures. There are however historical records and religious documents of that time which help us understand the background that preceded Jesus' coming. These books are usually referred to as the Apocrypha. During this period the nation tended to polarise either towards a more rebellious lifestyle against God's Law or to a more religious observance of it. When the voice of God is silent the same thing still happens with a polarisation between lawlessness on the one hand and legalism on the other.

The Temple   This was primarily a place for worship and sacrifice. Built on the summit of Mount Zion in Jerusalem, which had been dug away to leave a plateau of a thousand square feet, it was a magnificent structure of white marble plated with gold. It is said that when it shone in the sun its brilliance was so dazzling you could scarcely bear to look at it. Jesus' attitude to the Temple is very interesting, for on the one hand He greatly respected it and on the other, He seems to attach little permanent importance to it. This is evidenced by Him referring to it as the 'house of God' (Matthew 12:4, John 2:16), yet also saying that the Temple would soon be destroyed (Matthew 24:2). This was fulfilled in AD 70 when Titus led the Roman army into Jerusalem and destroyed everything as punishment on the Jews for their revolt against Rome. It is said that the heat of the flames caused the gold in the Temple to melt and in their frenzy to get at it the order was given by the Romans to pull down every stone of the Temple. Jesus had said over thirty years before,

> *'Not one stone here will be left on another, every stone shall be thrown down.'*   (Matthew 24:2)

On two separate occasions Jesus is seen cleansing the Temple and rebuking its officials for the way it had degenerated into a market place filled with thieves and robbers. The reason He said and did this is very interesting. The Passover for which Jesus had come to Jerusalem was the greatest of all the Jewish feasts. The Law laid down that every adult male who lived within fifteen miles of Jerusalem was bound to attend it. It has been estimated that more than two million Jews sometimes gathered in the Holy City to keep the Passover. When they arrived every Jew over nineteen years of age was required to pay the Temple tax to finance the on going ministry of the Temple. The tax was one half shekel, equivalent to almost two days wages for the average working man of the time. For ordinary purposes in Palestine all kinds of currency were valid, but not for the Temple tax which had to be paid in Galilean shekels or in shekels of the sanctuary. These were Jewish coins and so could be used as a gift to the Temple, but the other currencies were foreign and considered unclean. They might be used to pay ordinary debts, but not a debt to God.

Pilgrims arrived for Passover from all over the world with their own currency, so in the Temple courts were the money changers. There was nothing wrong with them being there if they were acting honestly. They fulfilled a necessary function. But they used their position to 'rip off' those from other nations. They made a charge for every half shekel they changed and another charge on every half shekel of change they had to give if a larger coin was tendered. The fact that the money changers received some commission was not wrong. What enraged Jesus was that those who came to seek God from foreign lands at the Passover were being fleeced, with a two shekel coin being charged half a shekel to change, equivalent to a whole day's wage.

There were also the sellers of oxen and sheep and doves. Frequently a visitor to the Temple wanted to make a sacrifice, but the Law said that only unblemished animals may be used. The Temple authorities appointed inspectors to examine the animals being offered, and for this they charged a fee. If the worshipper bought the animal outside the Temple it was guaranteed to be rejected. This meant that they had to purchase a sacrifice from the sellers in the Temple courts. The prices charged there were as much as twenty times more than what the animal would cost outside. Here was extortion at its worst. It was this corruption that so angered Jesus and caused Him to throw over the money changers' tables and drive out the animal sellers.

The pilgrims who had travelled from afar were often Gentiles and as such could only enter into the outer court of the Temple, the Court of the Gentiles. It was here that all the money changing and selling was going on. These Gentile pilgrims had come to seek the God of the Jews and when they came to the Temple to pray they were confronted by religious corruption. Jesus said that the Temple was to be a house of prayer for all nations.

Just one more observation. Jesus performs His first miracle at a wedding turning water into wine, then He leaves Cana and travels to Jerusalem and the next thing we read He is cleansing the Temple. He is obviously more pleased by a party where He is honoured than He is a religious establishment where He is not.

The Synagogue It was a most important institution in the life of any Jew. There was a difference between the Synagogues and the Temple. There was only one Temple but the Law laid down that wherever there were ten Jewish families there must be a Synagogue.

Here there was no sacrificial ritual or singing, it was the local centre for prayer and the study of the Law. On the Sabbath day the community would meet, men and women seated apart. The service consisted of three parts. The first part was for prayers. The second was readings from the Law and the Prophets, in which members from the congregation took part. The third part of the service was the address. The important fact to remember is that there was no one person to give this. The president of the Synagogue presided over the service arrangements and any distinguished person or stranger could be asked to speak. Anyone with a message to give was able to volunteer to give it, as long as the president of the Synagogue judged him a fit person to speak.

The synagogue was more than a place of worship, however. It was the local school, the community centre, and the place of local government. Its elders were the civic authorities of the community. It was the emergence of these synagogues during the intertestamental period that helped to unify and bind the Jewish communities together. What took place there influenced every area of their lives.

The Law From the time of Ezra in the 5th century BC an even greater emphasis was placed on studying and teaching the Law. The nation's downfall had been disobedience of God and His laws, so it was determined that the people would not make the same mistakes again. Hosea said that

God's people are destroyed from lack of knowledge (Hosea 4:6), so now there came a quest for knowledge. This intensive study meant that the Jews became known as, 'The people of the Book,' a worthy desire and title, but sadly it also brought with it an increasing number of traditions, which came to be as binding as the Law itself.

The Jews used the expression 'the Law' in four different ways.

1. They used it to mean the Ten Commandments.
2. The first five books of the Old Testament, which to them was the most important part of the Scriptures.
3. The phrase the Law and the Prophets meant the whole of Scripture.
4. Finally they used it to mean the oral or scribal law.

In the time of Jesus it was this scribal law that was most common and which both Jesus and later Paul utterly condemned. So what was this scribal law?

In the Old Testament the Law laid down great broad principles which a person was to take and interpret under God's guidance and apply to everyday situations in life. To the later Jews these principles did not seem enough. They held that the Law was divine and that in it God had said His last word and that therefore everything must be contained in it. They therefore argued that from the Law it must be possible to deduce a rule and a regulation for every possible situation in life. So arose the Scribes who made it the business of their lives to reduce these great truths of the Law to literally thousands of rules and regulations.

For example the Law said that the Sabbath day was to be kept holy, no work was to be done, so they sought to define work. They said to carry a burden on the Sabbath was to work. They defined what was a burden. In scribal law a burden was, food equal in weight to a dried fig, enough wine for mixing in a goblet, enough milk for one swallow, ink enough to write two letters of the alphabet and so on. They spent endless hours arguing over such details asking if a tailor committed a sin if he went out with a needle in his robe, whether a man might go out on the Sabbath wearing

49

artificial teeth and whether a father might lift his child on the Sabbath day. These things to them were the essence of religion, which degenerated into legalism.

To heal was considered work on the Sabbath. Healing was allowed if the person's life was in danger but only to stop things getting worse not to make them any better. Therefore a plain bandage might be put on a wound but no ointment. You realise now why Jesus came into confrontation with them.

The Scribes were the men who worked all these details out and the Pharisees were the men who had separated their lives from all ordinary activities to keep all these rules.

The Scribes As previously mentioned they were the interpreters and teachers of the Law, having taken over this role from the Priests and Levites after the exile. They were the professionals who were needed to prescribe exact regulations for every occasion. There were for example, 39 types of action prohibited on the Sabbath: reaping and threshing were forbidden, this included plucking ears of corn and rubbing the grain out in the hands (Luke 6:1–2). They clashed frequently with Jesus because He refused to adhere to all their man-made traditions and the interpretations of the Law, which they taught.

The Pharisees   Their name means 'separated ones.' These were the religious purists, a party which was an offshoot of the Hasidim, the 'faithful' or 'devoted' ones, who concentrated on control of religious, rather than political affairs. Their supreme concern and passion was to keep the Law, including all the traditions that had built up around it, as most of the Scribes also belonged to the Pharisee party. They were a group that began with high motives and had a strong following among the common people. Sadly they began to degenerate towards legalism and to a policy of separation from 'lesser mortals.' This led to hypocrisy and pride, as they were zealous in keeping the letter of the Law but missed entirely the spirit of it. Jesus denounced them with some of His strongest rebukes. He did not dispute their orthodoxy but rather the arrogance with which they held it.

The Sadducees   They were the other main party at the time of Jesus. These men were associated with the priestly families, and were either priests themselves or were related to them in some way. They were generally very wealthy as they also tended to come from the rich land owning class which in earlier days, by shrewd political manipulation, had secured a dominant position. Even though their influence had begun to diminish by Jesus' time, they still controlled a roughly equal proportion of seats in the Sanhedrin (the Jewish Supreme Council) with the Pharisees.

Their religious position and persuasion was opposed to the orthodoxy of the Pharisees, thus Paul was able to use this to his advantage when he was first on trial (Acts 23:6–10). They refused to accept any revelation beyond the first five books of Moses, Genesis to Deuteronomy, thus Jesus' answer about the resurrection (Luke 20:27–40) is taken from Exodus, a book that even the Sadducees accepted as from God. They also rejected belief in angels, demons, immortality and the supernatural. As an aristocratic minority often willing to compromise with the pagan rulers of Palestine, they enjoyed little popular support.

The Sanhedrin   This was the supreme court of the Jews. It was composed of Scribes, Pharisees, Sadducees and elders of the people. It numbered seventy and was presided over by the High Priest. It had complete jurisdiction over all religious and theological matters. During the time of Jesus it had no power to carry out the death sentence, this had to be passed by the Roman governor and carried out by the Roman authorities. It was for this reason that members brought Jesus before Pilate and falsely accused Him of treason against the Roman state.

The Zealots   While the other parties tried to make the best of Roman rule the Zealots, as they came to be called, were the freedom fighters, the revolutionaries of the Jewish people. They dreamt of and fought for a nation that was free and independent of Roman control, founding their desire and appeal on the belief that subjection to Rome was treason to God, the true King of Israel. They refused to give any earthly man the name and title of king.

Their founder was Judas the Galilean, who in AD 6 led an armed revolt against Rome (Acts 5:36–37). The rebellion was crushed and Judas killed, but his sons continued the struggle. It was this group that eventually sparked off the great rebellion which led to the Roman destruction of Jerusalem in AD 70. Masada was their final stronghold of resistance to Rome, it fell in AD 74. By Jesus' time, there had been many abortive revolts and two men in the Gospel accounts seem to be closely linked with this movement. One was Simon the Zealot who miraculously was able to work and minister alongside Matthew, a former tax collector. Simon would have formerly hated Matthew for working for the Romans, but such was the presence and influence of Jesus that former enemies now witnessed to the grace of God as they ministered together. The other man was probably Barabbas.

The Political World

The world into which Jesus was born was politically very volatile. Palestine was under the boot of Roman rule and occupation. There was constant intrigue and political manoeuvring both in Rome and Jerusalem among Roman governors and procurators who reported to the governors of Syria. Pilate is the best known of these procurators. This intrigue is clearly seen in the trials and death of Jesus. The religious parties were frightened of losing their influence, given to them by Roman rule, if Jesus continued to undermine their authority.

Pilate's fear of stepping out of line came about when he wanted to release Jesus.

> *'From then on, Pilate tried to set Jesus free, but the Jews kept shouting, "If you let this man go, you are no friend of Caesar. Anyone who claims to be a king opposes Caesar."'*
>
> (John 19:12)

At that time in Rome Sejanus, the prefect of the Praetorium guard, had staged an assassination attempt against Caesar. It had failed and retribution was swift, with conspiracy theories about who was involved circulating.

Jewish rule in Galilee under Roman authority was in the most part by the Herods, descendants of Herod Antipater, a half-Jewish adventurer who had been made 'king of the Jews' by Rome. Mostly procurators, on the other hand, ruled Judea.

Notes on Pilate

In 1961 a stone slab was discovered at Caesarea bearing the name Pontius Pilatus. Tacitus, the Roman writer, refers to the execution of Jesus by Pilate, and two Jewish writers, Josephus and Philo, relate several other incidents involving him. Philo, who was his contemporary, describes Pilate as 'by nature rigid, stubbornly harsh, spiteful and brutal.' He says that King Agrippa I described him in a letter to the Emperor Caligula as, 'a man of a very inflexible disposition, and very merciless as well as very obstinate.'

Pilate was evidently a middle class Roman with military administrative experience who in AD 26 was appointed to the office of procurator, i.e. Roman governor, of Judea by Emperor Tiberius. He served in this position for about ten years until AD 36. He thus possessed very wide powers, especially in financial and military matters. He appointed the high priests and controlled the Temple funds.

He antagonised the Jews almost as soon as he was appointed by allowing Roman troops to bring their regimental standards into Jerusalem. These contained representations of the Emperor and the Jews were furious because they felt the holy city had been desecrated by these idolatrous symbols. Pilate bowed to the political storm and ordered them removed. He also caused a revolt by using money from the Temple treasury to finance the building of an aqueduct to bring water from a spring 25 miles away into Jerusalem. Mass protests were met by force and many Jews died. This may well be the incident referred to in Luke 13:1.

Pilate's final blunder was to seize a number of Samaritans who had gathered on Mount Gerazim, their holy mountain, as a result of a rumour that sacred vessels from the tabernacle were hidden there. He had some of the ringleaders executed. In response the Samaritans protested to Vitellius, Governor of Syria and Pilate's superior, who ordered Pilate back to Rome to answer before the Emperor. The reigning emperor, Tiberius, died before Pilate reached Rome. We do not know the outcome of what happened, but Eusebius, a fourth century Christian historian, records a report that Pilate committed suicide.

The Social World

The Dispersion   By the time of Jesus Jews were scattered throughout the eastern Mediterranean. Since the Jewish exiles in 722, 597 and 587 BC some had been forcibly deported, scattered and displaced, so that by the first century AD there were a million Jews in Egypt alone. By Jesus' day between one half and two thirds of all Jews were living outside Palestine. These were known as the Diaspora, Jews of the dispersion.

Those Jews living in Palestine held mixed attitudes towards Jews of the dispersion. Those who had strongly maintained their Jewish faith were largely accepted. They paid the annual Temple tax and would make pilgrimages to the Temple in Jerusalem for the major festivals. Those who had decided to intermarry with the people among whom they were living, and had sacrificed and buried their Jewish identity, were generally despised.

The Samaritans feature in the Gospels as a people despised for being neither fully Jew nor fully Gentile. They regarded themselves as descendants of those Israelites who had been exiled after the fall of Samaria but most Jews would have nothing to do with them as they had intermarried with the newly imported alien population after Samaria fell in 722 BC. This throws much light on the way in which Jesus responded and dealt with the Samaritans in both His contact with them and His teaching involving them, such as the Parable of the Good Samaritan, and the woman at the well.

Greek language and culture After the death of Alexander the Great, who had conquered the entire eastern Mediterranean between 336 and 323 BC, Palestine was ruled by the Ptolemies, a succession of Hellenistic kings. They were happy to let the Jews govern themselves as far as their religion went and under their rule Greek language and culture came to dominate the commercial and educational life of Palestine.

The Hebrew Scriptures were translated into Greek and the common Greek dialect, Koine Greek, became an international language. This was the language in which the New Testament was written, though Aramaic remained the common language of the Jews in Palestine. The widespread use of Koine Greek, combined with the network of roads built and maintained by the Romans, enabled the Gospel message to spread quickly to the surrounding cities and nations. When Jesus was born in Bethlehem and the church birthed in Jerusalem the infrastructure was perfect to take the good news into all the world.

> *'But when the time had fully come, God sent his Son, born of a woman, born under law.'* (Galatians 4:4)

Some Famous Places

Bethlehem (*House of Bread*) The birth place of Jesus.

> *'But you, Bethlehem Ephrathah, though you are small among the clans of Judah, out of you will come for me one who will be ruler over Israel, whose origins are from of old, from ancient times.'* (Micah 5:2)

It was a little town six miles south of Jerusalem, standing high upon a grey limestone ridge some 2,500 feet high. It was here, in David's city, that the Jews expected the Messiah to be born.

'No room at the Inn.' It was here that Mary and Joseph came to register for the Roman census, Luke 2:1–3. They had

travelled almost 80 miles from Nazareth on what must have been a long, hard journey. Since Joseph and Mary came from the same family line it seems likely that they would have had relatives in Bethlehem. Yet the stigma of their circumstances went with them, Mary had conceived before marriage, which did not go unnoticed. It seems that no relation would take them in.

Nazareth   This lay in a hollow in the hills south of Galilee. Climbing its hills you could see the waters of the Mediterranean to the west. The plain, which skirted the coast, held the road from Damascus to Egypt, the land bridge to Africa. It was one of the greatest caravan routes in the world. Jesus spent most of His life, until He was thirty years old, here.

When Nathanael asks Andrew, *'Can any good thing come out of Nazareth?'* (John 1:46), it is helpful to bear in mind that there was often great rivalry between different towns, and that Nazareth is not even mentioned in the Old Testament.

Jerusalem   This is one of the world's great cities. It stands on the edge of the highest tablelands in Palestine, and is surrounded on the south eastern, the southern, and the western sides by deep ravines. Hence the fact that it was a formidable fortress and one of the main reasons King David made it the national capital. It was here that the great focal point of the nation's life was built, the magnificent Temple.

Capernaum   Jesus was rejected at Nazareth and so moved His ministry base to Capernaum (Matthew 4:13). It stood on the western shore of the Sea of Galilee and lay on the great highway from Damascus to Tyre. It was a wise and strategic move, from here He made many journeys throughout Galilee, occasionally travelling to Jerusalem and regions north of Galilee.

Caesarea Philippi   This district lies 25 miles north east of the Sea of Galilee. The area was scattered with temples of the ancient Syrian Baal worship, nearby rose a great hill in which there was a deep cavern, said to be the birth place of the god Pan, the god of nature. Caesarea Philippi was identified with the god so much that its original name was Panias. There also stood a great temple of white marble built by Herod the Great to honour the deity of Caesar. Some time later his son Philip further enriched and beautified it. He also changed its name to further honour the emperor, from Panias to Caesar, adding his own name to call the district Caesarea Philippi.

It was here that Jesus took His disciples and asked them what the people were saying about Him. Surrounded by all its shrines, where gods were said to become men and men to be gods, Jesus asks His disciples who they think He is. It is here that the breathtaking revelation comes from Peter that Jesus is the Son of God and Jesus declares He will build His church and all the powers of death and hell would not be able to prevail against it (Matthew 16:13–19).

Chapter 5

The Gospels –
One Story, Four Witnesses

*'The New Testament is the best book the
world has known or will know.'*
(*Charles Dickens*)

A five-year-old boy had just one line to say in his school's Christmas play, 'I bring you good tidings!' After many rehearsals he asked his mother what 'tidings' were. She explained that they were news. The performance began and the little angel became flustered. After a long embarrassing silence he finally shouted out, 'Hey, have I got news for you!'

Those early disciples took the Gospel everywhere, proclaiming, 'Hey, have we got good news for you.' They chose the Greek word *'euanggelion'* which we translate 'Gospel' or 'Good news' to describe the amazing truth of God's love and power. The word was originally a secular word, for it was often used with reference to the emperor's birthday. It was a holiday, a day of good news.

When we come to the four Gospels it is important to remember two obvious facts. The first is that Jesus did not write them. He never wrote a book, so these are not books by Jesus but books about Him, which contain a large collection of His teaching. The second fact to remember is that there are four of them. This helps us to understand and interpret them, especially when we come to the same events recorded in different ways. Some have argued that this undermines their trustworthiness, but good scholarship has demonstrated the historical reliability of the Gospel material. It is part of their genius as well as their genuineness that God has seen fit to give us four accounts, seen through the eyes of different witnesses, yet with a beautiful harmony and consistency.

We must remember that the witnesses responsible for the Gospels not only saw the truth, but they were changed by it. For this reason they invariably bring out those things that influenced them and others to leave all they had and follow Jesus. Not everything is recorded as is true of Luke with Acts. The writers paint a picture of the whole by elaborating on a few characteristic persons and experiences, which bring out crucial points in the development of the events.

Four people reporting the same events will see different aspects, as well as highlight particular incidents influenced not only by their own perspectives, but also by the people they are reporting to and the purpose they are recording them for. Anyway, if the four accounts were just repeating each other, why would we need to have four? One would have done. So why are there four?

Personality and Purpose

This is a good question. After all, we do not have four Acts of the Apostles, so why four accounts about Jesus? As I have just said each particular Gospel was written for a special purpose, to a specific group and community of people. Take Mark's Gospel, which was written first. It is not only the shortest, but the fastest moving. Mark records more miracles than any other Gospel. Note the word '**immediately**,' mentioned over 30 times, which is the key word in the Gospel. It begins with very little introduction, no birth narratives, no genealogy, the writer explodes into his testimony and the style is very vivid and picturesque and although much of the subject matter is found in Matthew and Luke (they quote all but 31 verses), it's not simply repetition, for it contains many details, often personal touches, not found in either of the others.

It is called Mark's Gospel because the author was John Mark. John was his Jewish name and Mark his Roman name. He was the young man who went with Paul and Barnabas on their first missionary journey, but for some reason he left them at Perga and went home. This displeased Paul so much he refused to let Mark go on the second missionary journey. Later in Paul's ministry Mark won his favour again and was considered an important co-worker.

Even though it was Mark who wrote the Gospel it was Peter who furnished the information, and some ancient traditions actually refer to it as Peter's Gospel. The style is very like Peter, full of action and encounter. He dives straight into his theme, 'Jesus the divine wonder worker'. It was written for mainly Gentile Christians, hence the scarce mention of Old Testament references and explanation of Jewish words and customs (see 3:17; 5:41; 7:1–4, 11, 34).

Although Matthew's Gospel was probably not the first to be written, it is appropriate that it is the one right next to the Old Testament and beginning the New as it was addressed primarily to the Jews to convince them of the truth regarding Jesus. This explains why there are 76 references to Jewish prophecies and 53 quotations from the Old Testament. He specially emphasises Jesus' mission to the Jews and the key word, which is frequently repeated, is '**fulfilled**.' This is to emphasise that the Old Testament prophecies were fulfilled in Christ. The word 'Kingdom' appears some 50 times as Matthew both presents and proves that Jesus of Nazareth is the kingly Messiah of Jewish prophecy. This is a good Gospel to recommend to Jews as Matthew clearly points out that Jesus did not come to destroy the Law but to fulfil it (Matthew 5:17–20).

Matthew was a tax collector before he became a disciple, so it is not surprising to find him presenting a well-documented and detailed account. Even though there is such a major Jewish emphasis, he records that Jesus' mission was to establish His Church. Matthew is the only Gospel to use the word 'church' (16:13–23; 18:17). By the time Matthew was written the church had become a great force and factor in the life of a Christian and society. He ends by emphasising that even though Jesus came first to the Jews, the good news of the Kingdom is to go into all the world as God's love reaches out to all nations (Matthew 28:19, 20).

Luke, a physician and travelling companion of Paul, was also a great church historian. He was a Gentile, and he has the unique distinction of being the only New Testament writer who was not a Jew. Indeed he is the only writer in the whole Bible who was not Jewish. Taken together, Luke's two books, the other being Acts, are longer than Paul's combined letters, making Luke the major contributor to the New Testament. He addresses his opening remarks to a man named Theophilus, with the title 'most excellent' which is normally used for a high official in the Roman government. He writes, therefore, a very detailed and thoroughly researched account of Jesus, to prove to his Roman and Gentile readers the absolute truthfulness and trustworthiness of the things that Theophilus in particular had been taught.

He presents Jesus as the friend of the poor and the outcast and has a universal emphasis that in Jesus all the barriers are down as He is for all men without class or distinction. God's love reaches out to all, Samaritans (Luke 9:51–56; 10:30–37), and Gentiles (Luke 2:32; 3:6; 4:25–27; 7:9; 13:29).

John's Gospel is commonly referred to as the fourth Gospel not only because it was the last one written but because it is different in nature and structure to the other three. In fact more than 90% of John is not found in the other Gospel accounts. He says nothing about the Christmas story, Jesus' birth, temptations, exorcisms (dealing with evil spirits), Gethsemane, the Last Supper and Jesus' Ascension. His teaching is different in style from the other three Gospels, they have many short pithy sayings and parables, John focuses more on long sermons, deep involved thoughtful discourses and arguments, as he concentrates more on Christian belief than behaviour.

In John, Jesus talks more about Himself than anyone else. There are the seven 'I AM' statements, that give divine distinction to who He is. Of the eight miracles recorded, six are unique to John. These are called signs, as each one points to who Jesus claimed to be. There is also a geographical shift as John talks more about Jesus in Judea and Samaria as well as in Galilee, whereas the others concentrated more on Galilee. The other Gospels mention far more about the latter part of Jesus' activity while John focuses more on His earlier ministry, and the last week of His life, with over half the space in his Gospel given to the events of Christ's life and teaching during the several days leading to the cross and resurrection.

The reasons for the different emphasis become apparent when you consider that this was the last Gospel written and it would be pointless for John merely to repeat everything recorded and now widely circulated in the other three Gospels. Some fifty to sixty years had passed since Jesus' death and resurrection and John had a long time to dwell upon all that had taken place. Besides, the church now was no longer primarily Jewish but was more Gentile and so we have recorded in John and nowhere else what is probably the most famous and well known statement in Scripture and probably the world. It has been translated into more languages than any other piece of literature ever written:

> *'God so loved the world that he gave his one and only Son, that whoever believes in him should not perish but have eternal life.'* (John 3:16)

John wrote with a definite purpose:

> *'But these are written that you may believe that Jesus is the Christ, the Son of God, and that by believing you may have life in his name.'* (John 20:31)

The Greek word for 'believe' means 'to go on believing who Jesus is and in His name.' Heresies had already started to creep into the church and two in particular were threatening to cause great confusion and division. One was denying Jesus' humanity and the other denying His deity.

Their technical terms are Docetism (Jesus only appeared to be human) and Gnosticism (you could only come to God through secret knowledge, God did not create the world, matter is essentially evil, good and evil are equal and Jesus was not divine). So John emphasises that Jesus was both God and man. The world was created through Jesus, the Word became flesh, Thomas addressed Him as, *'My Lord and my God.'* He tells us that Jesus was thirsty, hungry and tired, all human characteristics. Jesus is both divine and fully human and God loved the world not just a few with special know-ledge, and everyone who believes in Jesus will be saved.

There is one more insight that helps us understand why and what John wrote and that is the place from which he was writing. His Gospel was written from Ephesus in Turkey and in that great city two wrong views had developed regarding both Jesus and John the Baptist.

They were holding too high a view of John and too low a view of Jesus. When the Apostle Paul came to Ephesus (Acts 19:3), he came across a group and the only baptism they had heard of or known was John the Baptist's. It seems that a sect had grown around his memory and name, something that would have appalled him. Therefore every reference to John the Baptist puts him in his right place, lower than Jesus, by using the Baptist's own words to prove this. In John 3:27–30, John replied when told about the success of Jesus' ministry:

> *'A man can receive only what is given him from heaven. You yourselves can testify that I said, "I am not the Christ but am sent ahead of him." The bride belongs to the bridegroom. The friend who attends the bridegroom waits and listens for him, and is full of joy when he hears the bridegroom's voice. That joy is mine, and it is now complete. He must become greater; I must become less.'*

The table on the next page is a helpful though not exhaustive guide to understanding the four Gospels.

Even the introduction to each Gospel gives a summary interpretation of what the writer had in mind and why he has written in such a style with such meaning. It is obvious that the four Gospels begin in different places but they become even more meaningful when you understand where and why.

Gospel	Characteristic
Matthew	What Jesus said
Mark	What Jesus did
Luke	What Jesus felt
John	Who Jesus is
Matthew	Jesus is the Son of David
Mark	Jesus is the Servant of God and Man
Luke	Jesus is the Son of Man
John	Jesus is the Son of God
Matthew	Written primarily for the Jews
Mark	Written primarily for the Gentiles
Luke	Written primarily for the Gentiles and to Theophilus a Roman official
John	Written for the whole world

Mark gets into Jesus' ministry almost straightaway, while Matthew, writing for the Jews, goes back to Abraham. Luke, in his genealogy, traces back to Adam, whereas John goes back as far as the mind can go when he says, *'In the beginning was the Word.'*

When reading these accounts of Jesus, we need always to remember that each writer was inspired and aided by the Holy Spirit. David C.C. Watson in his book *Fact or Fantasy*, makes the interesting observation about the length of the four Gospels. He said that,

> 'Mark's Gospel would just about fit onto the middle pages of a full-size newspaper. Matthew is about half as long again with 15,000 words and Luke is about 10% more than Matthew. This is an astonishing fact when we consider what they might have been. Most modern biographies run to about 150,000 words, ten times longer than Matthew and the Jewish historian Josephus AD 90 took 750,000 words to write his *Antiquities and Wars of the Jews*.
>
> Equally fascinating is the actual number of Jesus' words recorded. If you took the time to make a detailed

count of every word spoken by Jesus, a red-letter Bible would help, you would find there are some 1,530 verses. Multiply this by 20 which is about the average number of words to a verse and you have a total of 30,600. This number includes many passages that overlap in the four Gospels, so 30,600 is a maximum number. Charles Haddon Spurgeon, the famous Baptist preacher during the last century, was a prolific speaker and writer. His recorded sermons from 1861–1891 fill 62 volumes of 700 pages each and it is said that in tract form they would reach from here to the moon.

During the three years of Jesus' ministry if He preached 15 times each week which was about the same as John Wesley, and spoke at about 120 words a minute multiplied by 20 hours for each week, Jesus would have spoken some six million words a year, a total of 18 million during the three years He ministered. Even if you think this estimate is too high and you halved it to nine million we have to conclude that there is much of what He said not recorded and He must have given the same teaching many different times and occasions.

"Jesus did many other miraculous signs in the presence of his disciples, which are not recorded in this book. But these are written that you may believe that Jesus is the Christ, the Son of God, and that by believing you may have life in his name." (John 20:30–31)

One very important reason for short Gospels and selected words has been discovered only this century. There are some 6,000 languages which require Bible translation and the Bible has been described by linguistical experts as the most translatable and comprehensive religious book that has ever been written.'

This condensing applies not only to what Jesus said but also to what He did. John ends his Gospel fully aware of everything else that had been written about Jesus by saying,

'Jesus did many other things as well. If every one of them were written down, I suppose that even the whole world would not have room for the books that would be written.'

(John 21:25)

This is beautifully expressed early in Jesus' ministry by John. His first miracle was at Cana in Galilee (John 2:1–11). From there He travelled to Capernaum, which was to become His base, staying a few days before going up to Jerusalem for the Passover. While there He drove the animals from the Temple and overturned the money changers' tables. He also did many miraculous signs,

'Now while he was in Jerusalem at the Passover Feast, many people saw the miraculous signs he was doing and believed in his name.' (John 2:23)

This is what Nicodemus refers to in John 3:2,

'He came to Jesus at night and said, "Rabbi, we know you are a teacher who has come from God. For no one could perform the miraculous signs you are doing if God were not with him."'

What all these miraculous signs were we do not know. Jesus' ministry was so full of them that they were too many to mention. The Gospels are not full biographies of Jesus. They give little information of His physical details or personal features and leave virtually all the first thirty years of His life unmentioned. The last week of His life is almost seven times longer than the record of His first year of ministry. The Gospels are primarily a proclamation of Good News, the Good News about Jesus Christ.

Chapter 6

The Four Gospels –
Why They Were Written

'Confucius said, "I know the way," Krishna said, "I see the way," Mohammed said, "I am a prophet of the way," Buddha said, "I am seeking the way," The New Age says, "We are on the way." Jesus said, "I AM the Way." '

A children's Sunday School class was asked by its teacher what they would do if Jesus walked into the classroom. One little girl said, 'Miss, I would take hold of my Bible, give it to Him and say. "Jesus, this is your life." '

We may smile at such a reply, not only because it reflects a child's response, but because it captures great spiritual truth. On one occasion Jesus said to the Pharisees who were opposing him,

> *'You diligently study the Scriptures because you think that by them you possess eternal life. These are the Scriptures that testify about me.'* (John 5:39)

These were men who not only diligently read and studied the Scriptures but also committed them to memory, yet Jesus rebuked them because despite all their knowledge they were spiritually blinded by their pride and prejudice as to who He was.

Throughout the Old Testament, clear testimony is given to Jesus, both in the Law with its types, offerings and sacrifices, and in the poetic and prophetic books where there are clear predictions and references concerning His birth, life, ministry, death, resurrection, second coming and universal reign.

What the Bible Scholar and historian F.F. Bruce says about this is very illuminating.

> 'The Old Testament was the church's first Bible. One of the extraordinary features of the church's expansion in the second century AD was the number of educated pagans who were converted not to Judaism but to Christianity. Jews and Christians alike at the time read the Old Testament but through different spectacles.'

Throughout the New Testament the apostles were constantly appealing to two areas of Jesus' life to establish His Messiahship. One was His resurrection and the other was fulfilled Messianic prophecy. In his book *Science Speaks*, Professor Peter Stoner devotes a whole chapter to the 'Christ of Prophecy.' He takes just eight prophecies out of hundreds that were fulfilled in Jesus, and shows through mathematical analysis that the possibility of them being fulfilled in any one person through chance, coincidence or complicity is totally beyond the realms of any possibility. Remember he is taking just eight of hundreds.

His conclusions, which have been examined by the American Scientific Affiliation and in general found to be dependable and accurate in regard to the scientific material presented, are staggering. Taking the predictions concerning, where the Messiah would be born (Micah 5:2), John the Baptist as the forerunner (Malachi 3:1), Jesus' entry riding into Jerusalem on a colt (Zechariah 9:9), His betrayal by a friend, causing wounds in His hands (Zechariah 13:6), betrayed for thirty pieces of silver (Zechariah 11:12), the thirty pieces of silver not being returned and cast to the potter in the house of the Lord (Zechariah 11:13), events leading to His crucifixion (Isaiah 53:7), the way He died (Psalm 22:16), the chance that any man would be able to fulfil just these eight predictions is a staggering 1 in 100,000,000,000,000,000.

Since there are over three hundred prophecies that speak of Christ's first coming, Stoner then goes on to calculate forty eight prophecies being fulfilled in just one man. His figures are a staggering 1 in 10 with 157 zeros. This is how it looks:

1 in
10,000,000,000,000,000,000,000,000,000,000,000,
000,000,000,000,000,000,000,000,000,000,000,000,
000,000,000,000,000,000,000,000,000,000,000,000,
000,000,000,000,000,000,000,000,000,000,000,000,
000,000,000,000,000

This brings us nicely to understanding why the Gospels were written in the first place.

Defending the Faith

Apologetics   Luke introduces his Gospel,

> *'Many have undertaken to draw up an account of the things that have been fulfilled among us, just as they were handed down to us by those who from the first were eyewitnesses and servants of the word. Therefore, since I myself have carefully investigated everything from the beginning, it seemed good also to me to write an orderly account for you, most excellent Theophilus, so that you may know the certainty of the things you have been taught.'*   (Luke 1:1–4)

Apologetics is not apologising for what the Christian faith teaches, quite the opposite, it is giving factual, intelligible reason for what is believed. Neither is it something passive and defensive, but rather is alive and active in challenging us to examine and give an account of our beliefs and world view in the light of God's Word and revelation in Jesus Christ.

C.S. Lewis, one of this century's greatest Christian apologists, wrote after his conversion from atheism,

> 'Anyone who is honestly trying to be a Christian will soon find his intelligence being sharpened. One of

the reasons why it needs no special education to be a Christian is that Christianity is an education itself. That is why an uneducated believer like John Bunyan was able to write a book, *Pilgrim's Progress*, that has astonished the whole world.'

He said on another occasion,

'If you are thinking of becoming a Christian it is going to take the whole of you, brains and all.'

Before the Gospels were written their accounts would have been passed on orally, as was traditionally the way such teachings were communicated. But as the church grew and both interest and opposition increased this was no longer sufficient. So as the apostles grew older they recorded their eye witness accounts to be written down and distributed to those in the rapidly expanding church and for those of future generations.

Defining The Faith

Teaching

'They devoted themselves to the apostles' teaching and to the fellowship, to the breaking of bread and to prayer.'

(Acts 2:42)

The initial explosive growth of the church was only the beginning. Within a few years the church in Jerusalem was numbered in tens of thousands. Within thirty years the Gospel had penetrated into Rome itself with even those in Caesar's own household followers of Jesus Christ (Philippians 4:22). Within 70 years it had succeeded in emptying and closing down so many pagan temples that their business in animals for sacrifice was no longer necessary. Jesus' command to His disciples was that they should 'make disciples.' Converts needed to be taught, heresy had to be exposed and truth conveyed.

Commenting on 2 Timothy 4:13, *'When you come, bring the*

cloak that I left with Carpus at Troas, and my scrolls, especially the parchments,' C.H. Spurgeon wrote,

> 'Paul is inspired, yet he wants books! He has been preaching at least for thirty years, yet he wants books. He has had a wider experience than most men, yet he wants books! He has been caught up into the third heaven and has heard things which it is unlawful to utter, he has written the major part of the New Testament, yet he wants books!'

Every revival in church history has brought with it an increased desire for learning and education among those converted. We owe our schools to the Gospel. How to educate the masses was no easy matter, but it was the church that took the lead and Sunday Schools were established. The 18th century revival under Wesley and Whitefield played a major part in this as these schools multiplied giving religious instruction to thousands. Yet they were only part of the answer as they met for only one day a week and specialised only in Bible teaching. By 1815 elementary education was becoming more and more widespread but it was entirely on private, mostly Christian, initiative.

Declaring the Faith

Evangelism   The Good News of Jesus was for the whole world. Indeed within a relatively short period of time those early disciples were being accused of, *'Turning the whole world upside down'* (Acts 17:6). Their message was all about Jesus and everywhere they went they proclaimed Him and demonstrated with the signs and wonders that accompanied their testimony that Jesus Christ is the Risen Lord.

One 20th century bishop lamented to a friend, 'When I read about the early church and the ministry of the Apostle Paul, there seems to have either been a rebellion or a revival everywhere he went. Everywhere I go people offer me a cup of tea.' It is only when the church is turned inside out the world is turned upside down.

John records towards the end of his Gospel the reason why he wrote it,

> *'These are written that you may believe that Jesus is the Christ, the Son of God, and that by believing you may have life in his name.'*　　　　　　　　　　　　　(John 20:31)

Chapter 7

The Four Gospels –
Why We Can Trust Them

'In 1778, Voltaire boasted that in 100 years
Christianity would be swept from existence.
Fifty years after his death the Geneva
Bible Society was printing and
distributing Bibles from his home.'

William Hume was an atheist who wrote a spurious Gospel to bring the New Testament into contempt. He maintained he could write a Gospel of his own that would be even better than the Gospel of John. When the book was published there was such an outcry that he did something he had not bothered to do before, he investigated the accounts in the Gospels so that he might be able to reply to his opponents' criticisms. While reading them a flood of light burst upon him that led to his conversion and then he wrote:

> 'The proudest heart that ever beat
> Hath been subdued in me.
> The vilest will that ever rose
> To scorn Thy word or aid Thy foes
> Is quelled, my God, by Thee.
>
> Thy will and not my will be done,
> My heart be ever Thine
> Confessing Thee the mighty Word
> I hail Thee, Christ, my God, my Lord
> And make Thy Name my sign.'

Archaeological Evidence

Sir William Ramsay was a Scottish archaeologist who didn't believe the Bible, and he was sure he could prove that the book of Acts was full of mistakes and could not be trusted. He didn't even believe that Luke wrote it. He said it was written one hundred years after Luke's time by someone who didn't even know what he was writing about. Ramsay thought the writer had just made up some of the stories because they would sound good and was firmly convinced of his belief. In 1880 he went on his first expedition to the places described in Acts. He was the first to find out that the city of Iconium was not part of the district of Lycaonia, as the experts in his day used to think. He also found that the people of Lycaonia even spoke their own language. But the book of Acts, which Ramsay didn't believe, had already explained that fact, in chapter 14:1–11.

Ramsay went on to become one of the world's greatest experts on life in New Testament times, and one of the greatest archaeologists who ever lived. His research led him to write many excellent books, which show how accurate and believable the New Testament is. In one of these books he announced that he had become a Christian. Regarding Luke's ability as a historian, Ramsay concluded after thirty years of study that, 'Luke is a historian of the first rank, not merely are his statements of fact trustworthy but this author should be placed along with the very greatest of historians.' He added, 'Luke's history is unsurpassed in respect of its trustworthiness.'

The Gospels are both trustworthy and life transforming. This is what C.H. Spurgeon, the great preacher of the last century, was referring to when he said, 'The Bible is like a lion. It needs no defence, let it loose, and it will defend itself.' Therefore, when we ask and seek to answer the question, 'Can we trust what the Bible says?' we come not with proud argument but rather with humble acknowledgement that God has not only inspired the original manuscripts of

Scripture but has also been watching over His word as it has been faithfully recorded down the centuries.

While it is therefore acknowledged that it is the original manuscripts that were inerrant as men wrote moved by the Holy Spirit, it can also be shown that a faithful and meticulous record has been kept and handed down to us today.

While I was compiling the chronological harmony of *The Life of Jesus* contained in the four Gospels, I was aware of just how perfectly the accounts affirmed each other. There was nothing that contradicted itself for even the more difficult passages to harmonise blended together when the details of background and language were researched. The next time someone tells you that the Bible is full of contradictions, ask them to show you where. They have usually never bothered reading or studying the Scriptures to find out, because if they had they would realise how perfectly everything flows together.

I am reminded of the tourist who was looking nonchalantly around a Florence art gallery, and exclaimed, 'Are these your masterpieces? I certainly don't see much in them.' 'Sir,' said the curator, 'It is not the pictures but the people who are on trial here.'

Historians have pointed out that on the basis of manuscript evidence alone, the writings of the New Testament were the most frequently copied and widely circulated books in ancient times. Although we do not possess the original manuscripts (Autographs) of the New Testament the faithful work of manuscript copyists over the centuries has ensured that we have the Gospel accounts in amazing accuracy. Even though it may be argued there are slight variant readings in a number of these manuscripts, there is not a single point of doctrine, which hangs on a disputed reading, and there is no ambiguity about what any text actually says.

The procedure for assessing the reliability of the New Testament is the same as for any other important ancient document when the original no longer exists. There are three vital factors. First, the bibliographical test – have the original manuscripts been handed down faithfully? Then there is the internal evidence test – what the Gospels tell us about themselves. Finally there is the external evidence test – an examination of other sources that shed light, such as contemporary ancient literature.

Following this process, which is the one used to check the authenticity of all ancient writings, we can come to an accurate decision regarding the accuracy of modern belief based upon ancient manuscripts. When we find several copies which are basically similar and fairly near in time to the original author, we are able to build a case for the reliability of their trustworthiness.

A time span which seems great to us will satisfy the experts, provided there are enough copies to enable them to cross-check. (Provided, also, that these copies were not all taken from the same earlier copy.)

Following is a table, which compares the New Testament with some other ancient manuscripts and accounts.

Author	When written	Earliest copy	Time span	Number of copies
Caesar	100–44 BC	AD 900	1,000 years	10
Plato's works	427–347 BC	AD 900	1,200 years	7
Aristotle's works	384–322 BC	AD 1100	1,400 years	49
Homer (*Iliad*)	900 BC	400 BC	500 years	643
New Testament[1]	AD 40–100	AD 125 [2]	25 years	Over 24,000

[1] This includes more than 5,300 known Greek manuscripts, over 10,000 Latin Vulgate manuscripts and at least 9,300 other early versions.
[2] In a Manchester university there is a fragment of the Gospel of John which experts have dated between AD 100 and AD 125.

In a recent book, Carsten Thiede, a German papyrologist, suggests that fragments catalogued as Magdalen GR 17 (portions of Matthew's Gospel 26:7–8; 26:31; 26:10; 32–33; 26:14–15; 22–23) at an Oxford University archive, date back not as earlier thought, to the second century, but into the first century. He has come to this conclusion after extensive investigation and is convinced that the manuscript dates back giving an eye witness account of the life and ministry of Jesus. If his research proves correct then the fragments will be the earliest examples ever found proving once again the incredible accuracy and authenticity of the New Testament and Gospel accounts.

Another table which follows shows the Early Church Fathers' quotation of the New Testament. They were writing and recalling these events within a comparatively short time after the last New Testament letter was completed.

Writer	Gospels	Acts	Paul's letters	General epistles	Revelation	Total
Justin Martyr	268	10	43	6	3	330
Irenaeus	1038	194	499	23	65	1819
Clement of Alexandria	1017	44	1127	207	11	2406
Origen	9231	349	7778	399	165	17922
Tertullian	3822	502	2609	120	205	7258
Hippolytus	734	42	387	27	188	1378
Eusebius	3258	211	1592	88	27	5176
Totals	**19368**	**1352**	**14035**	**870**	**664**	**36282**

Two men not mentioned in that list are also worth noting. The first is Papias, who became Bishop of Hierapolis in Asia Minor around AD 135. He wrote,

> 'And the elder said this also: Mark, having become the interpreter of Peter, wrote down accurately everything he remembered, without however recording in order what was either said or done by Christ. For neither did he hear the Lord, nor did he follow Him; but afterwards, as I said, followed Peter, who adapted his instructions to the needs of his hearers, but had no design of giving a connected account of the Lord's oracles.'

The other is a man named Tatian, born in Mesopotamia of Syrian parents in AD 110. He became a Christian while at Rome, through the teaching of Justin Martyr, but afterwards adopted a Gnostic heresy. His most famous book was a *Harmony of the Four Gospels* which became very popular but was later proscribed by the Bishops as being tainted with Tatian's Gnosticism, and so disappeared from view.

Whenever a prominent religious figure makes any statements that cast doubt on the Bible's accuracy or on Jesus' character, there is always a hype of publicity and comment within the media. Obviously controversy is news whereas orthodoxy isn't. Perhaps the most notable example of this is in the case of the late Bishop John Robinson who caused an avalanche of publicity and argument both in the social and religious world, when he published his book, *Honest to God*. To say the least it would not have been a publication the Apostle Paul would have enjoyed, yet it sold millions of copies.

Years later he wrote a much better book, *Can We Trust The New Testament?* It generated no publicity in the secular world, no comments by the media, no fanfare of support from the liberal theologians, and it has sold only a fraction of the number his other book did. Why? Probably because it was one of the most orthodox books he ever wrote and orthodoxy doesn't make the news. Sensation, even if it is not true, is often preferred to the truth that has been accepted and established. In this book John Robinson asserted that the New Testament books were written much sooner than the liberal school of thought suggested. He went on to say,

> 'The wealth of manuscripts, and above all the narrow interval of time between the writing and the earliest extant copies, make it by far the best attested text of any ancient writing in the world.'

The late Professor Fredric G. Kenyon, the director of the British Museum, was one of the most respected New Testament textual scholars this century. After a professional lifetime of in-depth review and analysis of the New Testament manuscripts, he concluded that the present text in our Bible is absolutely reliable. He wrote in his book *The Story of the Bible*,

> 'It is reassuring at the end to find that the general result of all these discoveries and all this study is to strengthen

the proof of the authenticity of the Scriptures, and our conviction that we have in our hands, in substantial integrity, the veritable Word of God.'

In his book *The Bible and Archaeology*, he went on to state,

'The interval between the dates of the original composition and the earliest extant evidence becomes so small as to be negligible, and the last foundation for any doubt that the Scriptures have come down to us substantially as they were written has now been removed.'

Michael Green concludes his chapter on 'Running away from History,' in his book *Runaway World* with the following story,

'I remember a research scientist once saying to me that he thought the story of Jesus mythical. I asked him when he had last read it. He had to admit that it was a very long time ago. I said to him something like this, "You are a scientist. You are accustomed to modifying your preconceived theories if the evidence warrants it. I suggest that you apply the same principle here. Examine the evidence at first hand. Be open to wherever it may lead you, and see what happens." I next met the man some months later at a Christian meeting. "I did what you suggested," he said, "and it has made a Christian of me."'

The evidence for the truth and trustworthiness of the Gospel story cannot compel you to believe if you refuse to do so. We all have a will and with it make choices. The evidence for the link between smoking and lung cancer is overwhelming. Every cigarette packet and poster carries a health warning, a death warning would be a better way to describe it. Yet despite the evidence many either refuse to acknowledge it or simply dismiss it. The story is told of one smoker, who was so annoyed over the warnings about smoking that he exclaimed, 'That does it, I'm going to quit reading those warnings for good.'

SECTION 2

The Life of Jesus and the Harmonisation of the Gospels

Chapter 8

Announcing the Birth of Jesus

*'In him was life,
and that life was the life of men.'*

***The Apostle John introduces his account of the life of
Jesus with the words***

In the beginning was the Word, and the Word was with God,
and the Word was God. He was with God in the beginning.
Through him all things were made; without him nothing was
made that has been made. In him was life, and that life
was the light of men. The light shines in the darkness, but
the darkness has not understood it. There came a man who
was sent from God; his name was John. He came as a witness
to testify concerning that light, so that through him all men
might believe. He himself was not the light; he came only as
a witness to the light. The true light that gives light to every
man was coming into the world.

He was in the world, and though the world was made
through him, the world did not recognise him. He came to
that which was his own, but his own did not receive him. Yet
to all who received him, to those who believed in his name,
he gave the right to become children of God, children born
not of natural descent, nor of human decision or a husband's
will, but born of God. The Word became flesh and made his
dwelling among us. We have seen his glory, the glory of the
One and Only, who came from the Father, full of grace and
truth.

John the Baptist testifies concerning him. He cries out, saying, 'This was he of whom I said, "He who comes after me has surpassed me because he was before me."' From the fullness of his grace we have all received one blessing after another. For the law was given through Moses; grace and truth came through Jesus Christ. No one has ever seen God, but God the One and Only, who is at the Father's side, has made him known.

The writer Luke introduces his history of the life of Jesus with a short introductory letter to Theophilus

Many have undertaken to draw up an account of the things that have been fulfilled among us, just as they were handed down to us by those who from the first were eyewitnesses and servants of the word. Therefore, since I myself have carefully investigated everything from the beginning, it seemed good also to me to write an orderly account for you, most excellent Theophilus, so that you may know the certainty of the things you have been taught. In the time of Herod king of Judea there was a priest named Zechariah, who belonged to the priestly division of Abijah; his wife Elizabeth was also a descendant of Aaron. Both of them were upright in the sight of God, observing all the Lord's commandments and regulations blamelessly. But they had no children, because Elizabeth was barren; and they were both well along in years.

The announcement of the birth of John the Baptist – around 5 BC

Once when Zechariah's division was on duty and he was serving as priest before God, he was chosen by lot, according to the custom of the priesthood, to go into the Temple of the Lord and burn incense. And when the time for the burning of incense came, all the assembled worshippers were praying outside. Then an angel of the Lord appeared to him, standing at the right side of the altar of incense. When Zechariah saw him, he was startled and was gripped with fear. But the angel said to him, 'Do not be afraid, Zechariah; your prayer has been heard. Your wife Elizabeth will bear you a son, and you are to give him the name John. He will be a joy and delight to you, and many will rejoice because of his birth, for he will be great in the sight of the Lord. He is never to take wine or other fermented drink, and he will be filled with the Holy Spirit even from birth. Many of the people of Israel will he bring back to the Lord their God. And he will go on before the Lord, in the spirit and power of Elijah, to turn the hearts of the fathers to their children and the disobedient to the wisdom of the righteous to make ready a people prepared for the Lord.'

Zechariah asked the angel, 'How can I be sure of this? I am an old man and my wife is well along in years.' The angel answered, 'I am Gabriel. I stand in the presence of God, and I have been sent to speak to you and to tell you this good news. And now you will be silent and not able to speak until the day this happens, because you did not believe my words, which will come true at their proper time.'

Meanwhile, the people were waiting for Zechariah and wondering why he stayed so long in the temple. When he came out, he could not speak to them. They realised he had seen a vision in the temple, for he kept making signs to them but remained unable to speak. When his time of service was completed, he returned home. After this his wife Elizabeth became pregnant and for five months remained in seclusion. 'The Lord has done this for me,' she said. 'In these days he has shown his favour and taken away my disgrace among the people.'

The announcement of the birth of Jesus

In the sixth month, God sent the angel Gabriel to Nazareth, a town in Galilee, to a virgin pledged to be married to a man named Joseph, a descendant of David. The virgin's name was Mary. The angel went to her and said, 'Greetings, you who are highly favoured! The Lord is with you.' Mary was greatly troubled at his words and wondered what kind of greeting this might be. But the angel said to her, 'Do not be afraid, Mary, you have found favour with God. You will be with child and give birth to a son, and you are to give him the name Jesus. He will be great and will be called the Son of the Most High. The Lord God will give him the throne of his father David, and he will reign over the house of Jacob forever; his kingdom will never end.' 'How will this be,' Mary asked the angel, 'Since I am a virgin?'

The angel answered, 'The Holy Spirit will come upon you, and the power of the Most High will overshadow you. So the holy one to be born will be called the Son of God. Even Elizabeth your relative is going to have a child in her old age, and she who was said to be barren is in her sixth month. For nothing is impossible with God.' 'I am the Lord's servant,' Mary answered. 'May it be to me as you have said.' Then the angel left her.

At that time Mary got ready and hurried to a town in the hill country of Judea, where she entered Zechariah's home and greeted Elizabeth. When Elizabeth heard Mary's greeting, the baby leaped in her womb, and Elizabeth was filled with the Holy Spirit. In a loud voice she exclaimed, 'Blessed are you among women, and blessed is the child you will bear! But why am I so favoured, that the mother of my Lord should come to me? As soon as the sound of your greeting reached my ears, the baby in my womb leaped for joy. Blessed is she who has believed that what the Lord has said to her will be accomplished!'

And Mary said,

> 'My soul glorifies the Lord
>   and my spirit rejoices in God my Saviour,
> for he has been mindful
>   of the humble state of his servant.
> From now on all generations will call me blessed,
>   for the Mighty One has done great things for me
>   holy is his name.
> His mercy extends to those who fear him,
>   from generation to generation.

He has performed mighty deeds with his arm;
> he has scattered those who are proud in their inmost
>> thoughts.
He has brought down rulers from their thrones
> but has lifted up the humble.
He has filled the hungry with good things
> but has sent the rich away empty.
He has helped his servant Israel,
> remembering to be merciful
to Abraham and his descendants forever,
> even as he said to our fathers.'

Mary stayed with Elizabeth for about three months and then returned home.

The birth of John the Baptist

When it was time for Elizabeth to have her baby, she gave birth to a son. Her neighbours and relatives heard that the Lord had shown her great mercy, and they shared her joy.

On the eighth day they came to circumcise the child, and they were going to name him after his father Zechariah, but his mother spoke up and said, 'No! He is to be called John.' They said to her, 'There is no one among your relatives who has that name.' Then they made signs to his father, to find out what he would like to name the child. He asked for a writing tablet, and to everyone's astonishment he wrote, 'His name is John.' Immediately his mouth was opened and his tongue was loosed, and he began to speak, praising God. The neighbours were all filled with awe, and throughout the hill country of Judea people were talking about all these things. Everyone who heard this wondered about it, asking, 'What then is this child going to be?' For the Lord's hand was with him.

His father Zechariah was filled with the Holy Spirit and prophesied,

> 'Praise be to the Lord, the God of Israel,
>> because he has come and has redeemed his people.

He has raised up a horn of salvation for us
   in the house of his servant David
(as he said through his holy prophets of long ago),
salvation from our enemies
   and from the hand of all who hate us
to show mercy to our fathers
   and to remember his holy covenant,
   the oath he swore to our father Abraham:
to rescue us from the hand of our enemies,
   and to enable us to serve him without fear
   in holiness and righteousness before him all our
      days.
And you, my child, will be called a prophet of the Most
    High;
   for you will go on before the Lord to prepare the way
      for him,
to give his people the knowledge of salvation
   through the forgiveness of their sins,
because of the tender mercy of our God,
   by which the rising sun will come to us from heaven
to shine on those living in darkness
   and in the shadow of death,
to guide our feet into the path of peace.'

And the child grew and became strong in spirit; and he lived in the desert until he appeared publicly to Israel.

Chapter 9

The Early Years

'You are to give him the name Jesus, because he will save his people from their sins.'

The birth of Jesus – around 4 BC

This is how the birth of Jesus Christ came about: His mother Mary was pledged to be married to Joseph, but before they came together, she was found to be with child through the Holy Spirit. Because Joseph her husband was a righteous man and did not want to expose her to public disgrace, he had in mind to divorce her quietly. But after he had considered this, an angel of the Lord appeared to him in a dream and said, 'Joseph son of David, do not be afraid to take Mary home as your wife, because what is conceived in her is from the Holy Spirit. She will give birth to a son, and you are to give him the name Jesus, because he will save his people from their sins.' All this took place to fulfil what the Lord had said through the prophet, 'The virgin will be with child and will give birth to a son, and they will call him Immanuel' which means, 'God with us.' When Joseph woke up, he did what the angel of the Lord had commanded him and took Mary home as his wife. But he had no union with her until she gave birth to a son. And he gave him the name Jesus.

In those days Caesar Augustus issued a decree that a census should be taken of the entire Roman world. (This was the first census that took place while Quirinius was governor of Syria.) Everyone went to his own town to register. So Joseph also went up from the town of Nazareth in Galilee to Judea, to Bethlehem the town of David, because he belonged to the house and line of David. He went there to register with Mary, who was pledged to be married to him and was expecting a child. While they were there, the time came for the baby to be born, and she gave birth to her firstborn, a son. She wrapped him in cloths and placed him in a manger, because there was no room for them in the inn. And there were shepherds living out in the fields nearby, keeping watch over their flocks at night. An angel of the Lord appeared to them, and the glory of the Lord shone around them, and they were terrified. But the angel said to them, 'Do not be afraid. I bring you good news of great joy that will be for all the people. Today, in the town of David, a Saviour has been born to you; he is Christ the Lord. This will be a sign to you: You will find a baby wrapped in cloths and lying in a manger.' Suddenly a great company of the heavenly host appeared with the angel, praising God and saying, 'Glory to God in the highest, and on earth peace to men on whom his favour rests.'

When the angels had left them and gone into heaven, the shepherds said to one another, 'Let's go to Bethlehem and see this thing that has happened, which the Lord has told us about.' So they hurried off and found Mary and Joseph, and the baby, who was lying in the manger. When they had seen him, they spread the word concerning what had been told them about this child, and all who heard it were amazed at what the shepherds said to them. But Mary treasured up all these things and pondered them in her heart. The shepherds returned, glorifying and praising God for all the things they had heard and seen, which were just as they had been told.

On the eighth day, when it was time to circumcise him, he was named Jesus, the name the angel had given him before he had been conceived. When the time of their purification according to the Law of Moses had been completed, Joseph and Mary took him to Jerusalem to present him to the Lord (as it is written in the Law of the Lord, 'Every firstborn male is to be consecrated to the Lord'), and to offer a sacrifice in keeping with what is said in the Law of the Lord: 'A pair of doves or two young pigeons.'

Now there was a man in Jerusalem called Simeon, who was righteous and devout. He was waiting for the consolation of Israel, and the Holy Spirit was upon him. It had been revealed to him by the Holy Spirit that he would not die before he had seen the Lord's Christ. Moved by the Spirit, he went into the temple courts. When the parents brought in the child Jesus to do for him what the custom of the Law required, Simeon took him in his arms and praised God, saying:

'Sovereign Lord, as you have promised,
  you now dismiss your servant in peace.
For my eyes have seen your salvation,
  which you have prepared in the sight of all people,
a light for revelation to the Gentiles
  and for glory to your people Israel.'

The child's father and mother marvelled at what was said about him. Then Simeon blessed them and said to Mary, his mother, 'This child is destined to cause the falling and rising of many in Israel, and to be a sign that will be spoken against, so that the thoughts of many hearts will be revealed. And a sword will pierce your own soul too.'

There was also a prophetess, Anna, the daughter of Phanuel, of the tribe of Asher. She was very old; she had lived with her husband seven years after her marriage, and then was a widow until she was eighty-four. She never left the temple but worshipped night and day, fasting and praying. Coming up to them at that very moment, she gave thanks to God and spoke about the child to all who were looking forward to the redemption of Jerusalem.

The Wisemen visit the child Jesus – around 3 BC

After Jesus was born in Bethlehem in Judea, during the time of King Herod, Magi from the east came to Jerusalem and asked, 'Where is the one who has been born king of the Jews? We saw his star in the east and have come to worship him.' When King Herod heard this he was disturbed, and all

Jerusalem with him. When he had called together all the people's chief priests and teachers of the law, he asked them where the Christ was to be born. 'In Bethlehem in Judea,' they replied, 'for this is what the prophet has written:

"But you, Bethlehem, in the land of Judah,
   are by no means least among the rulers of Judah;
for out of you will come a ruler
   who will be the shepherd of my people Israel."'

Then Herod called the Magi secretly and found out from them the exact time the star had appeared. He sent them to Bethlehem and said, 'Go and make a careful search for the child. As soon as you find him, report to me, so that I too may go and worship him.' After they had heard the king, they went on their way, and the star they had seen in the east went ahead of them until it stopped over the place where the child was. When they saw the star, they were overjoyed.

On coming to the house, they saw the child with his mother Mary, and they bowed down and worshipped him. Then they opened their treasures and presented him with gifts of gold and of incense and of myrrh. Having been warned in a dream not to go back to Herod, they returned to their country by another route.

When they had gone, an angel of the Lord appeared to Joseph in a dream. 'Get up,' he said, 'Take the child and his mother and escape to Egypt. Stay there until I tell you, for Herod is going to search for the child to kill him.' So he got up, took the child and his mother during the night and left for Egypt, where he stayed until the death of Herod. So was fulfilled what the Lord had said through the prophet, 'Out of Egypt I called my son.' When Herod realised that he had been outwitted by the Magi, he was furious, and he gave orders to kill all the boys in Bethlehem and its vicinity who were two years old and under, in accordance with the time he had learned from the Magi.

Then what was said through the prophet Jeremiah was fulfilled:

'A voice is heard in Ramah,
   weeping and great mourning,
Rachel weeping for her children
   and refusing to be comforted,
because they are no more.'

Around 2 BC

After Herod died, an angel of the Lord appeared in a dream to Joseph in Egypt and said, 'Get up, take the child and his mother and go to the land of Israel, for those who were trying to take the child's life are dead.' So he got up, took the child and his mother and went to the land of Israel. But when he heard that Archelaus was reigning in Judea in place of his father Herod, he was afraid to go there. Having been warned in a dream, he withdrew and returned to the district of Galilee, to live in their own town of Nazareth. So was fulfilled what was said through the prophets, 'He will be called a Nazarene.' And the child grew and became strong; he was filled with wisdom, and the grace of God was upon him.

Jesus' childhood – around AD 8

Every year his parents went to Jerusalem for the Feast of the Passover. When he was twelve years old, they went up to the Feast, according to the custom. After the Feast was over, while his parents were returning home, the boy Jesus stayed behind in Jerusalem, but they were unaware of it. Thinking he was in their company, they travelled on for a day. Then they began looking for him among their relatives and friends. When they did not find him, they went back to Jerusalem to look for him. After three days they found him in the temple courts, sitting among the teachers, listening to them and asking them questions. Everyone who heard him was amazed at his understanding and his answers. When his parents saw him, they were astonished. His mother said to him, 'Son, why have you treated us like this? Your father and I have been anxiously searching for you.' *'Why were you searching for me?'* he asked. *'Didn't you know I had to be in my Father's house?'* But they did not understand what he was saying to them. Then he went down to Nazareth with them and was obedient to them. But his mother treasured all these things in her heart. And Jesus grew in wisdom and stature, and in favour with God and men.

The ministry of John the Baptist – early AD 26

In the fifteenth year of the reign of Tiberius Caesar when Pontius Pilate was governor of Judea, Herod tetrarch of Galilee, his brother Philip tetrarch of Iturea and Traconitis, and Lysanias tetrarch of Abilene, during the high priesthood of Annas and Caiaphas, the word of God came to John son of Zechariah in the desert. He went into all the country around the Jordan, preaching a baptism of repentance for the forgiveness of sins.

As is written in the book of the words of Isaiah the prophet:

'A voice of one calling in the desert,
"Prepare the way for the Lord,
    make straight paths for him.
Every valley shall be filled in,
    every mountain and hill made low.
The crooked roads shall become straight,
    the rough ways smooth.
And all mankind will see God's salvation."'

And so John came, baptising in the desert region and preaching a baptism of repentance for the forgiveness of sins. The whole Judean countryside and all the people of Jerusalem went out to him. Confessing their sins, they were baptised by him in the Jordan River. John wore clothing made of camel's hair, with a leather belt around his waist, and he ate locusts and wild honey. He said to the crowds coming out to be baptised by him, 'You brood of vipers! Who warned you to flee from the coming wrath? Produce fruit in keeping with repentance. And do not begin to say to yourselves, "We have Abraham as our father." For I tell you that out of these stones God can raise up children for Abraham. The axe is already at the root of the trees, and every tree that does not produce good fruit will be cut down and thrown into the fire.' 'What should we do then?' the crowd asked.

John answered, 'The man with two tunics should share with him who has none, and the one who has food should do the same.' Tax collectors also came to be baptised. 'Teacher,' they asked, 'what should we do?' 'Don't collect any more than you are required to,' he told them. Then some soldiers asked him, 'And what should we do?' He replied, 'Don't extort money and don't accuse people falsely and be content with your pay.'

The people were waiting expectantly and were all wondering in their hearts if John might possibly be the Christ. John answered them all, 'I baptise you with water. But one more powerful than I will come, the thongs of whose sandals I am not worthy to untie. He will baptise you with the Holy Spirit and with fire. His winnowing fork is in his hand to clear his threshing floor and to gather the wheat into his barn, but he will burn up the chaff with unquenchable fire.' And with many other words John exhorted the people and preached the good news to them.

Jesus' baptism and temptations – autumn/winter AD 26

At that time, when all the people were being baptised, Jesus came from Nazareth in Galilee and was baptised by John in the Jordan. But John tried to deter him, saying, 'I need to be baptised by you, and do you come to me?' Jesus replied, *'Let it be so now; it is proper for us to do this to fulfil all righteousness.'* Then John consented. As soon as Jesus was baptised, he went up out of the water. As he was praying heaven was opened, and he saw the Spirit of God descending on him in bodily form like a dove. And a voice from heaven said, 'You are my Son, whom I love, with you I am well pleased.' Now Jesus himself was about thirty years old when he began his ministry. He was the son, so it was thought, of Joseph.

Jesus, full of the Holy Spirit, returned from the Jordan and was immediately led by the Spirit into the desert for forty days where he was to be tempted by the devil. During this time he was with wild animals, and angels came and attended to him. He ate nothing during those days, and at the end of them he was hungry. The devil came and said to him, 'If you are the Son of God, tell these stones to become bread.' Jesus answered, *'It is written: "Man does not live on bread alone, but on every word that comes from the mouth of God."'* Then the devil led him to Jerusalem, the holy city and had him stand on the highest point of the temple. 'If you are the Son of God,' he said, 'Throw yourself down from here. For it is written:

> "He will command his angels concerning you
>   to guard you carefully;
> they will lift you up in their hands,
>   so that you will not strike your foot against a
>   stone."'

Jesus answered him, *'It is also written: "Do not put the Lord your God to the test."'* Again, the devil took him to a very high mountain and showed him in an instant all the kingdoms of the world and their splendour. 'All this I will give you,' he said. 'I will give you all their authority and splendour, for it has been given to me, and I can give it to anyone I want to. So if you will bow down and worship me, it will all be yours.' Jesus said to him, *'Away from me, Satan! For it is written: "Worship the Lord your God, and serve him only."'* When the devil had finished all this tempting, he left him until an opportune time, and angels came and attended to Jesus.

Chapter 10

Jesus' Early Ministry

*'For God so loved the world
that he gave his one and only son.'*

Now this was John the Baptist's testimony when the Jews of Jerusalem sent priests and Levites to ask him who he was. He did not fail to confess, but confessed freely, 'I am not the Christ.' They asked him, 'Then who are you? Are you Elijah?' He said, 'I am not.' 'Are you the Prophet?' He answered, 'No.' Finally they said, 'Who are you? Give us an answer to take back to those who sent us. What do you say about yourself?' John replied in the words of Isaiah the prophet, 'I am the voice of one calling in the desert, "Make straight the way for the Lord."' Now some Pharisees who had been sent questioned him, 'Why then do you baptise if you are not the Christ, nor Elijah, nor the Prophet?' 'I baptise with water,' John replied, 'but among you stands one you do not know. He is the one who comes after me, the thongs of whose sandals I am not worthy to untie.' This all happened at Bethany on the other side of the Jordan, where John was baptising.

The first disciples – early AD 27

The next day John saw Jesus coming toward him and said, 'Look, the Lamb of God, who takes away the sin of the world! This is the one I meant when I said, "A man who comes after me has surpassed me because he was before me." I myself did not know him, but the reason I came baptising with water was that he might be revealed to Israel.' Then John gave this testimony, 'I saw the Spirit come down from heaven as a dove and remain on him. I would not have known him, except that the one who sent me to baptise with water told me, "The man on whom you see the Spirit come down and remain is he who will baptise with the Holy Spirit." I have seen and I testify that this is the Son of God.'

The following day John was there again with two of his disciples. When he saw Jesus passing by, he said, 'Look, the Lamb of God!' When the two disciples heard him say this, they followed Jesus. Turning around, Jesus saw them following and asked, *'What do you want?'* They said, 'Rabbi' (which means Teacher), 'where are you staying?' *'Come,'* he replied, *'and you will see.'* So they went and saw where he was staying and spent that day with him. It was about the tenth hour.

Andrew, Simon Peter's brother, was one of the two who heard what John had said and who had followed Jesus. The first thing Andrew did was to find his brother Simon and tell him, 'We have found the Messiah' (that is, the Christ). And he brought him to Jesus. Jesus looked at him and said, *'You are Simon son of John. You will be called Cephas'* (which, when translated, is Peter).

The next day Jesus decided to leave for Galilee. Finding Philip, he said to him, *'Follow me.'* Philip, like Andrew and Peter, was from the town of Bethsaida. Philip found Nathanael and told him, 'We have found the one Moses wrote about in the Law, and about whom the prophets also wrote, Jesus of Nazareth, the son of Joseph.' 'Nazareth! Can anything good come from there?' Nathanael asked. 'Come and see,' said Philip.

When Jesus saw Nathanael approaching, he said of him, *'Here is a true Israelite, in whom there is nothing false.'* 'How do you know me?' Nathanael asked. Jesus answered, *'I saw you while you were still under the fig tree before Philip called you.'* Then Nathanael declared, 'Rabbi, you are the Son of God; you are the King of Israel.' Jesus said, *'You believe because I told you I saw you under the fig tree. You shall see greater things than that.'* He then added, *'I tell you the truth, you shall see heaven open, and the angels of God ascending and descending on the Son of Man.'*

The first miracle

On the third day a wedding took place at Cana in Galilee. Jesus' mother was there, and Jesus and his disciples had also been invited to the wedding. When the wine was gone, Jesus' mother said to him, 'They have no more wine.' *'Dear woman, why do you involve me?'* Jesus replied. *'My time has not yet come.'* His mother said to the servants, 'Do whatever he tells you.' Nearby stood six stone water jars, the kind used by the Jews for ceremonial washing, each holding from twenty to thirty gallons. Jesus said to the servants, *'Fill the jars with water';* so they filled them to the brim. Then he told them, *'Now draw some out and take it to the master of the banquet.'* They did so, and the master of the banquet tasted the water that had been turned into wine. He did not realise where it had come from, though the servants who had drawn the water knew. Then he called the bridegroom aside and said, 'Everyone brings out the choice wine first and then the cheaper wine after the guests have had too much to drink; but you have saved the best till now.' This, the first of his miraculous signs, Jesus performed at Cana in Galilee. He thus revealed his glory and his disciples put their faith in him.

After this he went down to Capernaum with his mother and brothers and his disciples. There they stayed for a few days. When it was almost time for the Jewish Passover, Jesus went up to Jerusalem. In the temple courts he found men selling cattle, sheep and doves, and others sitting at tables exchanging money. So he made a whip out of cords, and drove all from the temple area, both sheep and cattle; he scattered the coins of the money changers and overturned their tables. To those who sold doves he said, *'Get these out of here! How dare you turn my Father's house into a market!'* His disciples remembered that it is written; 'Zeal for your house will consume me.'

Then the Jews demanded of him, 'What miraculous sign can you show us to prove your authority to do all this?' Jesus answered them, *'Destroy this temple, and I will raise it again in three days.'* The Jews replied, 'It has taken forty-six years to build this Temple, and you are going to raise it in three days?' But the Temple he had spoken of was his body. After he was raised from the dead, his disciples recalled what he had said. Then they believed the Scripture and the words that Jesus had spoken.

Now while he was in Jerusalem at the Passover Feast, many people saw the miraculous signs he was doing and believed in his name. But Jesus would not entrust himself to them, for he knew all men. He did not need man's testimony about man, for he knew what was in a man.

Jesus is visited by Nicodemus

Now there was a man of the Pharisees named Nicodemus, a member of the Jewish ruling council. He came to Jesus at night and said, 'Rabbi, we know you are a teacher who has come from God. For no one could perform the miraculous signs you are doing if God were not with him.' In reply Jesus declared, *'I tell you the truth, no one can see the kingdom of God unless he is born again.'* 'How can a man be born when he is old?' Nicodemus asked. 'Surely he cannot enter a second time into his mother's womb to be born!'

Jesus answered, *'I tell you the truth, no one can enter the kingdom of God unless he is born of water and the Spirit. Flesh gives birth to flesh, but the Spirit gives birth to spirit. You should not be surprised at my saying, "You must be born again." The wind blows wherever it pleases. You hear its sound, but you cannot tell where it comes from or where it is going. So it is with everyone born of the Spirit.'*

'How can this be?' Nicodemus asked.

'You are Israel's teacher,' said Jesus, *'and do you not under-stand these things? I tell you the truth, we speak of what we know, and we testify to what we have seen, but still you people do not accept our testimony. I have spoken to you of earthly things and*

you do not believe; how then will you believe if I speak of heavenly things? No one has ever gone into heaven except the one who came from heaven, the Son of Man. Just as Moses lifted up the snake in the desert, so the Son of Man must be lifted up, that everyone who believes in him may have eternal life.

'For God so loved the world that he gave his one and only Son, that whoever believes in him shall not perish but have eternal life. For God did not send his Son into the world to condemn the world, but to save the world through him. Whoever believes in him is not condemned, but whoever does not believe stands condemned already because he has not believed in the name of God's one and only Son. This is the verdict: light has come into the world, but men loved darkness instead of light because their deeds were evil. Everyone who does evil hates the light, and will not come into the light for fear that his deeds will be exposed. But whoever lives by the truth comes into the light, so that it may be seen plainly that what he has done has been done through God.'

After this, Jesus and his disciples went out into the Judean countryside, where he spent some time with them, and baptised. Now John also was baptising at Aenon near Salim, because there was plenty of water, and people were constantly coming to be baptised. (This was before John was put in prison.)

An argument developed between some of John's disciples and a certain Jew over the matter of ceremonial washing. They came to John and said to him, 'Rabbi, that man who was with you on the other side of the Jordan, the one you testified about well, he is baptising, and everyone is going to him.'

To this John replied, 'A man can receive only what is given him from heaven. You yourselves can testify that I said, "I am not the Christ but am sent ahead of him." The bride belongs to the bridegroom. The friend who attends the bridegroom waits and listens for him, and is full of joy when he hears the bridegroom's voice. That joy is mine, and it is now complete. He must become greater; I must become less.

'The one who comes from above is above all; the one who is from the earth belongs to the earth, and speaks as one from the earth. The one who comes from heaven is above all. He testifies to what he has seen and heard, but no one accepts his testimony. The man who has accepted it has certified that God is truthful. For the one whom God has sent speaks the words of God, for God gives the Spirit without limit. The Father loves the Son and has placed everything in his hands. Whoever believes in the Son has eternal life, but whoever rejects the Son will not see life, for God's wrath remains on him.'

The Pharisees heard that Jesus was gaining and baptising more disciples than John, although in fact it was not Jesus who baptised, but his disciples. When the Lord learned of this, and then that John had been put in prison, he left Judea and went back once more to Galilee. Now John had rebuked Herod the tetrach because of Herodias, his brother's wife, and all the other evil things he had done, and Herod added to his evil by having John locked up.

The story of the 'Bad' Samaritan

Now Jesus had to go through Samaria. So he came to a town in Samaria called Sychar, near the plot of ground Jacob had given to his son Joseph. Jacob's well was there, and Jesus, tired as he was from the journey, sat down by the well. It was about the sixth hour. When a Samaritan woman came to draw water, Jesus said to her, *'Will you give me a drink?'* (His disciples had gone into the town to buy food.) The Samaritan woman said to him, 'You are a Jew and I am a Samaritan woman. How can you ask me for a drink?' (For Jews do not associate with Samaritans.) Jesus answered her, *'If you knew the gift of God and who it is that asks you for a drink, you would have asked him and he would have given you living water.'* 'Sir,' the woman said, 'you have nothing to draw with and the well is deep. Where can you get this living water? Are you greater than our father Jacob, who gave us the well and drank from it himself, as did also his sons and his flocks and herds?'

Jesus answered, *'Everyone who drinks this water will be thirsty again, but whoever drinks the water I give him will never thirst.*

Indeed, the water I give him will become in him a spring of water welling up to eternal life.' The woman said to him, 'Sir, give me this water so that I won't get thirsty and have to keep coming here to draw water.' He told her, *'Go, call your husband and come back.'* 'I have no husband,' she replied. Jesus said to her, *'You are right when you say you have no husband. The fact is, you have had five husbands, and the man you now have is not your husband. What you have just said is quite true.'*

'Sir,' the woman said, 'I can see that you are a prophet. Our fathers worshipped on this mountain, but you Jews claim that the place where we must worship is in Jerusalem.' Jesus declared, *'Believe me, woman, a time is coming when you will worship the Father neither on this mountain nor in Jerusalem. You Samaritans worship what you do not know; we worship what we do know, for salvation is from the Jews. Yet a time is coming and has now come when the true worshippers will worship the Father in spirit and truth, for they are the kind of worshippers the Father seeks. God is spirit, and his worshippers must worship in spirit and in truth.'* The woman said, 'I know that Messiah (called Christ) is coming. When he comes, he will explain everything to us.' Then Jesus declared, *'I who speak to you am he.'*

Just then his disciples returned and were surprised to find him talking with a woman. But no one asked, 'What do you want?' or 'Why are you talking with her?' Then, leaving her water jar, the woman went back to the town and said to the people, 'Come, see a man who told me everything I ever did. Could this be the Christ?' They came out of the town and made their way toward him.

Meanwhile his disciples urged him, 'Rabbi, eat something.' But he said to them, *'I have food to eat that you know nothing about.'* Then his disciples said to each other, 'Could someone have brought him food?'

'My food,' said Jesus, *'Is to do the will of him who sent me and to finish his work. Do you not say, "Four months more and then the harvest"? I tell you, open your eyes and look at the fields! They are ripe for harvest. Even now the reaper draws his wages, even now he harvests the crop for eternal life, so that the sower and the reaper may be glad together. Thus the saying "One sows and*

another reaps" is true. I sent you to reap what you have not worked for. Others have done the hard work, and you have reaped the benefits of their labour.'

Many of the Samaritans from that town believed in him because of the woman's testimony, 'He told me everything I ever did.' So when the Samaritans came to him, they urged him to stay with them, and he stayed two days. And because of his words many more became believers. They said to the woman, 'We no longer believe just because of what you said; now we have heard for ourselves, and we know that this man really is the Saviour of the world.'

Chapter 11

The Great Galilean Ministry

*'The Spirit of the Lord is on me
because he has anointed me
to preach good news to the poor.'*

December AD 27

After the two days he left for Galilee. (Now Jesus himself had pointed out that a prophet has no honour in his own country.) When he arrived in Galilee, he came in the power of the Spirit, and news about him spread through the whole countryside. The Galileans welcomed him. They had seen all that he had done in Jerusalem at the Passover Feast, for they also had been there. He taught in their synagogues and everyone praised him.

Once more he visited Cana, where he had turned the water into wine. And there was a certain royal official whose son lay sick at Capernaum. When this man heard that Jesus had arrived in Galilee from Judea, he went to him and begged him to come and heal his son, who was close to death. *'Unless you people see miraculous signs and wonders,'* Jesus told him, *'you will never believe.'* The royal official said, 'Sir, come down before my child dies.' Jesus replied, *'You may go. Your son will live.'*

The man took Jesus at his word and departed. While he was still on the way, his servants met him with the news that his boy was living. When he inquired as to the time when his son got better, they said to him, 'The fever left him yesterday at the seventh hour.' Then the father realised that this was the exact time at which Jesus had said to him, *'Your son will live.'* So he and all his household believed. This was the second miraculous sign that Jesus performed, having come from Judea to Galilee.

Jesus returns to his home town

He went to Nazareth, where he had been brought up, and on the Sabbath day he went into the synagogue, as was his custom. And he stood up to read. The scroll of the prophet Isaiah was handed to him. Unrolling it, he found the place where it is written:

> *'The Spirit of the Lord is on me,*
> *because he has anointed me*
> *to preach good news to the poor.*
> *He has sent me to proclaim freedom for the prisoners*
> *and recovery of sight for the blind,*
> *to release the oppressed,*
> *to proclaim the year of the Lord's favour.'*

Then he rolled up the scroll, gave it back to the attendant and sat down. The eyes of everyone in the synagogue were fastened on him, and he began by saying to them, *'Today this Scripture is fulfilled in your hearing.'* All spoke well of him and were amazed at the gracious words that came from his lips. 'Isn't this Joseph's son?' they asked.

Jesus said to them, *'Surely you will quote this proverb to me: "Physician, heal yourself! Do here in your home town what we have heard that you did in Capernaum." I tell you the truth,'* he continued, *'no prophet is accepted in his home town. I assure you that there were many widows in Israel in Elijah's time, when the sky was shut for three and a half years and there was a severe famine throughout the land. Yet Elijah was not sent to any of them, but to a widow in Zarephath in the region of Sidon. And there were many in Israel with leprosy in the time of Elisha the prophet, yet not one of them was cleansed, only Naaman the Syrian.'*

All the people in the synagogue were furious when they heard this. They got up, drove him out of the town, and took him to the brow of the hill on which the town was built, in order to throw him down the cliff. But he walked right through the crowd and went on his way.

So leaving Nazareth, he went and lived in Capernaum, which was by the lake in the area of Zebulun and Naphtali to fulfil what was said through the prophet Isaiah:

> 'Land of Zebulun and land of Naphtali,
>   the way to the sea, along the Jordan,
>   Galilee of the Gentiles
> the people living in darkness
>   have seen a great light;
> on those living in the land of the shadow of death
>   a light has dawned.'

The call of Peter, Andrew, James and John

Jesus went into Galilee proclaiming the good news of God. *'The time has come,'* he said. *'The kingdom of God is near. Repent and believe the good news!'*

As Jesus was walking beside the Sea of Galilee, he saw two brothers, Simon called Peter and his brother Andrew. They were casting a net into the lake, for they were fishermen. *'Come, follow me,'* Jesus said, *'and I will make you fishers of men.'* At once they left their nets and followed him. Going on from there, he saw two other brothers, James son of Zebedee and his brother John. They were in a boat with their father Zebedee, preparing their nets. Jesus called them, and immediately they left the boat and their father and followed him.

Jesus went throughout Galilee, teaching in their synagogues, preaching the good news of the Kingdom, and healing every disease and sickness among the people. News about him spread all over Syria, and people brought to him all who were ill with various diseases, those suffering severe pain, the demon-possessed, those having seizures, and the paralysed, and he healed them. Large crowds from Galilee, the Decapolis, Jerusalem, Judea and the region across the Jordan followed him.

They went to Capernaum, and when the Sabbath came, Jesus went into the synagogue and began to teach the people. The people were amazed at his teaching, because he taught them as one who had authority, not as the teachers of the law. Just then a man in their synagogue who was possessed by an evil spirit cried out, 'Ha! What do you want with us, Jesus of Nazareth? Have you come to destroy us? I know who you are, the Holy One of God!' *'Be quiet!'* said Jesus sternly. *'Come out of him!'* The evil spirit shook the man violently throwing him down before them all and came out of him with a shriek without injuring him. The people were all so amazed that they asked each other, 'What is this? A new teaching, and with authority! He even gives orders to evil spirits and they obey him.' News about him spread quickly over the whole region of Galilee.

As soon as they left the synagogue, they went with James and John to the home of Simon and Andrew. Simon's mother-in-law was in bed suffering with a high fever, and they told Jesus about her, asking him to help. So he went to her, and bending over her took her hand and rebuked the fever, and it left her. He helped her get up and immediately she began to wait on them. That evening after sunset the people brought to Jesus all the sick. There were many with various kinds of diseases and those who were demon-possessed. The whole town gathered at the door, and Jesus laying his hands on each one, healed them. He also drove out many demons, and they came out of people, shouting, 'You are the Son of God!' But he rebuked them and would not allow them to speak because they knew he was the Christ. This was to fulfil what was spoken through the prophet Isaiah, 'He took up our infirmities and carried our diseases.'

Very early in the morning, while it was still dark, Jesus got up, left the house and went off to a solitary place, where he prayed. Simon and his companions went to look for him, and when they found him, they exclaimed, 'Everyone is looking for you!' When the people who were looking for him found him they tried to keep him from leaving them. Jesus said to his disciples, *'Let us go somewhere else to the nearby villages and the other towns, so I can preach there also the good news of the kingdom of God, because that is why I was sent.'* So he travelled throughout Galilee, preaching in their synagogues and driving out demons.

One day as Jesus was standing by the Lake of Gennesaret, with the people crowding around him and listening to the word of God, he saw at the water's edge two boats, left there by the fishermen, who were washing their nets. He got into one of the boats, the one belonging to Simon, and asked him to put out a little from shore. Then he sat down and taught the people from the boat. When he had finished speaking, he said to Simon, *'Put out into deep water, and let down the nets for a catch.'* Simon answered, 'Master, we've worked hard all night and haven't caught anything. But because you say so, I will let down the nets.' When they had done so, they caught such a large number of fish that their nets began to break. So they signalled their partners in the other boat to come and help them, and they came and filled both boats so full that they began to sink. When Simon Peter saw this, he fell at Jesus' knees and said, 'Go away from me, Lord; I am a sinful man!'

For he and all his companions were astonished at the catch of fish they had taken, and so were James and John, the sons of Zebedee, Simon's partners. Then Jesus said to Simon, *'Don't be afraid; from now on you will catch men.'* So they pulled their boats up on shore, left everything and followed him.

A remarkable cure

While Jesus was in one of the towns, a man came along who was covered with leprosy. When he saw Jesus, he fell with his face to the ground and begged him, 'Lord, if you are willing, you can make me clean.' Filled with compassion, Jesus reached out his hand and touched the man. *'I am willing,'* he said. *'Be clean!'* And immediately the leprosy left him and he was cured. Then Jesus ordered him, *'Don't tell anyone, but go, show yourself to the priest and offer the sacrifices that Moses commanded for your cleansing, as a testimony to them.'* Instead he went out and began to talk freely, spreading the news all the more so crowds of people came to hear him and to be healed of their sicknesses. As a result, Jesus could no longer enter a town openly and often withdrew to lonely places to pray.

A few days later, Jesus stepped into a boat and came to his own town of Capernaum once more. When the people including the Pharisees and teachers of the law heard that he had come home, they came to hear him from every village of Galilee and from Judea and Jerusalem. So many gathered that there was no room left, not even outside the door, and he preached the word to them. And the power of the Lord was present for him to heal the sick.

Four men came, bringing to him a paralytic, lying on a mat and tried to take him into the house to lay before Jesus. Since they could not get him to Jesus because of the crowd, they went up on the roof and made an opening above Jesus by digging through the roof. Then they lowered him on his mat through the tiles into the middle of the crowd, right in front of Jesus.

When Jesus saw their faith, he said to the paralytic, *'Son, your sins are forgiven.'* At this point some teachers of the law were sitting there, thinking to themselves, 'Why does this fellow talk like that? He's blaspheming! Who can forgive sins but God alone?' Immediately Jesus knew in his spirit that this was what they were thinking, and he said to them, *'Why are you thinking these things, entertaining such evil thoughts in your hearts? Which is easier: to say to the paralytic, "Your sins are forgiven," or to say, "Get up, take your mat and walk"? But that you may know that the Son of Man has authority on earth to forgive sins.'* He said to the paralytic, *'I tell you, get up, take your mat and go home.'* Immediately he stood up in front of them, took what he had been lying on and walked out in full view of them all and went home praising God. When the crowd saw this they were filled with awe and amazed and praised

God, who had given such authority to men, saying, 'We have never seen anything like this, we have seen remarkable things today'

The call of Matthew the tax collector

Once again Jesus went out beside the lake. A large crowd came to him, and he began to teach them. As he walked along, he saw Levi (Matthew) son of Alphaeus sitting at the tax collector's booth. *'Follow me,'* Jesus told him, and Levi got up, left everything and followed him. Then Levi held a great banquet for Jesus at his house, and a large crowd of tax collectors and others were eating with him and his disciples, for there were many who followed him. But when the Pharisees and the teachers of the law who belonged to their sect saw him they complained to his disciples, 'Why do you and your teacher eat and drink with tax collectors and "sinners"?' On hearing this, Jesus answered them, *'It is not the healthy who need a doctor, but the sick. But go and learn what this means: "I desire mercy, not sacrifice." For I have not come to call the righteous, but sinners to repentance.'*

Now John the Baptist's disciples and the Pharisees were fasting, so some of the people came along with some of John's own disciples and asked Jesus, 'How is it that John's disciples and the disciples of the Pharisees are fasting, but yours go on eating and drinking?'

Jesus answered, *'How can you make the guests of the bridegroom fast while he is with them? They cannot, so long as they have him with them. But the time will come when the bridegroom will be taken from them, and on that day they will fast. No one sews a patch of unshrunk cloth on an old garment. If he does, the new piece will pull away from the old, making the tear worse, and the patch from the new will not match the old. And neither do men pour new wine into old wineskins. If they do the wine will burst the skins, the wine will run out and the wineskins will be ruined. No, new wine must be poured into new wineskins, so both are preserved. And no one after drinking old wine wants the new, for he says, "The old is better."'*

Jesus heads for Jerusalem – April AD 28

Some time later, Jesus went up to Jerusalem for a feast of the Jews. Now there is in Jerusalem near the Sheep Gate a pool, which in Aramaic is called Bethesda and which is surrounded by five covered colonnades. Here a great number of disabled people used to lie, the blind, the lame, the paralysed and they waited for the moving of the waters. (From time to time an angel of the Lord would come down and stir up the waters. The first one into the pool after each such disturbance would be cured of whatever disease he had.) One who was there had been an invalid for thirty-eight years. When Jesus saw him lying there and learned that he had been in this condition for a long time, he asked him, *'Do you want to get well?'* 'Sir,' the invalid replied, 'I have no one to help me into the pool when the water is stirred. While I am trying to get in, someone else goes down ahead of me.' Then Jesus said to him, *'Get up! Pick up your mat and walk.'* At once the man was cured; he picked up his mat and walked.

The day on which this took place was a Sabbath, and so the Jews said to the man who had been healed, 'It is the Sabbath; the law forbids you to carry your mat.' But he replied, 'The man who made me well said to me, *"Pick up your mat and walk."'* So they asked him, 'Who is this fellow who told you to pick it up and walk?' The man who was healed had no idea who it was, for Jesus had slipped into the crowd that was there. Later Jesus found him at the temple and said to him, *'See, you are well again. Stop sinning or something worse may happen to you.'* The man went away and told the Jews that it was Jesus who had made him well.

Because Jesus was doing these things on the Sabbath, the Jews persecuted him. Jesus said to them, *'My Father is always at his work to this very day, and I, too, am working.'* For this reason the Jews tried all the harder to kill him; not only was he breaking the Sabbath, but he was even calling God his own Father, making himself equal with God. Jesus gave them this answer, *'I tell you the truth, the Son can do nothing by himself; he can do only what he sees his Father doing, because whatever the Father does the Son also does. For the Father loves the Son and shows him all he does. Yes, to your amazement he will show him even greater things than these. For just as the Father raises the dead and gives them life, even so the Son gives life to whom he is pleased to give it. Moreover, the Father judges no one, but has entrusted all judgement to the Son, that all may honour the Son just as they honour the Father. He who does not honour the Son does not honour the Father, who sent him. I tell you the truth, whoever hears my word and believes him who sent me has eternal life and will not be condemned; he has crossed over from death to life. I tell you the truth, a time is coming and has now come when the dead will hear the voice of the Son of God and those who hear will live. For as the Father has life in himself, so he has granted the Son to have life in himself. And he has given him authority to judge because he is the Son of Man.*

'Do not be amazed at this, for a time is coming when all who are in their graves will hear his voice and come out. Those who have done good will rise to live, and those who have done evil will rise to be condemned. By myself I can do nothing; I judge only as I hear, and my judgement is just, for I seek not to please myself but him who sent me. If I testify about myself, my testimony is not valid. There is another who testifies in my favour, and I know that his testimony about me is valid. You have sent to John and he has testified to the truth. Not that I accept human testimony; but I mention it that you may be saved.

'John was a lamp that burned and gave light, and you chose for a time to enjoy his light. I have testimony weightier than that of John. For the very work that the Father has given me to finish, and which I am doing, testifies that the Father has sent me. And the Father who sent me has himself testified concerning me. You have never heard his voice nor seen his form, nor does his word dwell in you, for you do not believe the one he sent. You diligently study the Scriptures because you think that by them you possess eternal life. These are the Scriptures that testify about me, yet you refuse to come to me to have life.

'I do not accept praise from men, but I know you. I know that you do not have the love of God in your hearts. I have come in my Father's name, and you do not accept me; but if someone else

comes in his own name, you will accept him. How can you believe if you accept praise from one another, yet make no effort to obtain the praise that comes from the only God? But do not think I will accuse you before the Father. Your accuser is Moses, on whom your hopes are set. If you believed Moses, you would believe me, for he wrote about me. But since you do not believe what he wrote, how are you going to believe what I say?'*

Jesus clashes with the religious legalists

One Sabbath Jesus was going through the grain fields, and his disciples began to pick some heads of grain, rub them in their hands and eat the kernels. When some of the Pharisees saw this they said to him, 'Look! Your disciples are doing what is unlawful on the Sabbath?' Jesus answered them, *'Have you never read what David did when he and his companions were hungry? He entered the house of God, and he and his companions ate the consecrated bread, which was not lawful for them to do, but only for the priests. Or haven't you read in the Law that on the Sabbath the priests in the temple desecrate the day yet are innocent? I tell you that one greater than the temple is here. If you had known what these words mean, "I desire mercy, not sacrifice," you would not have condemned the innocent.'* Then Jesus said to them, *'The Son of Man is Lord of the Sabbath.'*

Going on from that place he went into the synagogue and was teaching, and a man was there whose right hand was shrivelled. The Pharisees and the teachers of the law were looking for a reason to accuse Jesus, so they watched him closely to see if he would heal on the Sabbath. They asked him, 'Is it lawful to heal on the Sabbath?' But Jesus knew what they were thinking and said to the man with the shrivelled hand, *'Get up and stand in front of everyone.'* So he got up and stood there. Then Jesus said to them, *'I ask you, which is lawful on the Sabbath, to do good or to do evil, to save life or to destroy it?'* But they remained silent. He looked around at them all in anger and, deeply distressed at their stubborn hearts, said to the man, *'Stretch out your hand.'* He did so, and his hand was completely restored. But they were furious and began to discuss with one another and plot with the Herodians how they might kill Jesus.

The appointment of the Twelve Apostles

Jesus withdrew with his disciples to the lake, and a large crowd from Galilee followed. When they heard all he was doing, many people came to him from Judea, Jerusalem, Idumea, and the regions across the Jordan and around Tyre and Sidon. Because of the crowd he told his disciples to have a small boat ready for him, to keep the people from crowding him, for he had healed many, so that those with diseases were pushing forward to touch him. Whenever the evil spirits saw him, they fell down before him and cried out, 'You are the Son of God.' But he gave them strict orders not to tell who he was. All these things were happening to fulfil what was spoken through the prophet Isaiah:

> 'Here is my servant whom I have chosen,
>   the one I love, in whom I delight;
> I will put my Spirit on him,
>   and he will proclaim justice to the nations.
> He will not quarrel or cry out;
>   no one will hear his voice in the streets.
> A bruised reed he will not break,
>   and a smouldering wick he will not snuff out,
> till he leads justice to victory.
>   In his name the nations will put their hope.'

One of those days Jesus went out to a mountainside to pray, and spent the night praying to God. When morning came, he called his disciples to him and chose twelve of them, designating them apostles, that they might be with him and that he might send them out to preach and to have authority to drive out demons and to heal every disease. These are the twelve he appointed: first, Simon (whom he named Peter), his brother Andrew, James son of Zebedee and his brother John (to whom he gave the name Boanerges, which means Sons of Thunder) Philip, Bartholomew, Matthew, Thomas, James son of Alphaeus, Simon who was called the Zealot, Thaddaeus, and Judas Iscariot, who became a traitor and betrayed him. He went down with them and stood on a level place. A large crowd of his disciples was there and a great number of people from all over Judea, from Jerusalem, and from the coast of Tyre and Sidon, who had come to hear him and to be healed of their diseases. Those troubled by evil spirits were cured, and the people all tried to touch him, because power was coming from him and healing them all.

Chapter 12

The Sermon on the Mount

'Blessed are the pure in heart
for they shall see God'

When he saw the crowds, he went up on the mountainside and sat down. His disciples came to him, and he looked at them and began to teach them, saying;

'Blessed are the poor in spirit,
for theirs is the kingdom of heaven.
Blessed are those who mourn,
for they will be comforted.
Blessed are the meek,
for they will inherit the earth.
Blessed are those who hunger and thirst for righteousness,
for they will be filled.
Blessed are you who weep now,
for you will laugh.
Blessed are the merciful,
for they will be shown mercy.
Blessed are the pure in heart,
for they will see God.
Blessed are the peacemakers,
for they will be called sons of God.
Blessed are those who are persecuted because of
righteousness,
for theirs is the kingdom of heaven.

'Blessed are you when people insult you, persecute you and falsely say all kinds of evil against you because of me. Rejoice in

that day, leap for joy and be glad, because great is your reward in heaven, for in the same way they persecuted the prophets who were before you.

    'But woe to you who are rich,
      for you have already received your comfort.
    Woe to you who are well fed now,
      for you will go hungry.
    Woe to you who laugh now,
      for you will mourn and weep.
    Woe to you when all men speak well of you,
      for that is how their fathers treated the false prophets.

'You are the salt of the earth. But if the salt loses its saltiness, how can it be made salty again? It is no longer good for anything, except to be thrown out and trampled by men. You are the light of the world. A city on a hill cannot be hidden. Neither do people light a lamp and put it under a bowl. Instead they put it on its stand, and it gives light to everyone in the house. In the same way, let your light shine before men, that they may see your good deeds and praise your Father in heaven.

'Do not think that I have come to abolish the Law or the Prophets; I have not come to abolish them but to fulfil them. I tell you the truth, until heaven and earth disappear, not the smallest letter, not the least stroke of a pen, will by any means disappear from the Law until everything is accomplished. Anyone who breaks one of the least of these commandments and teaches others to do the same will be called least in the kingdom of heaven, but whoever practices and teaches these commands will be called great in the kingdom of heaven. For I tell you that unless your right-eousness surpasses that of the Pharisees and the teachers of the law, you will certainly not enter the kingdom of heaven.

'You have heard that it was said to the people long ago, "Do not murder, and anyone who murders will be subject to judgement." But I tell you that anyone who is angry with his brother will be subject to judgement. Again, anyone who says to his brother, "Raca," is answerable to the Sanhedrin. But anyone who says, "You fool!" will be in danger of the fire of hell. Therefore, if you are offering your gift at the altar and there remember that your

brother has something against you, leave your gift there in front of the altar. First go and be reconciled to your brother; then come and offer your gift.

'Settle matters quickly with your adversary who is taking you to court. Do it while you are still with him on the way, or he may hand you over to the judge, and the judge may hand you over to the officer, and you may be thrown into prison. I tell you the truth, you will not get out until you have paid the last penny.

'You have heard that it was said, "Do not commit adultery." But I tell you that anyone who looks at a woman lustfully has already committed adultery with her in his heart. If your right eye causes you to sin, gouge it out and throw it away. It is better for you to lose one part of your body than for your whole body to be thrown into hell. And if your right hand causes you to sin, cut it off and throw it away. It is better for you to lose one part of your body than for your whole body to go into hell.

'It has been said, "Anyone who divorces his wife must give her a certificate of divorce." But I tell you that anyone who divorces his wife, except for marital unfaithfulness, causes her to become an adulteress, and anyone who marries the divorced woman commits adultery.

'Again, you have heard that it was said to the people long ago, "Do not break your oath, but keep the oaths you have made to the Lord." But I tell you, do not swear at all: either by heaven, for it is God's throne; or by the earth, for it is his footstool; or by Jerusalem, for it is the city of the Great King. And do not swear by your head, for you cannot make even one hair white or black. Simply let your "Yes" be "Yes," and your "No," "No"; anything beyond this comes from the evil one.

'You have heard that it was said, "Eye for eye, and tooth for tooth." But I tell you, do not resist an evil person. If someone strikes you on the right cheek, turn to him the other also. And if someone wants to sue you and take your tunic, let him have your cloak as well. Do to others as you would have them do to you. If someone forces you to go one mile, go with him two miles. Give to everyone who asks you, and do not demand back when someone takes what belongs to you, and do not turn away from the one who wants to borrow from you.

'You have heard that it was said, "love your neighbours and hate your enemy." But I tell you: love your enemies, do good to those who hate you. Bless those who curse you and pray for those who persecute you, that you may be sons of your Father in heaven. He causes his sun to rise on the evil and the good, and sends rain on the righteous and the unrighteous. If you love those who love you, what reward will you get? Are not even the tax collectors and sinners doing that? And if you greet and do good only to your brothers, what are you doing more than others? Do not even pagans do that? And if you lend to those from whom you expect repayment, what credit is that to you? Even "sinners" lend to "sinners," expecting to be repaid in full. But love your enemies, do good to them, and lend to them without expecting to get anything back. Then your reward will be great, and you will be sons of the Most High, because he is kind to the ungrateful and wicked. Be merciful, just as your Father is merciful. And be perfect, even, as your heavenly Father is perfect.'

Giving, praying and fasting

'Be careful not to do your "acts of righteousness" before men, to be seen by them. If you do, you will have no reward from your Father in heaven. So when you give to the needy, do not announce it with trumpets, as the hypocrites do in the synagogues and on the streets, to be honoured by men. I tell you the truth, they have received their reward in full. But when you give to the needy, do not let your left hand know what your right hand is doing, so that your giving may be in secret. Then your Father, who sees what is done in secret, will reward you.

'And when you pray, do not be like the hypocrites, for they love to pray standing in the synagogues and on the street corners to be seen by men. I tell you the truth, they have received their reward in full. But when you pray, go into your room, close the door and pray to your Father, who is unseen. Then your Father, who sees what is done in secret, will reward you. And when you pray, do not keep on babbling like pagans, for they think they will be heard because of their many words. Do not be like them, for your Father knows what you need before you ask him.

'This, then, is how you should pray:

"Our Father in heaven,
hallowed be your name,
your kingdom come,
your will be done
   on earth as it is in heaven.
Give us today our daily bread.
Forgive us our debts,
   as we also have forgiven our debtors.
And lead us not into temptation,
but deliver us from the evil one.
For Thine is the kingdom,
the power and the glory,
for ever and ever, Amen."

'For if you forgive men when they sin against you, your heavenly Father will also forgive you. But if you do not forgive men their sins, your Father will not forgive your sins.

'When you fast, do not look sombre as the hypocrites do, for they disfigure their faces to show men they are fasting. I tell you the truth, they have received their reward in full. But when you fast, put oil on your head and wash your face, so that it will not be obvious to men that you are fasting, but only to your Father, who is unseen; and your Father, who sees what is done in secret, will reward you.'

Teaching on money

'Do not store up for yourselves treasures on earth, where moth and rust destroy, and where thieves break in and steal. But store up for yourselves treasures in heaven, where moth and rust do not destroy, and where thieves do not break in and steal. For where your treasure is, there your heart will be also.

'The eye is the lamp of the body. If your eyes are good, your whole body will be full of light. But if your eyes are bad, your whole body will be full of darkness. If then the light within you is darkness, how great is that darkness!

'No one can serve two masters. Either he will hate the one and *love the other, or he will be devoted to the one and despise the other. You cannot serve both God and Money.'*

Teaching on worry

'Therefore I tell you, do not worry about your life, what you will eat or drink; or about your body, what you will wear. Is not life more important than food, and the body more important than clothes? Look at the birds of the air; they do not sow or reap or store away in barns, and yet your heavenly Father feeds them. Are you not much more valuable than they? Who of you by worrying can add a single hour to his life? And why do you worry about clothes? See how the lilies of the field grow. They do not labour or spin. Yet I tell you that not even Solomon in all his splendour was dressed like one of these. If that is how God clothes the grass of the field, which is here today and tomorrow is thrown into the fire, will he not much more clothe you, O you of little faith? So do not worry, saying, "What shall we eat?" or "What shall we drink?" or "What shall we wear?" For the pagans run after all these things, and your heavenly Father knows that you need them. But seek first his kingdom and his righteousness, and all these things will be given to you as well. Therefore do not worry about tomorrow, for tomorrow will worry about itself. Each day has enough trouble of its own.

'Do not judge, or you too will be judged. Do not condemn, and you will not be condemned. Forgive and you will be forgiven. Give and it will be given to you. A good measure, pressed down, shaken together and running over, will be poured into your lap. For in the same way you judge others, you will be judged, and with the measure you use, it will be measured to you.'

Love, judgement and discernment

He also told them this parable, *'Can a blind man lead a blind man? Will they both not fall into a pit? A student is not above his teacher, but everyone who is fully trained will be like his teacher.*

'Why do you look at the speck of sawdust in your brother's eye and pay no attention to the plank in your own eye? How can you

say to your brother, "Let me take the speck out of your eye," when all the time you fail to see the plank in your own eye? You hypocrite, first take the plank out of your own eye, and then you will see clearly to remove the speck from your brother's eye.

'Do not give dogs what is sacred; do not throw your pearls to pigs. If you do, they may trample them under their feet, and then turn and tear you to pieces.

'Ask and it will be given to you; seek and you will find; knock and the door will be opened to you. For everyone who asks receives; he who seeks finds; and to him who knocks, the door will be opened. Which of you, if his son asks for bread, will give him a stone? Or if he asks for a fish, will give him a snake? If you, then, though you are evil, know how to give good gifts to your children, how much more will your Father in heaven give good gifts to those who ask him! So in everything, do to others what you would have them do to you, for this sums up the Law and the Prophets.

'Enter through the narrow gate. For wide is the gate and broad is the road that leads to destruction, and many enter through it. But small is the gate and narrow the road that leads to life, and only a few find it.

'Watch out for false prophets. They come to you in sheep's clothing, but inwardly they are ferocious wolves. By their fruit you will recognise them for every tree is recognised by its own fruit. Do people pick grapes from thorn bushes, or figs from thistles? Likewise every good tree bears good fruit, but a bad tree bears bad fruit. A good tree cannot bear bad fruit, and a bad tree cannot bear good fruit. Every tree that does not bear good fruit is cut down and thrown into the fire. Thus, by their fruit you will recognise them. For the good man brings good things out of the good stored up in his heart, and the evil man brings evil things out of the evil stored up in his heart. For out of the overflow of his heart his mouth speaks.

'Not everyone who says to me, "Lord, Lord," will enter the kingdom of heaven, but only he who does the will of my Father who is in heaven. Many will say to me on that day, "Lord, Lord, did we not prophesy in your name, and in your name drive out demons and perform many miracles?" Then I will tell them plainly, "I never knew you. Away from me, you evildoers!"

'Therefore everyone who hears these words of mine and puts them into practice is like a wise man who built his house by digging down deep and laying the foundation on the rock. The rain came down, the streams rose, the winds blew and the torrent struck against that house; yet it did not fall, because it had been founded on the rock. But everyone who hears these words of mine and does not put them into practice is like a foolish man who built his house on sand without a foundation. The moment the rain came down, the streams rose, the winds blew and the torrent struck that house, it fell with a great crash and its destruction was complete.'

Chapter 13

Jesus Comes Down the Mountain

'Come to me all you who are weary ...
and I will give you rest.'

When Jesus had finished saying these things, the crowds were amazed at his teaching, because he taught as one who had authority, and not as their teachers of the law. When he came down from the mountainside, large crowds followed him. He went and entered Capernaum where a centurion's servant, whom his master valued highly, was sick, lying paralysed in terrible suffering and about to die. The centurion heard of Jesus and sent some elders of the Jews to him, asking him to come and heal his servant. When they came to Jesus, they pleaded earnestly with him, 'This man deserves to have you do this, because he loves our nation and has built our synagogue.' So Jesus went with them. He was not far from the house when the centurion sent friends to say to him, 'Lord, don't trouble yourself, for I do not deserve to have you come under my roof. That is why I did not even consider myself worthy to come to you. But say the word, and my servant will be healed. For I myself am a man under authority, with soldiers under me. I tell this one, "Go," and he goes; and that one, "Come," and he comes. I say to my servant, "Do this," and he does it.'

When Jesus heard this, he was amazed at him, and turning to the crowd following him, he said, *'I tell you, I have not found anyone in Israel with such great faith. I say to you that many will come from the east and the west, and will take their places at the feast with Abraham, Isaac and Jacob in the kingdom of heaven. But the subjects of the kingdom will be thrown outside, into the darkness, where there will be weeping and gnashing of teeth.'* Then Jesus said, *'Go! It will be done just as you believed it would.'* The men who had been sent returned to the house and found the servant well, he was healed at that very hour.

Jesus raises the dead

Soon afterward, Jesus went to a town called Nain, and his disciples and a large crowd went along with him. As he approached the town gate, a dead person was being carried out, the only son of his mother, and she was a widow. And a large crowd from the town was with her. When the Lord saw her, his heart went out to her and he said, *'Don't cry.'* Then he went up and touched the coffin, and those carrying it stood still. He said, *'Young man, I say to you, get up!'* The dead man sat up and began to talk, and Jesus gave him back to his mother. They were all filled with awe and praised God. 'A great prophet has appeared among us,' they said. 'God has come to help his people.' This news about Jesus spread throughout Judea and the surrounding country.

John the Baptist's bewilderment

John the Baptist's disciples told him about all these things. Calling two of them, he sent them to the Lord to ask, 'Are you the one who was to come, or should we expect someone else?' When the men came to Jesus, they said, 'John the Baptist sent us to you to ask, "Are you the one who was to come, or should we expect someone else?" ' At that very time Jesus cured many who had diseases, sicknesses and evil spirits, and gave sight to many who were blind. So he replied to the messengers, *'Go back and report to John what you have seen and heard: the blind receive sight, the lame walk, those who have leprosy are cured, the deaf hear, the dead are raised, and the good news is preached to the poor. Blessed is the man who does not fall away on account of me.'*

After John's messengers left, Jesus began to speak to the crowd about John, *'What did you go out into the desert to see? A reed swayed by the wind? If not, what did you go out to see? A man dressed in fine clothes? No, those who wear expensive clothes and indulge in luxury are in palaces. But what did you go out to see? A prophet? Yes, I tell you, and more than a prophet. This is the one about whom it is written:*

> *' "I will send my messenger ahead of you,*
> *who will prepare your way before you."*

'I tell you, among those born of women there is no one greater than John; yet the one who is least in the kingdom of God is greater than he.' (All the people, even the tax collectors, when they heard Jesus' words, acknowledged that God's way was right, because they had been baptised by John. But the Pharisees and experts in the law rejected God's purpose for themselves, because they had not been baptised by John.)

'To what, then, can I compare the people of this generation? What are they like? They are like children sitting in the market-place and calling out to each other:

> *' "We played the flute for you,*
> *and you did not dance;*
> *we sang a dirge,*
> *and you did not cry."*

'For John the Baptist came neither eating bread nor drinking wine, and you say, "He has a demon." The Son of Man came eating and drinking, and you say, "Here is a glutton and a drunkard, a friend of tax collectors and sinners." But wisdom is proved right by all her children.'

Then Jesus began to denounce the cities in which most of his miracles had been performed, because they did not repent. *'Woe to you, Korazin! Woe to you, Bethsaida! If the miracles that were performed in you had been performed in Tyre and Sidon, they would have repented long ago in sackcloth and ashes. But I tell you, it will be more bearable for Tyre and Sidon on the day of judgement than for you. And you, Capernaum, will you be lifted up to the skies? No, you will go down to the depths. If the miracles that were performed in you had been performed in Sodom, it would have remained to this day. But I tell you that it will be more bearable for Sodom on the day of judgement than for you.'*

At that time Jesus said, *'I praise you, Father, Lord of heaven and earth, because you have hidden these things from the wise and learned, and revealed them to little children. Yes, Father, for this was your good pleasure. All things have been committed to me by my Father. No one knows the Son except the Father, and no one knows the Father except the Son and those to whom the Son chooses to reveal him. Come to me, all you who are weary and burdened, and I will give you rest. Take my yoke upon you and learn from me, for I am gentle and humble in heart, and you will find rest for your souls. For my yoke is easy and my burden is light.'*

Dinner with a Pharisee and feet washed by a prostitute

Now one of the Pharisees invited Jesus to have dinner with him, so he went to the Pharisee's house and reclined at the table. When a woman who had lived a sinful life in that town learned that Jesus was eating at the Pharisee's house, she brought an alabaster jar of perfume, and as she stood behind him at his feet weeping, she began to wet his feet with her tears. Then she wiped them with her hair, kissed them and poured perfume on them.

When the Pharisee who had invited him saw this, he said to himself, 'If this man were a prophet, he would know who is touching him and what kind of woman she is, that she is a sinner.' Jesus answered him, *'Simon, I have something to tell you.'* 'Tell me, teacher,' he said. *'Two men owed money to a certain moneylender. One owed him five hundred denarii, and the other fifty. Neither of them had the money to pay him back, so he cancelled the debts of both. Now which of them will love him more?'* Simon replied, 'I suppose the one who had the bigger debt cancelled.' *'You have judged correctly,'* Jesus said.

Then he turned toward the woman and said to Simon, *'Do you see this woman? I came into your house. You did not give me any water for my feet, but she wet my feet with her tears and wiped them with her hair. You did not give me a kiss, but this woman, from the time I entered, has not stopped kissing my feet. You did not put oil on my head, but she has poured perfume on my feet. Therefore, I tell you, her many sins have been forgiven, for she loved much. But he who has been forgiven little loves little.'* Then Jesus said to her, *'Your sins are forgiven.'* The other guests began to say among themselves, 'Who is this who even forgives sins?' Jesus said to the woman, *'Your faith has saved you; go in peace.'*

Demons, deliverance and the devil's defeat

After this, Jesus travelled about from one town and village to another, proclaiming the good news of the kingdom of God. The Twelve were with him, and also some women who had been cured of evil spirits and diseases: Mary (called Magdalene) from whom seven demons had come out; Joanna the wife of Cuza, the manager of Herod's household; Susanna; and many others. These women were helping to support them out of their own means.

Then Jesus entered a house, and again a crowd gathered, so that he and his disciples were not even able to eat. When his family heard about this, they went to take charge of him, for they said, 'He is out of his mind.'

Then they brought him a demon-possessed man who was blind and mute, and Jesus drove out the demon that was mute and healed him, so that he could both talk and see. All the people were astonished and said, 'Could this be the Son of David?' But when the Pharisees heard this, they said, 'It is only by Beelzebub, the prince of demons, that this fellow drives out demons.' Jesus knew their thoughts and he spoke to them in parables, *'Every kingdom divided against itself will be ruined, and every city or household divided against itself will not stand but fall. If Satan drives out Satan, he is divided against himself. How then can his kingdom stand? I say this because you claim that I drive out demons by Beelzebub.*

'Now if I drive out demons by Beelzebub, by whom do your people drive them out? So then, they will be your judges. But if I

drive out demons by the finger of God, which is the power of the Spirit, then the kingdom of God has come upon you. Or again, when a strong man fully armed, guards his own house, his possessions are safe. But when someone stronger attacks and overpowers him and ties him up, he takes away the armour in which the man trusted and is able to carry off his possessions and divide the spoils. He who is not with me is against me, and he who does not gather with me scatters. And so I tell you, every sin and blasphemy will be forgiven men, but the blasphemy against the Spirit will not be forgiven. Anyone who speaks a word against the Son of Man will be forgiven, but anyone who speaks against the Holy Spirit will not be forgiven, either in this age or in the age to come, he is guilty of an eternal sin.' He said this because they were saying, 'He has an evil spirit.'

'Make a tree good and its fruit will be good, or make a tree bad and its fruit will be bad, for a tree is recognised by its fruit. You brood of vipers, how can you who are evil say anything good? For out of the overflow of the heart the mouth speaks. The good man brings good things out of the good stored up in him, and the evil man brings evil things out of the evil stored up in him. But I tell you that men will have to give account on the day of judgement for every careless word they have spoken. For by your words you will be acquitted, and by your words you will be condemned.

'When an evil spirit comes out of a man, it goes through arid places seeking rest and does not find it. Then it says, "I will return to the house I left." When it arrives, it finds the house unoccupied, swept clean and put in order. Then it goes and takes with it seven other spirits more wicked than itself, and they go in and live there. And the final condition of that man is worse than the first. This is how it will be with this wicked generation.'

Sign seekers

As the crowds increased some of the Pharisees and teachers of the law said to him, 'Teacher, we want to see a miraculous sign from you.' He answered, *'A wicked and adulterous generation asks for a miraculous sign! But none will be given it except the sign of the prophet Jonah. For as Jonah was a sign to the*

Ninevites and three days and three nights in the belly of a huge fish, so the Son of Man will be three days and three nights in the heart of the earth. The men of Nineveh will stand up at the judgement with this generation and condemn it; for they repented at the preaching of Jonah, and now one greater than Jonah is here. The Queen of the South will rise at the judgement with this generation and condemn it; for she came from the ends of the earth to listen to Solomon's wisdom, and now one greater than Solomon is here.

'No one lights a lamp and puts it in a place where it will be hidden, or under a bowl. Instead he puts it on its stand, so that those who come in may see the light. Your eye is the lamp of your body. When your eyes are good, your whole body also is full of light. But when they are bad, your body is full of darkness. See to it then, that the light within you is not darkness. Therefore, if your whole body is full of light, and no part of it dark, it will be completely lighted, as when the light of a lamp shines on you.'

As Jesus was saying these things, a woman in the crowd called out, 'Blessed is the mother who gave you birth and nursed you.' He replied, *'Blessed rather are those who hear the word of God and obey it.'* While Jesus was still talking to the crowd, his mother and brothers stood outside, wanting to speak to him, but they were unable to get near him because of the crowd. So they sent someone in to call him and said to him, 'Your mother and brothers are standing outside, wanting to speak to you.' He replied to him, *'Who is my mother, and who are my brothers?'* Pointing to his disciples, he said, *'Here are my mother and my brothers. For whoever does the will of my Father in heaven by hearing his Word and putting it into practice is my brother and sister and mother.'*

Parables of the Kingdom of God

That same day Jesus went out of the house and sat by the lake. Such large crowds gathered around him that he got into a boat and sat in it out on the lake, while all the people stood on the shore. Then he told them many things in parables, saying, *'Listen! A farmer went out to sow his seed. As he was*

scattering the seed, some fell along the path, and the birds came
and ate it up. Some fell on rocky places, where it did not have
much soil. It sprang up quickly, because the soil was shallow. But
when the sun came up, the plants were scorched, and they
withered because they had no root. Other seed fell among thorns,
which grew up and choked the plants. Still other seed fell on good
soil, where it produced a crop multiplying a hundred, sixty or thirty
times what was sown. He who has ears, let him hear.'

When he was alone, the twelve and the others around him
asked him, 'Why do you speak to the people in parables?' He
replied, *'The knowledge of the secrets of the kingdom of heaven
has been given to you, but not to them on the outside. Whoever has
will be given more, and he will have an abundance. Whoever does
not have, even what he has will be taken from him. This is why I
speak to them in parables:*

> *' "Though seeing, they do not see;*
>   *though hearing, they do not hear or understand."*

'In them is fulfilled the prophecy of Isaiah:

> *' "You will be ever hearing but never understanding;*
>   *you will be ever seeing but never perceiving.*
> *For this people's heart has become calloused;*
>   *they hardly hear with their ears,*
>   *and they have closed their eyes.*
> *Otherwise they might see with their eyes,*
>   *hear with their ears,*
>   *understand with their hearts and turn,*
> *and I would heal them."*

*'But blessed are your eyes because they see, and your ears
because they hear. For I tell you the truth, many prophets and
righteous men longed to see what you see but did not see it, and to
hear what you hear but did not hear it.'*

Then Jesus said to them, *'Don't you understand? How then
will you understand any parable? The seed is the word of God.
Those along the path are the ones who hear. When anyone hears
the message about the kingdom and does not understand it, the
evil one comes and snatches away what was sown in his heart so*

131

that they may not believe and be saved. This is the seed sown along the path. The one who received the seed that fell on rocky places is the man who hears the word and at once receives it with joy. But since he has no root, he lasts only a short time. When trouble or persecution comes because of the word, he quickly falls away.

'The one who received the seed that fell among the thorns is the man who hears the word, but the worries of this life and the deceitfulness of wealth choke it, making it unfruitful. But the one who received the seed that fell on good soil stands for the man with a good and noble heart who hears the word, understands and retains it, and by persevering produces a crop, yielding a hundred, sixty or thirty times what was sown.'

He said to them, *'Do you bring a lamp to put it under a bowl or a bed to hide it? Instead, don't you put it on its stand so that those who come in can see the light? There is nothing hidden that will not be disclosed, and nothing concealed that will not be known or brought out into the open. Therefore consider carefully how you listen, with the measure you use it will be measured to you and even more. Whoever has will be given more, whoever does not have, even what he thinks he has will be taken from him.'*

He also said, *'This is what the kingdom of God is like. A man scatters seed on the ground. Night and day, whether he sleeps or gets up, the seed sprouts and grows, though he does not know how. All by itself the soil produces grain, first the stalk, then the head, then the full kernel in the head. As soon as the grain is ripe, he puts the sickle to it, because the harvest has come.'*

Jesus told them another parable, *'The kingdom of heaven is like a man who sowed good seed in his field. But while everyone was sleeping, his enemy came and sowed weeds among the wheat, and went away. When the wheat sprouted and formed heads, then the weeds also appeared.*

'The owner's servants came to him and said, "Sir, didn't you sow good seed in your field? Where then did the weeds come from?" "An enemy did this," he replied. The servants asked him, "Do you want us to go and pull them up?" "No," he answered, "because while you are pulling the weeds, you may root up the wheat with them. Let both grow together until the harvest. At that

time I will tell the harvesters: first collect the weeds and tie them in bundles to be burned; then gather the wheat and bring it into my barn."'

He told them another parable, 'The kingdom of heaven is like a mustard seed, which a man took and planted in his field. Though it is the smallest of all your seeds, yet when it grows, it is the largest of garden plants and becomes a tree, so that the birds of the air come and perch in its big branches in the shade.'

He told them still another parable, 'The kingdom of heaven is like yeast that a woman took and mixed into a large amount of flour until it worked all through the dough.'

Jesus spoke all these things to the crowd in parables; he did not say anything to them without using a parable. So was fulfilled what was spoken through the prophet Isaiah:

> 'I will open my mouth in parables,
> I will utter things hidden since the creation of the
> world.'

Then he left the crowd and went into the house. His disciples came to him and said, 'Explain to us the parable of the weeds in the field.' He answered, 'The one who sowed the good seed is the Son of Man. The field is the world, and the good seed stands for the sons of the kingdom. The weeds are the sons of the evil one, and the enemy who sows them is the devil. The harvest is the end of the age, and the harvesters are angels. As the weeds are pulled up and burned in the fire, so it will be at the end of the age. The Son of Man will send out his angels, and they will weed out of his kingdom everything that causes sin and all who do evil. They will throw them into the fiery furnace, where there will be weeping and gnashing of teeth. Then the righteous will shine like the sun in the kingdom of their Father. He who has ears, let him hear.

'The kingdom of heaven is like treasure hidden in a field. When a man found it, he hid it again, and then in his joy went and sold all he had and bought that field. Again, the kingdom of heaven is like a merchant looking for fine pearls. When he found one of great value, he went away and sold everything he had and bought it. Once again, the kingdom of heaven is like a net that was let down into the lake and caught all kinds of fish. When it was full, the fishermen pulled it up on the shore. Then they sat down and collected the good fish in baskets, but threw the bad away. This is how it will be at the end of the age. The angels will come and separate the wicked from the righteous and throw them into the fiery furnace, where there will be weeping and gnashing of teeth.

'Have you understood all these things?' Jesus asked, 'Yes,' they replied. He said to them, *'Therefore every teacher of the law who has been instructed about the kingdom of heaven is like the owner of a house who brings out of his storeroom new treasures as well as old.'* When Jesus had finished these parables, he moved on from there.

The calming of the storm and healing of the Gadarene demoniac

That day when evening came, Jesus seeing the crowds around him gave orders to his disciples, saying, *'Let us go over to the other side of the lake.'* Then he got into the boat and his disciples followed him. So leaving the crowd behind, they took him along. There were also other boats with them. As they sailed, he fell asleep. Without warning a furious squall came upon the lake, and the waves swept over the boat, so that it was nearly swamped and they were in great danger. Jesus was in the stern, sleeping on a cushion. The disciples woke him saying, 'Master, Teacher, don't you care if we drown? Lord, save us! We're going to drown!' He replied, *'You of little faith, why are you so afraid?'* Then he got up, rebuked the wind and said to the raging waves, *'Quiet! Be still!'* Then the wind died down and it was completely calm. He said to his disciples, *'Where is your faith?'* They were terrified and amazed asking each other, 'Who is this man? He commands even the winds and the waves and they obey him!'

When he arrived at the other side in the country of the Gerasenes, which is across the lake from Galilee, Jesus stepped ashore and two demon-possessed men came running from the tombs to meet him. They were so violent that no one could pass that way. 'What do you want with us, Son of God?' they shouted. 'Have you come here to torture us before the appointed time?' One of these men came from the town, but for a long time had not lived in a house, but had lived in the tombs. Many times the demons had seized him, and though he was chained hand and foot and kept under guard, he had broken his chains and had been driven by the demons into solitary places. Night and day among the tombs and in the hills he would cry out and cut himself with stones. When he saw Jesus, he cried out and fell at his feet, shouting at the top of his voice, 'What do you want with me, Jesus, Son of the Most High God? I beg you, don't torture me!' For Jesus had commanded, *'Come out of this man, you evil spirit!'*

Jesus asked him, *'What is your name?'* 'My name is Legion,' he replied, because many demons had gone into him. They begged him repeatedly not to send them out of the area and order them to go into the Abyss. A large herd of pigs was feeding on the nearby hillside. The demons begged Jesus, 'Send us among the pigs, allow us to go into them,' and he gave them permission. When the demons came out, they went into the pigs, and the herd rushed down the steep bank into the lake and were drowned.

When those tending the pigs saw what had happened, they ran off and reported this in the town and countryside, including what had happened to the demon possessed men. Then the whole town went out to meet Jesus. When they came to him, they found the man who had been possessed by the legion of demons, sitting at Jesus' feet, dressed and in his right mind; and they were afraid. Those who had seen it told the people how the demon-possessed man had been cured and about the pigs as well. Then all the people of the region of the Gerasenes asked Jesus to leave them, because they were overcome with fear. So he got into the boat and left.

As he was getting back into the boat the man from whom the demons had gone out begged to go with him, but Jesus sent him away, saying, *'Return home to your family and tell them how much the Lord has done for you and how he has had mercy on you.'* So the man went away and began to tell in the Decapolis how much Jesus had done for him. And all the people were amazed.

More miracles

Now when Jesus returned, having again crossed over by boat to the other side of the lake, a large crowd welcomed him, for they were all expecting him. Then a man named Jairus, a ruler of the synagogue, came and fell at Jesus' feet, pleading earnestly with him to come to his house saying, 'My little daughter is dying. Please come and put your hands on her so that she will be healed and live.' She was his only daughter, just twelve years of age. As Jesus was on his way, the crowds almost crushed him. A woman was there who had been subject to bleeding for twelve years. She had suffered a great deal under the care of many doctors and had spent all she had, yet instead of getting better she grew worse for no one could heal her. When she heard about Jesus, she came up behind him in the crowd and touched his cloak, because she thought, 'If I just touch his clothes, I will be healed.' Immediately her bleeding stopped and she felt in her body that she was freed from her suffering.

At once Jesus realised that power had gone out from him. He turned around in the crowd and asked, *'Who touched my clothes?'* When they all denied it, Peter answered, 'Master, the people are crowding and pressing against you.' And his disciples said, 'And you ask, who touched me?' But Jesus kept looking around to see who had done it. He said, *'Someone touched me; I know that power has gone out from me.'* Then the woman, knowing what had happened and seeing that she could not go unnoticed, came trembling and fell at his feet. In the presence of all the people, she told why she had touched him and how she had been instantly healed. Then he said to her, *'Take heart daughter, your faith has healed you. Go in peace and be freed from your suffering.'*

While Jesus was still speaking, some men came from the house of Jairus, the synagogue ruler. 'Your daughter is dead,' they said. 'Don't bother the teacher any more.' Hearing this, Jesus ignored what they said to Jairus, saying, *'Don't be afraid; just believe, and she will be healed.'* He did not let anyone follow him except Peter, James and John the brother of James. When they arrived at the house of Jairus, Jesus saw a commotion, with people crying and wailing loudly. He did not let anyone go in with him except Peter, John and James, and the child's father and mother. *'Stop wailing,'* Jesus said. *'She is not dead but asleep.'* They laughed at him, knowing that she was dead. After he put them all out, he took the child's father and mother and the disciples who were with him, and went in where the child was. He took her by the hand and said to her, *'Talitha koum!'* (which means, 'Little girl, I say to you, get up!'). Immediately her spirit returned, and at once she stood up and walked around. Then Jesus told them to give her something to eat. At this they were completely astonished. He gave them strict orders not to tell anyone what had happened.

As Jesus went on from there, two blind men followed him, calling out, 'Have mercy on us, Son of David!' When he had gone indoors, the blind men came to him, and he asked them, *'Do you believe that I am able to do this?'* 'Yes, Lord,' they replied. Then he touched their eyes and said, *'According to your faith will it be done to you,'* and their sight was restored. Jesus warned them sternly, *'See that no one knows about this.'* But they went out and spread the news about him all over that region. While they were going out, a man who was demon-possessed and could not talk was brought to Jesus. And when the demon was driven out, the man who had been mute spoke. The crowd was amazed and said, 'Nothing like this has ever been seen in Israel.' But the Pharisees said, 'It is by the prince of demons that he drives out demons.'

Chapter 14

The Year of Opposition

'Lord, to whom shall we go?
You have the words of eternal life.'

Jesus left there and went to his home town, accompanied by his disciples. When the Sabbath came, he began to teach in the synagogue, and many who heard him were amazed. 'Where did this man get these things?' they asked. 'What's this wisdom that has been given him, that he even does miracles! Isn't this the carpenter? Isn't this Mary's son and the brother of James, Joseph, Judas and Simon? Aren't all his sisters here with us?' And they took offence at him. Jesus said to them, *'Only in his home town, among his relatives and in his own house is a prophet without honour.'* He could not do any miracles there, except lay his hands on a few sick people and heal them. And he was amazed at their lack of faith.

Jesus went through all the towns and villages, teaching in their synagogues, preaching the good news of the Kingdom and healing every disease and sickness. When he saw the crowds, he had compassion on them, because they were harassed and helpless, like sheep without a shepherd. Then he said to his disciples, *'The harvest is plentiful but the workers are few. Ask the Lord of the harvest, therefore, to send out workers into his harvest field.'*

The mission of the Twelve – February AD 29

Jesus called his twelve disciples to him and gave them authority to drive out evil spirits and to heal every disease and sickness and to preach the Kingdom of God. He sent them out with the following instructions, *'Do not go among the Gentiles or enter any town of the Samaritans. Go rather to the lost sheep of Israel. As you go, preach this message: "The kingdom of heaven is near." Heal the sick, raise the dead, cleanse those who have leprosy, drive out demons. Freely you have received, freely give. Do not take along any gold or silver or copper in your belts; take no bag for the journey, or extra tunic, or sandals or a staff; for the worker is worth his keep. Whatever town or village you enter, search for some worthy person there and stay at his house until you leave. As you enter the home, give it your greeting. If the home is deserving, let your peace rest on it; if it is not, let your peace return to you. If anyone will not welcome you or listen to your words, shake the dust off your feet when you leave that home or town as a testimony against them. I tell you the truth, it will be more bearable for Sodom and Gomorrah on the day of judgement than for that town. I am sending you out like sheep among wolves. Therefore be as shrewd as snakes and as innocent as doves.*

'Be on your guard against men; they will hand you over to the local councils and flog you in their synagogues. On my account you will be brought before governors and kings as witnesses to them and to the Gentiles. But when they arrest you, do not worry about what to say or how to say it. At that time you will be given what to say, for it will not be you speaking, but the Spirit of your Father speaking through you. Brother will betray brother to death, and a father his child; children will rebel against their parents and have them put to death. All men will hate you because of me, but he who stands firm to the end will be saved. When you are persecuted in one place, flee to another. I tell you the truth, you will not finish going through the cities of Israel before the Son of Man comes.

'A student is not above his teacher, nor a servant above his master. It is enough for the student to be like his teacher, and the servant like his master. If the head of the house has been called Beelzebub, how much more the members of his household!

'So do not be afraid of them. There is nothing concealed that will not be disclosed, or hidden that will not be made known. What I tell you in the dark, speak in the daylight; what is whispered in your ear, proclaim from the roofs. Do not be afraid

of those who kill the body but cannot kill the soul. Rather, be afraid of the One who can destroy both soul and body in hell. Are not two sparrows sold for a penny? Yet not one of them will fall to the ground apart from the will of your Father. And even the very hairs of your head are all numbered. So don't be afraid; you are worth more than many sparrows.

'Whoever acknowledges me before men, I will also acknowledge him before my Father in heaven. But whoever disowns me before men, I will disown him before my Father in heaven. Do not suppose that I have come to bring peace to the earth. I did not come to bring peace, but a sword. For I have come to turn a man against his father, a daughter against her mother, a daughter-in-law against her mother-in-law. A man's enemies will be the members of his own household.

'Anyone who loves his father or mother more than me is not worthy of me; anyone who loves his son or daughter more than me is not worthy of me; and anyone who does not take his cross and follow me is not worthy of me. Whoever finds his life will lose it, and whoever loses his life for my sake will find it. He who receives you receives me, and he who receives me receives the one who sent me.

'Anyone who receives a prophet because he is a prophet will receive a prophet's reward, and anyone who receives a righteous man because he is a righteous man will receive a righteous man's reward. And if anyone gives even a cup of cold water to one of these little ones because he is my disciple, I tell you the truth, he will certainly not lose his reward.'

After Jesus had finished instructing his twelve disciples, he went on from there to teach and preach in the towns of Galilee, while the disciples went out preaching the gospel, telling the people to repent. They drove out many demons and anointed many sick people with oil and healed them.

Herod has John the Baptist beheaded

King Herod heard about this, for Jesus' name had become well known. And he was perplexed because some were saying, 'John the Baptist has been raised from the dead, and that is why miraculous powers are at work in him.' Others said, 'He is Elijah.' And still others claimed, 'He is a prophet, like one of the prophets of long ago.' But when Herod heard this, he said, 'I beheaded John. Who, then, is this man I hear such things about?' And he said to his attendants, 'This is John the Baptist; he has risen from the dead! That is why miraculous powers are at work in him.' He was greatly puzzled.

Herod had liked to hear John preach but had given orders to have him arrested, bound and put in prison. He had done this because of Herodias, his brother Philip's wife, whom he had married. For John had been saying to Herod, 'It is not lawful for you to have your brother's wife.' So Herodias nursed a grudge against John and wanted to kill him. But she was not able to, because Herod feared John and protected him, knowing him to be a righteous and holy man. He was also afraid of the people, because they considered John to be a prophet.

Finally the opportune time came for Herodias. On his birthday Herod gave a banquet for his high officials and military commanders and the leading men of Galilee. When the daughter of Herodias, Salome, came in and danced, she greatly pleased Herod and his dinner guests. The king said to her, 'Ask me for anything you want, and I'll give it to you.' And he promised her with an oath, 'Whatever you ask I will give you, up to half my kingdom.'

She went out and said to her mother, 'What shall I ask for?' 'The head of John the Baptist,' she answered. At once the girl hurried in to the king with the request, 'I want you to give me right now the head of John the Baptist on a platter.' The king was greatly distressed, but because of his oaths and his dinner guests, he did not want to refuse her. So he immediately sent an executioner with orders to bring John's head. The man went, beheaded John in the prison, and brought back his head on a platter. He presented it to the girl, and she gave it to her mother. On hearing of this, John's disciples came and took his body and laid it in a tomb. Then they went and told Jesus.

The feeding of the five thousand – April AD 29

Then the apostles returned and gathered around Jesus and reported to him all they had done and taught. Because so many people were coming and going that they did not even have a chance to eat, he said to them, *'Come with me by yourselves to a quiet place and get some rest.'* Then he took them with him and they withdrew by themselves to find a solitary place. They headed towards a town called Bethsaida, crossing by boat to the far shore of the Sea of Galilee.

Many who saw them leaving recognised them and ran on foot from all the towns because they had seen all the miraculous signs he had performed on the sick and got there ahead of them. When Jesus landed he saw a great crowd had followed him and he had compassion on them, because they were like sheep without a shepherd. He welcomed them and spoke to them about the Kingdom of God, and healed those who needed healing. He went up on the hillside and sat down with his disciples. (The Jewish Passover Feast was near.) Jesus lifted up his eyes and saw a great crowd coming towards him. His disciples said to him, 'This is a remote place, and it is already very late, send the people away so they can go to the surrounding countryside and villages and buy themselves something to eat and find lodging.'

But he answered, *'They do not need to go away. You give them something to eat.'* He said to Philip, *'Where shall we buy bread for these people to eat?'* He asked this only to test him, for he already had in mind what he was going to do. Philip answered him, 'Eight months wages would not buy enough bread for each one to have a bite! Are we to go and spend that much on bread and give it to them to eat?' *'How many loaves do you have?'* Jesus asked. *'Go and see.'*

Another of his disciples, Andrew, Simon Peter's brother, spoke up, 'Here is a boy with five small barley loaves and two small fish, but how far will they go among so many?' Jesus said, *'Bring them here to me and have the people sit down in groups of about fifty each.'* There was plenty of green grass in that place, so they sat down in groups of hundreds and fifties.

Jesus then took the five loaves and the two fish and looking up to heaven, he gave thanks and broke the loaves. Then he gave them to his disciples to set before the people. He also divided the two fish among them all and they all ate as much as they wanted and were satisfied.

Jesus said to his disciples, *'Gather the pieces that are left over. Let nothing be wasted.'* So they gathered them and filled twelve baskets with the pieces of the five barley loaves and two fish left over by those who had eaten.

The number of men that had eaten was five thousand, besides women and children. After the people saw the miraculous sign that Jesus did, they began to say, 'Surely this is the Prophet who is to come into the world.'

Immediately Jesus made his disciples leave him to get into the boat and go on ahead of him to Bethsaida, while he stayed behind to dismiss the crowd because he knew that they intended to come and make him king by force, so he withdrew by himself to a mountain to pray.

By now it was evening and his disciples went down to the lake, where they got into the boat and set off across the lake for Capernaum. It was dark, the boat was in the middle of the lake and Jesus was alone on land. He saw the disciples straining at the oars, because the wind was against them. A strong wind was blowing and the waters grew rough. About the fourth watch of the night he went out to them, walking on the lake, they had rowed three or three and a half miles. They saw Jesus approaching the boat, walking on the water. He was about to pass them by. They thought he was a ghost. They cried out in fear, because they all saw him and were terrified. Immediately he spoke to them and said, *'Take courage! It is I don't be afraid.'* 'Lord, if it's you,' Peter replied, 'tell me to come to you on the water.' *'Come,'* he said. Then Peter got down out of the boat, walked on the water and came to Jesus. But when he saw the wind, he was afraid and, beginning to sink, cried out, 'Lord, save me!' Immediately Jesus reached out his hand and caught him. *'You of little faith,'* he said, *'why did you doubt?'*

And when they climbed into the boat to be with the others, the wind died down. They were completely amazed, and worshipped him saying, 'Truly you are the Son of God.' For they had not understood about the loaves; their hearts were hardened. And immediately the boat reached the shore where they were heading.

Jesus, the Bread of Life

The next day, when the men of that place recognised Jesus, they sent word to all the surrounding country. People brought all their sick to him and begged him to let the sick just touch the edge of his cloak, and all who touched him were healed.

The crowd that had stayed on the opposite shore of the lake realised that only one boat had been there, and that Jesus had not entered it with his disciples, but that they had gone away alone. Then some boats from Tiberius landed near the place where the people had eaten the bread after the Lord had given thanks. Once the crowd realised that neither Jesus nor his disciples were there, they got into the boats and went to Capernaum in search of Jesus. When they found him on the other side of the lake, they asked him, 'Rabbi, when did you get here?' Jesus answered, *'I tell you the truth, you are looking for me, not because you saw miraculous signs but because you ate the loaves and had your fill. Do not work for food that spoils, but for food that endures to eternal life, which the Son of Man will give you. On him God the Father has placed his seal of approval.'* Then they asked him, 'What must we do to do the works God requires?' Jesus answered, *'The work of God is this: to believe in the one he has sent.'*

So they asked him, 'What miraculous sign then will you give that we may see it and believe you? What will you do? Our forefathers ate the manna in the desert; as it is written: "He gave them bread from heaven to eat."' Jesus said to them, *'I tell you the truth, it is not Moses who has given you the bread from heaven, but it is my Father who gives you the true bread from heaven. For the bread of God is he who comes down from heaven and gives life to the world.'* 'Sir,' they said, 'From now on give us this bread.'

Then Jesus declared, *'I am the bread of life. He who comes to me will never go hungry, and he who believes in me will never be thirsty. But as I told you, you have seen me and still you do not believe. All that the Father gives me will come to me, and whoever comes to me I will never drive away. For I have come down from heaven not to do my will but to do the will of him who sent me. And this is the will of him who sent me, that I shall lose none of all that he has given me, but raise them up at the last day. For my Father's will is that everyone who looks to the Son and believes in him shall have eternal life, and I will raise him up at the last day.'*

At this the Jews began to grumble about him because he said, *'I am the bread that came down from heaven.'* They said, 'Is this not Jesus, the son of Joseph, whose father and mother we know? How can he now say, *"I came down from heaven"*?'

'Stop grumbling among yourselves,' Jesus answered. *'No one can come to me unless the Father who sent me draws him, and I will raise him up at the last day. It is written in the Prophets: "They will all be taught by God." Everyone who listens to the Father and learns from him comes to me. No one has seen the Father except the one who is from God; only he has seen the Father. I tell you the truth, he who believes has everlasting life. I am the bread of life. Your forefathers ate the manna in the desert, yet they died. But here is the bread that comes down from heaven, which a man may eat and not die. I am the living bread that came down from heaven. If anyone eats of this bread, he will live forever. This bread is my flesh, which I will give for the life of the world.'*

Then the Jews began to argue sharply among themselves, 'How can this man give us his flesh to eat?' Jesus said to them, *'I tell you the truth, unless you eat the flesh of the Son of Man and drink his blood, you have no life in you. Whoever eats my flesh and drinks my blood has eternal life, and I will raise him up at the last day. For my flesh is real food and my blood is real drink. Whoever eats my flesh and drinks my blood remains in me, and I in him. Just as the living Father sent me and I live because of the Father, so the one who feeds on me will live because of me. This is the bread that came down from heaven. Your forefathers ate manna and died, but he who feeds on this bread will live forever.'*

On hearing it, many of his disciples said, 'This is a hard teaching. Who can accept it?' Aware that his disciples were grumbling about this, Jesus said to them, *'Does this offend you? What if you see the Son of Man ascend to where he was before! The Spirit gives life; the flesh counts for nothing. The words I have spoken to you are spirit and they are life. Yet there are some of you who do not believe.'* For Jesus had known from the beginning which of them did not believe and who would betray him. He went on to say, *'This is why I told you that no one can come to me unless the Father has enabled him.'* From this time many of his disciples turned back and no longer followed him. *'You do not want to leave too, do you?'* Jesus asked the Twelve.

Simon Peter answered him, 'Lord, to whom shall we go? You have the words of eternal life. We believe and know that you are the Holy One of God.' Then Jesus replied, *'Have I not chosen you, the Twelve? Yet one of you is a devil!'* (He meant Judas, the son of Simon Iscariot, who, though one of the Twelve, was later to betray him.) After this, Jesus went around in Galilee, purposely staying away from Judea because the Jews there were waiting to take his life.

Jesus condemns religious legalism

Then some of the Pharisees and some of the teachers of the law who had come from Jerusalem gathered around Jesus and saw some of his disciples eating food with hands that were 'unclean,' that is, unwashed. (The Pharisees and all the Jews do not eat unless they give their hands a ceremonial washing, holding to the tradition of the elders. When they come from the marketplace they do not eat unless they wash. And they observe many other traditions, such as the washing of cups, pitchers and kettles.)

So the Pharisees and teachers of the law asked Jesus, 'Why don't your disciples live according to the tradition of the elders instead of eating their food with "unclean' hands?'

He replied, *'Isaiah was right when he prophesied about you hypocrites; as it is written:*

' "These people honour me with their lips,
but their hearts are far from me.
They worship me in vain;
their teachings are but rules taught by men."

'You have let go of the commands of God and are holding on to the traditions of men.'

And he said to them, *'You have a fine way of setting aside the commands of God in order to observe your own traditions! For Moses said, "Honour your father and your mother," and, "Anyone who curses his father or mother must be put to death." But you say that if a man says to his father or mother: "Whatever help you might otherwise have received from me is Corban"* (that is, a gift devoted to God), *then you no longer let him do anything for his father or mother. Thus you nullify the word of God by your tradition that you have handed down. And you do many things like that.'*

Again Jesus called the crowd to him and said, *'Listen to me, everyone, and understand this. Nothing outside a man can make him "unclean" by going into him. Rather, it is what comes out of a man that makes him "unclean." '*

After he had left the crowd and entered the house, his disciples came to him and asked, *'Do you know that the Pharisees were offended when they heard this?'*

He replied, *'Every plant that my heavenly Father has not planted will be pulled up by the roots. Leave them; they are blind guides. If a blind man leads a blind man, both will fall into a pit.'* Peter said, 'Explain the parable to us.' *'Are you so dull?'* Jesus asked them. *'Don't you see that nothing that enters a man from the outside can make him "unclean"? For it doesn't go into his heart but into his stomach, and then out of his body.'* (In saying this, Jesus declared all foods 'clean.')

He went on, *'What comes out of a man is what makes him "unclean." For from within, out of men's hearts, come evil thoughts, sexual immorality, theft, murder, adultery, greed, malice, deceit, lewdness, envy, slander, arrogance and folly. All these evils come from inside and make a man "unclean."'*

Jesus travels out of Palestine

Jesus left that place and went to the vicinity of Tyre and Sidon. He entered a house and did not want anyone to know it; yet he could not keep his presence secret. In fact, as soon as she heard about him, a Canaanite woman whose little daughter was possessed by an evil spirit came and fell at his feet. The woman was a Greek, born in Syrian Phoenicia. She begged Jesus to drive the demon out of her daughter. 'Lord, Son of David, have mercy on me! My daughter is suffering terribly from demon possession.' Jesus did not answer her a word. So his disciples came to him and urged him, 'Send her away, for she keeps crying out after us.' He answered her, *'I was sent only to the lost sheep of Israel.'*

The woman came and knelt before him. 'Lord, help me!' she said. *'First let the children eat all they want,'* he told her, *'For it is not right to take the children's bread and toss it to their dogs.'* 'Yes, Lord,' she replied, 'But even the dogs eat the children's crumbs that fall from the master's table.' Then he told her, *'Woman, you have great faith. For such a reply, you may go; your request is granted, the demon has left your daughter.'* And her daughter was healed from that very hour. She went home and found her child lying on the bed, and the demon gone.

Then Jesus left the vicinity of Tyre and went through Sidon, down to the Sea of Galilee and into the region of the Decapolis. Then he went up into the hills and sat down. Great crowds came to him, bringing the lame, the blind, the crippled, the dumb and many others, and laid them at his feet; and he healed them. Some people brought to him a man who was deaf and could hardly talk, and they begged him to place his hand on the man. After he took him aside, away from the crowd, Jesus put his fingers into the man's ears. Then he spat and touched the man's tongue. He looked up to heaven and with a deep sigh said to him, *'Ephphatha!'* (which means, 'Be opened!'). At this, the man's ears were opened, his tongue was loosened and he began to speak plainly.

Jesus commanded them not to tell anyone. But the more he did so, the more they kept talking about it. People were overwhelmed with amazement when they saw the dumb speaking, the crippled made well, the lame walking and the blind seeing. 'He has done everything well,' they said. 'He even makes the deaf hear and the mute speak.' And they praised the God of Israel.

The feeding of the four thousand

During those days another large crowd gathered. Since they had nothing to eat, Jesus called his disciples to him and said, *'I have compassion for these people; they have already been with me three days and have nothing to eat. I do not want to send them home hungry, they will collapse on the way, because some of them have come a long distance.'*

His disciples answered, 'But where in this remote place can anyone get enough bread to feed such a crowd?' *'How many loaves do you have?'* Jesus asked. 'Seven,' they replied, 'and a few small fish.'

He told the crowd to sit down on the ground. When he had taken the seven loaves and given thanks, he broke them and gave them to his disciples to set before the people, and they did so. They had a few small fish as well; he gave thanks for them also and told the disciples to distribute them. The people ate and were satisfied. Afterward the disciples picked up seven basketfuls of broken pieces that were left over. About four thousand men were present. And having sent them away, he got into the boat with his disciples and went to the region of Dalmanutha.

The Pharisees and Sadducees came and began to question Jesus. To test him, they asked him for a sign from heaven. He sighed deeply and said, *'When evening comes, you say, "It will be fair weather, for the sky is red," and in the morning, "Today it will be stormy, for the sky is overcast." You know how to interpret the appearance of the sky, but you cannot interpret the signs of the* times. *Why does this generation ask for a miraculous sign? Because it is wicked and adulterous. I tell you the truth, no sign will be given to it except the sign of Jonah'* Then he left them, got back into the boat and crossed to the other side.

The disciples had forgotten to bring bread, except for one loaf they had with them in the boat. *'Be careful,'* Jesus warned them. *'Watch out for the yeast of the Pharisees and Sadducees and that of Herod.'* They discussed this with one another and said, 'It is because we have no bread.'

Aware of their discussion, Jesus asked them, *'You of little faith. Why are you talking among yourselves about having no bread? Do you still not see or understand? Are your hearts hardened? Do you have eyes but fail to see, and ears but fail to hear? And don't you remember? When I broke the five loaves for the five thousand, how many basketfuls of pieces did you pick up?'*

'Twelve,' they replied. *'And when I broke the seven loaves for the four thousand, how many basketfuls of pieces did you pick up?'* They answered, 'Seven.' He said to them, *'How is it you don't understand that I was not talking to you about bread? But be on your guard against the yeast of the Pharisees and Sadducees.'* Then they understood that he was not telling them to guard against the yeast used in bread, but against the teaching of the Pharisees and Sadducees.

They came to Bethsaida, and some people brought a blind man and begged Jesus to touch him. He took the blind man by the hand and led him outside the village. When he had spat on the man's eyes and put his hands on him, Jesus asked, *'Do you see anything?'* He looked up and said, 'I see people; they look like trees walking around. 'Once more Jesus put his hands on the man's eyes. Then his eyes were opened, his sight was restored, and he saw everything clearly. Jesus sent him home, saying, *'Don't go into the village.'*

Chapter 15

Who Do You Say That I Am?

*'You are the Christ,
the Son of the Living God.'*

Jesus and his disciples went on to the villages around Caesarea Philippi to spend some time praying with them in private. On the way he asked them, *'Who do people say the Son of Man is?'* They replied, 'Some say John the Baptist; others say Elijah, and still others, Jeremiah or one of the prophets of long ago has come back to life.' *'But what about you?'* he asked. *'Who do you say I am?'* Simon Peter answered, 'You are the Christ, the Son of the living God.'

Jesus replied, *'Blessed are you, Simon son of Jonah, for this was not revealed to you by man, but by my Father in heaven. And I tell you that you are Peter, and on this rock I will build my church, and the gates of Hades will not overcome it. I will give you the keys of the kingdom of heaven; whatever you bind on earth will be bound in heaven, and whatever you loose on earth will be loosed in heaven.'* Then he strictly warned his disciples not to tell anyone that he was the Christ.

From that time on Jesus began to explain to his disciples that he must go to Jerusalem and suffer many things at the hands of the elders, chief priests and teachers of the law, and that he must be killed and on the third day be raised to life.

Peter took him aside and began to rebuke him. 'Never, Lord!' he said. 'This shall never happen to you!' Jesus turned and said to Peter, *'Get behind me, Satan! You are a stumbling block to me; you do not have in mind the things of God, but the things of men.'*

Then Jesus said to his disciples, *'If anyone would come after me, he must deny himself and take up his cross and follow me. For whoever wants to save his life will lose it, but whoever loses his life for me will save it. What good will it be for a man if he gains the whole world, yet loses and forfeits his soul? Or what can a man give in exchange for his soul? If anyone is ashamed of me and my words in this adulterous and sinful generation, the Son of Man will be ashamed of him when he comes in his Father's glory with the holy angels, and then he will reward each person according to what he has done. I tell you the truth, some who are standing here will not taste death before they see the Son of Man coming in his kingdom and the kingdom of God come with power.'*

The Transfiguration of Jesus

After six days Jesus took Peter, James and John with him and led them up a high mountain, where they were all alone. There he was transfigured before them. His face shone like the sun, and his clothes became dazzling white, whiter than anyone in the world could bleach them, as bright as a flash of lightening. Just then there appeared before them Moses and Elijah in glorious splendour, talking with Jesus. They spoke about his departure, which he was about to bring to fulfilment in Jerusalem. Peter and his companions were very sleepy, but when they became fully awake, they saw Jesus' glory and the two men standing with him. As the men were leaving Jesus, Peter said to him, 'Rabbi, it is good for us to be here. If you wish I will put up three shelters, one for you, one for Moses and one for Elijah.' (He did not know what he was saying, they were so frightened.)

While he was still speaking, a bright cloud appeared and enveloped them, and they were afraid as they entered the cloud, and a voice came from the cloud saying, 'This is my Son, whom I love and have chosen, with him I am well pleased. Listen to him!' When the disciples heard this they fell face down to the ground, terrified. But Jesus came and touched them. *'Get up,'* he said. *'Don't be afraid.'* Suddenly, when they looked around, they no longer saw anyone with them except Jesus.

As they were coming down the mountain the next day Jesus gave them orders, *'Don't tell anyone what you have seen, until the Son of Man has been raised from the dead.'* They kept the matter to themselves, discussing what 'rising from the dead' meant. And they asked him, 'Why do the teachers of the law say that Elijah must come first?' Jesus replied, *'To be sure, Elijah does come first, and restores all things. Why then is it written that the Son of Man must suffer much and be rejected? But I tell you, Elijah has come, and they did not recognise him, but have done to him everything they wished, just as it is written about him. In the same way the Son of Man is going to suffer at their hands.'* Then the disciples understood that he was talking to them about John the Baptist.

When they came to the other disciples, they saw a large crowd around them and the teachers of the law arguing with them. As soon as all the people saw Jesus, they were overwhelmed with wonder and ran to greet him. *'What are you arguing with them about?'* he asked. A man in the crowd approached Jesus and knelt before him. 'Lord, have mercy on my son, I beg you to look at him, for he is my only child. He is possessed by a spirit that has robbed him of speech. He has seizures and is suffering greatly. Whenever it seizes him, he suddenly screams, it throws him to the ground in convulsions, he foams at the mouth, gnashes his teeth and becomes rigid. It scarcely ever leaves him and is destroying him. I asked your disciples to drive out the spirit, but they could not.'

'O unbelieving and perverse generation,' Jesus replied, *'How long shall I stay with you? How long shall I put up with you? Bring the boy here to me.'*

So they brought him. When the spirit saw Jesus, it immediately threw the boy into a convulsion. He fell to the ground and rolled around, foaming at the mouth. Jesus asked the boy's father, *'How long has he been like this?'* 'From childhood,' he answered. 'It has often thrown him into fire or water to kill him. But if you can do anything, take pity on us and help us.' '"*If you can*"?' said Jesus. *'Everything is possible for him who believes.'* Immediately the boy's father exclaimed, 'I do believe; help me overcome my unbelief!' When Jesus saw that a crowd was running to the scene, he rebuked the evil spirit. *'You deaf and mute spirit,'* he said, *'I command you, come out of him and never enter him again.'* The spirit shrieked, convulsed him violently and came out. The boy looked so much like a corpse that many said, 'He's dead.' But Jesus took him by the hand and lifted him to his feet, and he stood up and was healed from that moment and Jesus gave him back to his father. And they were all amazed at the greatness of God.

After Jesus had gone indoors, his disciples asked him privately, 'Why couldn't we drive it out?' He replied, *'Because you have so little faith and this kind can only come out by prayer and fasting. I tell you the truth, if you have faith as small as a mustard seed, you can say to this mountain, "Move from here to there" and it will move. Nothing will be impossible to you.'*

They left that place and passed through Galilee. Jesus did not want anyone to know where they were, because he was teaching his disciples. While everyone was marvelling at all that Jesus did, he said to his disciples, *'Listen carefully to what I am about to tell you, the Son of Man is going to be betrayed into the hands of men. They will kill him, and after three days he will rise.'* The disciples were filled with grief because they did not understand what he meant, it was hidden from them, so they did not grasp it, and were afraid to ask him about it.

After Jesus and his disciples arrived in Capernaum, the collectors of the two-drachma tax came to Peter and asked, 'Doesn't your teacher pay the temple tax?' 'Yes, he does,' he replied. When Peter came into the house, Jesus was first to speak. *'What do you think, Simon?'* he asked. *'From whom do the kings of the earth collect duty and taxes, from their own sons or from others?'* 'From others,' Peter answered. *'Then the sons are exempt,'* Jesus said to him. *'But so that we may not offend them, go to the lake and throw out your line. Take the first fish you catch; open its mouth and you will find a four drachma coin. Take it and give it to them for my tax and yours.'*

Who is the greatest?

When he was in the house, he asked them, *'What were you arguing about on the road?'* But they kept quiet because on the way they had argued about who was the greatest, for they were asking and wanted to know who is the greatest in the kingdom of heaven. Sitting down, Jesus called the Twelve and said, *'If anyone wants to be first, he must be the very last, and the servant of all.'* He took a little child and had him stand among them. And he said, *'I tell you the truth, unless you change and become like little children, you will never enter the kingdom of heaven.'* Taking him in his arms, he said to them, *'Therefore, whoever humbles himself like this child is the greatest in the kingdom of heaven. And whoever welcomes one of these little children in my name welcomes me; and whoever welcomes me does not welcome me but the one who sent me.'*

'Teacher,' said John, 'we saw a man driving out demons in your name and we told him to stop, because he was not one of us.' *'Do not stop him,'* Jesus said. *'No one who does a miracle in my name can in the next moment say anything bad about me, for whoever is not against us is for us. I tell you the truth, anyone who gives you a cup of water in my name because you belong to Christ will certainly not lose his reward.*

'But if anyone causes one of these little ones who believe in me to sin, it would be better to have a large millstone hung around his neck and to be drowned in the depths of the sea. Woe to the world because of the things that cause people to sin! Such things must come, but woe to the man through whom they come! If your hand or your foot causes you to sin cut it off and throw it away. It is better for you to enter life maimed or crippled than to have two hands or two feet and be thrown into eternal fire. And if your eye causes you to sin, gouge it out and throw it away. It is better for you to enter life in the kingdom of God with one eye than to have two eyes and be thrown into the fire of hell, where,

> *' "their worm does not die,*
> *and the fire is not quenched."*

'Everyone will be salted with fire. Salt is good, but if it loses its

saltiness, how can you make it salty again? Have salt in yourselves, and be at peace with each other. See that you do not look down on one of these little ones. For I tell you that their angels in heaven always see the face of my Father in heaven.

'What do you think? If a man owns a hundred sheep, and one of them wanders away, will he not leave the ninety-nine on the hills and go to look for the one that wandered off? And if he finds it, I tell you the truth, he is happier about that one sheep than about the ninety-nine that did not wander off. In the same way your Father in heaven is not willing that any of these little ones should be lost.

'If your brother sins against you, go and show him his fault, just between the two of you. If he listens to you, you have won your brother over. But if he will not listen, take one or two others along, so that "every matter may be established by the testimony of two or three witnesses." If he refuses to listen to them, tell it to the church; and if he refuses to listen even to the church, treat him as you would a pagan or a tax collector.

'I tell you the truth, whatever you bind on earth will be bound in heaven, and whatever you loose on earth will be loosed in heaven.

'Again, I tell you that if two of you on earth agree about anything you ask for, it will be done for you by my Father in heaven. For where two or three come together in my name, there am I with them.'

How many times should we forgive?

Then Peter came to Jesus and asked, 'Lord, how many times shall I forgive my brother when he sins against me? Up to seven times?' Jesus answered, *'I tell you, not seven times, but seventy-seven times. Therefore, the kingdom of heaven is like a king who wanted to settle accounts with his servants. As he began the settlement, a man who owed him ten thousand talents was brought to him. Since he was not able to pay, the master ordered that he and his wife and his children and all that he had, be sold to repay the debt. The servant fell on his knees before him. "Be patient with me," he begged, "and I will pay back everything." The servant's master took pity on him, cancelled the debt and let him go.*

'But when that servant went out, he found one of his fellow servants who owed him a hundred denarii. He grabbed him and began to choke him. "Pay back what you owe me!" he demanded. His fellow servant fell to his knees and begged him, "Be patient with me, and I will pay you back." But he refused. Instead, he went off and had the man thrown into prison until he could pay the debt.

'When the other servants saw what had happened, they were greatly distressed and went and told their master everything that had happened. Then the master called the servant in. "You wicked servant," he said, "I cancelled all that debt of yours because you begged me to. Shouldn't you have had mercy on your fellow servant just as I had on you?" In anger his master turned him over to the jailers to be tortured, until he should pay back all he owed. This is how my heavenly Father will treat each of you unless you forgive your brother from your heart.'

October AD 29

When the Jewish Feast of Tabernacles was near, Jesus' brothers said to him, 'You ought to leave here and go to Judea, so that your disciples may see the miracles you do. No one who wants to become a public figure acts in secret. Since you are doing these things, show yourself to the world.' For even his own brothers did not believe in him.

Therefore Jesus told them, *'The right time for me has not yet come; for you any time is right. The world cannot hate you, but it hates me because I testify that what it does is evil. You go to the Feast. I am not yet going up to this Feast, because for me the right time has not yet come.'* Having said this, he stayed in Galilee until after his brothers had left for the Feast. Then he also went, but not publicly, but in secret for the time was approaching for him to be taken up to heaven so he departed from Galilee and resolutely set out for Jerusalem. He sent messengers on ahead, who went into a Samaritan village to get things ready for him, but the people there did not welcome him, because he was heading for Jerusalem.

When the disciples James and John saw this, they asked,

'Lord, do you want us to call fire down from heaven to destroy them?' But Jesus turned and rebuked them, and they went to another village. As they were walking along the road, a man said to him, 'I will follow you wherever you go.' To which Jesus replied, *'Foxes have holes and the birds of the air have nests, but the Son of Man has no place to lay his head.'* He said to another man, one of his disciples, *'Follow me.'* But the man replied, 'Lord, first let me go and bury my father.' Jesus said to him, *'Let the dead bury their own dead, but you go and proclaim the kingdom of God.'* Still another said, 'I will follow you, Lord, but first let me go back and say good bye to my family.' Jesus replied, *'No one who puts his hand to the plough and looks back is fit for service in the kingdom of God.'*

Now at the Feast the Jews were watching for him and asking, 'Where is that man?' Among the crowds there was widespread whispering about him. Some said, 'He is a good man.' Others replied, 'No, he deceives the people.' But no one would say anything publicly about him for fear of the Jews.

Not until halfway through the Feast did Jesus go up to the temple courts and begin to teach. The Jews were amazed and asked, 'How did this man get such learning without having studied?' Jesus answered, *'My teaching is not my own. It comes from him who sent me. If anyone chooses to do God's will, he will find out whether my teaching comes from God or whether I speak on my own. He who speaks on his own does so to gain honour for himself, but he who works for the honour of the one who sent him is a man of truth; there is nothing false about him. Has not Moses given you the Law? Yet not one of you keeps the Law. Why are you trying to kill me?'* 'You are demon-possessed,' the crowd answered. 'Who is trying to kill you?'

Jesus said to them, *'I did one miracle, and you are all astonished. Yet, because Moses gave you circumcision (though actually it did not come from Moses, but from the patriarchs), you circumcise a child on the Sabbath. Now if a child can be circumcised on the Sabbath so that the law of Moses may not be broken, why are you angry with me for healing the whole man* on the Sabbath? Stop judging by mere appearances, and make a right judgement.'

At that point some of the people of Jerusalem began to ask, 'Isn't this the man they are trying to kill? Here he is, speaking publicly, and they are not saying a word to him. Have the authorities really concluded that he is the Christ? But we know where this man is from; when the Christ comes, no one will know where he is from.'

Then Jesus, still teaching in the temple courts, cried out, *'Yes, you know me, and you know where I am from. I am not here on my own, but he who sent me is true. You do not know him, but I know him because I am from him and he sent me.'* At this they tried to seize him, but no one laid a hand on him, because his time had not yet come. Still, many in the crowd put their faith in him. They said, 'When the Christ comes, will he do more miraculous signs than this man?' The Pharisees heard the crowd whispering such things about him. Then the chief priests and the Pharisees sent temple guards to arrest him.

Jesus said, *'I am with you for only a short time, and then I go to the one who sent me. You will look for me, but you will not find me; and where I am, you cannot come.'* The Jews said to one another, 'Where does this man intend to go that we cannot find him? Will he go where our people live scattered among the Greeks, and teach the Greeks? What did he mean when he said, *"You will look for me, but you will not find me and where I am, you cannot come"*?'

Jesus, the Life Giver

On the last and greatest day of the Feast, Jesus stood and said in a loud voice, *'If anyone is thirsty, let him come to me and drink. Whoever believes in me, as the Scripture has said, streams of living water will flow from within him.'* By this he meant the Spirit, whom those who believed in him were later to receive. Up to that time the Spirit had not been given, since Jesus had not yet been glorified. On hearing his words some of the people said, 'Surely this man is the Prophet.' Others said, 'He is the Christ.' Still others asked, 'How can the Christ come from Galilee? Does not the Scripture say that the Christ will come from David's family and from Bethlehem, the town where David lived?' Thus the people were divided because of Jesus. Some wanted to seize him, but no one laid a hand on him.

Finally the temple guards went back to the chief priests and Pharisees, who asked them, 'Why didn't you bring him in?' 'No one ever spoke the way this man does,' the guards declared. 'You mean he has deceived you also?' the Pharisees retorted. 'Has any of the rulers or any of the Pharisees believed in him? No! But this mob that knows nothing of the law, there is a curse on them.' Nicodemus, who had gone to Jesus earlier and who was one of their own number, asked, 'Does our law condemn anyone without first hearing him to find out what he is doing?' They replied, 'Are you from Galilee, too? Look into it, and you will find that a prophet does not come out of Galilee.' Then each went to his own home. But Jesus went to the Mount of Olives.

A woman caught in the act of adultery

At dawn he appeared again in the temple courts, where all the people gathered around him, and he sat down to teach them. The teachers of the law and the Pharisees brought in a woman caught in adultery. They made her stand before the group and said to Jesus, 'Teacher, this woman was caught in the act of adultery. In the Law Moses commanded us to stone such women. Now what do you say?' They were using this question as a trap, in order to have a basis for accusing him. But Jesus bent down and started to write on the ground with his finger.

When they kept on questioning him, he straightened up and said to them, *'If any one of you is without sin, let him be the first to throw a stone at her.'* Again he stooped down and wrote on the ground. At this, those who heard began to go away one at a time, the older ones first, until only Jesus was left, with the woman still standing there. Jesus straightened up and asked her, *'Woman, where are they? Has no one condemned you?'* 'No one, sir,' she said. *'Then neither do I condemn you,'* Jesus declared. *'Go now and leave your life of sin.'*

Chapter 16

Jesus, the Light of the World

*'I have come that they may have life,
and life to the full.'*

When Jesus spoke again to the people, he said, *'I am the light of the world. Whoever follows me will never walk in darkness, but will have the light of life.'*

The Pharisees challenged him, 'Here you are, appearing as your own witness; your testimony is not valid.' Jesus answered, *'Even if I testify on my own behalf, my testimony is valid, for I know where I came from and where I am going. But you have no idea where I come from or where I am going. You judge by human standards; I pass judgement on no one. But if I do judge, my decisions are right, because I am not alone. I stand with the Father, who sent me. In your own Law it is written that the testimony of two men is valid. I am one who testifies for myself; my other witness is the Father, who sent me.'*

Then they asked him, 'Where is your father?' *'You do not know me or my Father,'* Jesus replied. *'If you knew me, you would know my Father also.'* He spoke these words while teaching in the temple area near the place where the offerings were put. Yet no one seized him, because his time had not yet come.

Once more Jesus said to them, *'I am going away, and you will look for me, and you will die in your sin. Where I go, you cannot come.'*

This made the Jews ask, 'Will he kill himself? Is that why he says, *"Where I go, you cannot come"*?' But he continued, *'You are from below; I am from above. You are of this world; I am not of this world. I told you that you would die in your sins; if you do not believe that I am the one I claim to be, you will indeed die in your sins.'* 'Who are you?' they asked. *'Just what I have been claiming all along,'* Jesus replied. *'I have much to say in judgement of you. But he who sent me is reliable, and what I have heard from him I tell the world.'*

They did not understand that he was telling them about his Father. So Jesus said, *'When you have lifted up the Son of Man, then you will know that I am the one I claim to be and that I do nothing on my own but speak just what the Father has taught me. The one who sent me is with me; he has not left me alone, for I always do what pleases him.'* Even as he spoke, many put their faith in him.

To the Jews who had believed him, Jesus said, *'If you hold to my teaching, you are really my disciples. Then you will know the truth, and the truth will set you free.'*

They answered him, 'We are Abraham's descendants and have never been slaves of anyone. How can you say that we shall be set free?' Jesus replied, *'I tell you the truth, everyone who sins is a slave to sin. Now a slave has no permanent place in the family, but a son belongs to it forever. So if the Son sets you free, you will be free indeed. I know you are Abraham's descendants. Yet you are ready to kill me, because you have no room for my word. I am telling you what I have seen in the Father's presence, and you do what you have heard from your father.'* 'Abraham is our father,' they answered. *'If you were Abraham's children,'* said Jesus, *'then you would do the things Abraham did. As it is, you are determined to kill me, a man who has told you the truth that I heard from God. Abraham did not do such things. You are doing the things your own father does.'*

'We are not illegitimate children,' they protested. 'The only Father we have is God himself.' Jesus said to them, *'If God were your Father, you would love me, for I came from God and now am here. I have not come on my own; but he sent me. Why is my language not clear to you? Because you are unable to hear what I say. You belong to your father, the devil, and you want to carry out your father's desire. He was a murderer from the beginning, not holding to the truth, for there is no truth in him.*

When he lies, he speaks his native language, for he is a liar and the father of lies. Yet because I tell the truth, you do not believe me! Can any of you prove me guilty of sin? If I am telling the truth, why don't you believe me? He who belongs to God hears what God says. The reason you do not hear is that you do not belong to God.'

The Jews answered him, 'Aren't we right in saying that you are a Samaritan and demon-possessed?' *'I am not possessed by a demon,'* said Jesus, *'But I honour my Father and you dishonour me. I am not seeking glory for myself; but there is one who seeks it, and he is the judge. I tell you the truth, if anyone keeps my word, he will never see death.'*

At this the Jews exclaimed, 'Now we know that you are demon-possessed! Abraham died and so did the prophets, yet you say that if anyone keeps your word, he will never taste death. Are you greater than our father Abraham? He died, and so did the prophets. Who do you think you are?'

Jesus replied, *'If I glorify myself, my glory means nothing. My Father, whom you claim as your God, is the one who glorifies me. Though you do not know him, I know him. If I said I did not, I would be a liar like you, but I do know him and keep his word. Your father Abraham rejoiced at the thought of seeing my day; he saw it and was glad.'* 'You are not yet fifty years old,' the Jews said to him, 'And you have seen Abraham!' *'I tell you the truth,'* Jesus answered, *'Before Abraham was born, I am!'*

At this, they picked up stones to stone him, but Jesus hid himself, slipping away from the Temple grounds.

Blind eyes open

As he went along, he saw a man blind from birth. His disciples asked him, 'Rabbi, who sinned, this man or his parents, that he was born blind?' *'Neither this man nor his parents sinned,'* said Jesus, *'But this happened so that the work of God might be displayed in his life. As long as it is day, we must do the work of him who sent me. Night is coming, when no one can work. While I am in the world, I am the light of the world.'* Having said this, he spat on the ground, made some mud with the saliva, and put it on the man's eyes. *'Go,'* he told him, *'Wash in the Pool of Siloam'* (this word means Sent). So the man went and washed, and came home seeing.

His neighbours and those who had formerly seen him begging asked, 'Isn't this the same man who used to sit and beg?' Some claimed that he was. Others said, 'No, he only looks like him.' But he himself insisted, 'I am the man.' 'How then were your eyes opened?' they demanded.

He replied, 'The man they call Jesus made some mud and put it on my eyes. He told me to go to Siloam and wash. So I went and washed, and then I could see.' 'Where is this man?' they asked him. 'I don't know,' he said.

They brought to the Pharisees the man who had been blind. Now the day on which Jesus had made the mud and opened the man's eyes was a Sabbath. Therefore the Pharisees also asked him how he had received his sight. 'He put mud on my eyes,' the man replied, 'And I washed, and now I see.' Some of the Pharisees said, 'This man is not from God, for he does not keep the Sabbath.' But others asked, 'How can a sinner do such miraculous signs?' So they were divided. Finally they turned again to the blind man, 'What have you to say about him? It was your eyes he opened.'

The man replied, 'He is a prophet.' The Jews still did not believe that he had been blind and had received his sight until they sent for the man's parents. 'Is this your son?' they asked. 'Is this the one you say was born blind? How is it that now he can see?'

'We know he is our son,' the parents answered, 'And we know he was born blind. But how he can see now, or who opened his eyes, we don't know. Ask him. He is of age; he will speak for himself.' His parents said this because they were afraid of the Jews, for already the Jews had decided that anyone who acknowledged that Jesus was the Christ would be put out of the synagogue. That was why his parents said, 'He is of age; ask him.'

A second time they summoned the man who had been blind. 'Give glory to God,' they said. 'We know this man is a sinner.' He replied, 'Whether he is a sinner or not, I don't know. One thing I do know. I was blind but now I see!'

Then they asked him, 'What did he do to you? How did he open your eyes?' He answered, 'I have told you already and you did not listen. Why do you want to hear it again? Do you want to become his disciples, too?' Then they hurled insults at him and said, 'You are this fellow's disciple! We are disciples of Moses! We know that God spoke to Moses, but as for this fellow, we don't even know where he comes from.' The man answered, 'Now that is remarkable! You don't know where he comes from, yet he opened my eyes. We know that God does not listen to sinners. He listens to the godly man who does his will. Nobody has ever heard of opening the eyes of a man born blind. If this man were not from God, he could do nothing.' To this they replied, 'You were steeped in sin at birth; how dare you lecture us!' And they threw him out.

Jesus heard that they had thrown him out, and when he found him, he said, *'Do you believe in the Son of Man?'* 'Who is he, sir?' the man asked. 'Tell me so that I may believe in him.' Jesus said, *'You have now seen him; in fact, he is the one speaking with you.'* Then the man said, 'Lord, I believe,' and he worshipped him.

None so blind as those who will not see

Jesus said, *'For judgement I have come into this world, so that the blind will see and those who see will become blind.'* Some Pharisees who were with him heard him say this and asked, 'What? Are we blind too?' Jesus said, *'If you were blind, you would not be guilty of sin; but now that you claim you can see, your guilt remains. I tell you the truth, the man who does not enter the sheep pen by the gate, but climbs in by some other way, is a thief and a robber. The man who enters by the gate is the shepherd of his sheep. The watchman opens the gate for him, and the sheep listen to his voice. He calls his own sheep by name and leads them out. When he has brought out all his own, he goes on ahead of them, and his sheep follow him because they know his voice. But they will never follow a stranger; in fact, they will run away from him because they do not recognise a stranger's voice.'* Jesus used this figure of speech, but they did not understand what he was telling them.

Jesus, the Good Shepherd

Therefore Jesus said again, *'I tell you the truth, I am the gate for the sheep. All who ever came before me were thieves and robbers, but the sheep did not listen to them. I am the gate; whoever enters through me will be saved. He will come in and go out, and find pasture. The thief comes only to steal and kill and destroy; I have come that they may have life, and have it to the full. I am the good shepherd. The good shepherd lays down his life for the sheep. The hired hand is not the shepherd who owns the sheep. So when he sees the wolf coming, he abandons the sheep and runs away. Then the wolf attacks the flock and scatters it. The man runs away because he is a hired hand and cares nothing for the sheep.*

'I am the good shepherd; I know my sheep and my sheep know me just as the Father knows me and I know the Father and I lay down my life for the sheep. I have other sheep that are not of this sheep pen. I must bring them also. They too will listen to my voice, and there shall be one flock and one shepherd. The reason my Father loves me is that I lay down my life only to take it up again. No one takes it from me, but I lay it down of my own accord. I have authority to lay it down and authority to take it up again. This command I received from my Father.'

At these words the Jews were again divided. Many of them said, 'He is demon-possessed and raving mad. Why listen to him?' But others said, 'These are not the sayings of a man possessed by a demon. Can a demon open the eyes of the blind?'

Then came the Feast of Dedication at Jerusalem. It was winter, and Jesus was in the temple area walking in Solomon's Colonnade. The Jews gathered around him, saying, 'How long will you keep us in suspense? If you are the Christ, tell us plainly.' Jesus answered, *'I did tell you, but you do not believe. The miracles I do in my Father's name speak for me, but you do not believe because you are not my sheep. My sheep listen to my voice; I know them, and they follow me. I give them eternal life, and they shall never perish; no one can snatch them out of my hand. My Father, who has given them to me, is greater than all; no one can snatch them out of my Father's hand. I and the Father are one.'*

Again the Jews picked up stones to stone him, but Jesus said to them, *'I have shown you many great miracles from the Father. For which of these do you stone me?'* 'We are not stoning you for any of these,' replied the Jews, 'But for blasphemy, because you, a mere man, claim to be God.' Jesus answered them, *'Is it not written in your Law, "I have said you are gods"? If he called them "gods," to whom the word of God came and the Scripture cannot be broken, what about the one whom the Father set apart as his very own and sent into the world? Why then do you accuse me of blasphemy because I said, "I am God's Son"? Do not believe me unless I do what my Father does. But if I do it, even though you do not believe me, believe the miracles, that you may know and understand that the Father is in me, and I in the Father.'* Again they tried to seize him, but he escaped their grasp. Then Jesus went back across the Jordan to the place where John had been baptising in the early days. Here he stayed and many people came to him. They said, 'Though John never performed a miraculous sign, all that John said about this man was true.' And in that place many believed in Jesus.

The mission of the seventy two

After this the Lord appointed seventy-two others and sent them two by two ahead of him to every town and place where he was about to go. He told them, *'The harvest is plentiful, but the workers are few. Ask the Lord of the harvest, therefore, to send out workers into his harvest field. Go! I am sending you out like lambs among wolves. Do not take a purse or bag or sandals; and do not greet anyone on the road.*

'When you enter a house, first say, "Peace to this house." If a man of peace is there, your peace will rest on him; if not, it will return to you. Stay in that house, eating and drinking whatever they give you, for the worker deserves his wages. Do not move around from house to house.

'When you enter a town and are welcomed, eat what is set before you. Heal the sick who are there and tell them, "The kingdom of God is near you." But when you enter a town and are not welcomed, go into its streets and say, "Even the dust of your town that sticks to our feet we wipe off against you. Yet be sure of this: The kingdom of God is near." I tell you, it will be more bearable on that day for Sodom than for that town.

'Woe to you, Korazin! Woe to you, Bethsaida! For if the miracles that were performed in you had been performed in Tyre and Sidon, they would have repented long ago, sitting in sackcloth and ashes. But it will be more bearable for Tyre and Sidon at the judgement than for you. And you, Capernaum, will you be lifted up to the skies? No, you will go down to the depths. He who listens to you listens to me; he who rejects you rejects me; but he who rejects me rejects him who sent me.'

The seventy-two returned with joy and said, 'Lord, even the demons submit to us in your name.' He replied, 'I saw Satan fall like lightning from heaven. I have given you authority to trample on snakes and scorpions and to overcome all the power of the enemy; nothing will harm you. However, do not rejoice that the spirits submit to you, but rejoice that your names are written in heaven.'

At that time Jesus, full of joy through the Holy Spirit, said, 'I praise you, Father, Lord of heaven and earth, because you have hidden these things from the wise and learned, and revealed them to little children. Yes, Father, for this was your good pleasure. All things have been committed to me by my Father. No one knows who the Son is except the Father, and no one knows who the Father is except the Son and those to whom the Son chooses to reveal him.'

Then he turned to his disciples and said privately, 'Blessed are the eyes that see what you see. For I tell you that many prophets and kings wanted to see what you see but did not see it, and to hear what you hear but did not hear it.'

The parable of the Good Samaritan

On one occasion an expert in the law stood up to test Jesus. 'Teacher,' he asked, 'What must I do to inherit eternal life?'

'*What is written in the Law?*' he replied. '*How do you read it?*' He answered, 'Love the Lord your God with all your heart and with all your soul and with all your strength and with all your mind and, love your neighbours as yourself.' '*You have answered correctly,*' Jesus replied. '*Do this and you will live.*' But he wanted to justify himself, so he asked Jesus, 'And who is my neighbour?'

In reply Jesus said, '*A man was going down from Jerusalem to Jericho, when he fell into the hands of robbers. They stripped him of his clothes, beat him and went away, leaving him half dead. A priest happened to be going down the same road, and when he saw the man, he passed by on the other side. So too, a Levite, when he came to the place and saw him, passed by on the other side. But a Samaritan, as he travelled, came where the man was; and when he saw him, he took pity on him. He went to him and bandaged his wounds, pouring on oil and wine. Then he put the man on his own donkey, took him to an inn and took care of him. The next day he took out two silver coins and gave them to the innkeeper. "Look after him," he said, "And when I return, I will reimburse you for any extra expense you may have." Which of these three do you think was a neighbour to the man who fell into the hands of robbers?*'

The expert in the law replied, 'The one who had mercy on him.' Jesus told him, '*Go and do likewise.*'

As Jesus and his disciples were on their way, he came to a village where a woman named Martha opened her home to him. She had a sister called Mary, who sat at the Lord's feet listening to what he said. But Martha was distracted by all the preparations that had to be made. She came to him and asked, 'Lord, don't you care that my sister has left me to do the work by myself? Tell her to help me!' '*Martha, Martha,*' the Lord answered, '*You are worried and upset about many things, but only one thing is needed. Mary has chosen what is better, and it will not be taken away from her.*'

Jesus teaches his disciples how to pray

One day Jesus was praying in a certain place. When he

finished, one of his disciples said to him, 'Lord, teach us to pray, just as John taught his disciples.'

He said to them,

> *'When you pray, say:*
> *"Father,*
> *hallowed be your name,*
> *your kingdom come,*
> *Give us each day our daily bread.*
> *Forgive us our sins,*
> *for we also forgive everyone who sins against us.*
> *And lead us not into temptation." '*

Then he said to them, *'Suppose one of you has a friend, and he goes to him at midnight and says, "Friend, lend me three loaves of bread, because a friend of mine on a journey has come to me, and I have nothing to set before him." Then the one inside answers, "Don't bother me. The door is already locked, and my children are with me in bed. I can't get up and give you anything." I tell you, though he will not get up and give him the bread because he is his friend, yet because of the man's boldness he will get up and give him as much as he needs.*

'So I say to you: Ask and it will be given to you; seek and you will find; knock and the door will be opened to you. For everyone who asks receives; he who seeks finds; and to him who knocks, the door will be opened.

'Which of you fathers, if your son asks for bread will give him a stone or if he asks for a fish will give him a snake instead? Or if he asks for an egg, will give him a scorpion? If you then, though you are evil, know how to give good gifts to your children, how much more will your Father in heaven give the Holy Spirit to those who ask him!'

A confrontation with legalism

A Pharisee invited Jesus to eat with him; so he went in and reclined at the table. But the Pharisee, noticing that Jesus did not first wash before the meal, was surprised. Then the Lord said to him, *'Now then, you Pharisees clean the outside of the cup* and dish, but inside you are full of greed and wickedness. You foolish people! Did not the one who made the outside make the inside also? But give what is inside the dish to the poor, and everything will be clean for you.

'Woe to you Pharisees, because you give God a tenth of your mint, rue and all other kinds of garden herbs, but you neglect justice and the love of God. You should have practised the latter without leaving the former undone.

'Woe to you Pharisees, because you love the most important seats in the synagogues and greetings in the marketplaces.

'Woe to you, because you are like unmarked graves, which men walk over without knowing it.'

One of the experts in the law answered him, 'Teacher, when you say these things, you insult us also.' Jesus replied, 'And you experts in the law, woe to you, because you load people down with burdens they can hardly carry, and you yourselves will not lift one finger to help them.

'Woe to you, because you build tombs for the prophets, and it was your forefathers who killed them. So you testify that you approve of what your forefathers did; they killed the prophets, and you build their tombs. Because of this, God in his wisdom said, "I will send them prophets and apostles, some of whom they will kill and others they will persecute." Therefore this generation will be held responsible for the blood of all the prophets that has been shed since the beginning of the world, from the blood of Abel to the blood of Zechariah, who was killed between the altar and the sanctuary. Yes, I tell you, this generation will be held responsible for it all. Woe to you experts in the law, because you have taken away the key to knowledge. You yourselves have not entered, and you have hindered those who were entering.'

When Jesus left there, the Pharisees and the teachers of the law began to oppose him fiercely and to besiege him with questions, waiting to catch him in something he might say.

Meanwhile, when a crowd of many thousands had gathered, so that they were trampling on one another, Jesus began to speak first to his disciples, saying, 'Be on your guard against the yeast of the Pharisees, which is hypocrisy. There is *nothing concealed that will not be disclosed, or hidden that will not be made known. What you have said in the dark will be heard in the daylight, and what you have whispered in the ear in the inner rooms will be proclaimed from the roofs.*

'I tell you, my friends, do not be afraid of those who kill the body and after that can do no more. But I will show you whom you should fear: Fear him who, after the killing of the body, has power to throw you into hell. Yes, I tell you, fear him. Are not five sparrows sold for two pennies? Yet not one of them is forgotten by God. Indeed, the very hairs of your head are all numbered. Don't be afraid; you are worth more than many sparrows.

'I tell you, whoever acknowledges me before men, the Son of Man will also acknowledge him before the angels of God. But he who disowns me before men will be disowned before the angels of God. And everyone who speaks a word against the Son of Man will be forgiven, but anyone who blasphemes against the Holy Spirit will not be forgiven.

'When you are brought before synagogues, rulers and author-ities, do not worry about how you will defend yourselves or what you will say, for the Holy Spirit will teach you at that time what you should say.'

The rich fool

Someone in the crowd said to him, 'Teacher, tell my brother to divide the inheritance with me.' Jesus replied, *'Man, who appointed me a judge or an arbiter between you?'* Then he said to them, *'Watch out! Be on your guard against all kinds of greed; a man's life does not consist in the abundance of his possessions.'* And he told them this parable, *'The ground of a certain rich man produced a good crop. He thought to himself, "What shall I do? I have no place to store my crops." Then he said, "This is what I'll do. I will tear down my barns and build bigger ones, and there I will store all my grain and my goods. And I'll say to myself, 'You have plenty of good things laid up for many years. Take life easy; eat, drink and be merry.' " But God said to him, "You fool! This very night your life will be demanded from you. Then who will get what you have prepared for yourself?"*

'This is how it will be with anyone who stores up things for himself but is not rich toward God.' Then Jesus said to his disciples, 'Therefore I tell you, do not worry about your life, what you will eat; or about your body, what you will wear. Life is more than food, and the body more than clothes. Consider the ravens: They do not sow or reap, they have no storeroom or barn; yet God feeds them. And how much more valuable you are than birds! Who of you by worrying can add a single hour to his life? Since you cannot do this very little thing, why do you worry about the rest?

'Consider how the lilies grow. They do not labour or spin. Yet I tell you, not even Solomon in all his splendour was dressed like one of these. If that is how God clothes the grass of the field, which is here today, and tomorrow is thrown into the fire, how much more will he clothe you, O you of little faith! And do not set your heart on what you will eat or drink; do not worry about it. For the pagan world runs after all such things, and your Father knows that you need them. But seek his kingdom, and these things will be given to you as well.

'Do not be afraid, little flock, for your Father has been pleased to give you the kingdom. Sell your possessions and give to the poor. Provide purses for yourselves that will not wear out, a treasure in heaven that will not be exhausted, where no thief comes near and no moth destroys. For where your treasure is, there your heart will be also.'

Are you ready for Jesus' return?

'Be dressed ready for service and keep your lamps burning, like men waiting for their master to return from a wedding banquet, so that when he comes and knocks they can immediately open the door for him. It will be good for those servants whose master finds them watching when he comes. I tell you the truth, he will dress himself to serve, will have them recline at the table and will come and wait on them. It will be good for those servants whose master finds them ready, even if he comes in the second or third watch of the night. But understand this: If the owner of the house had known at what hour the thief was coming, he would not have let his house be broken into. You also must be ready, because the Son of Man will come at an hour when you do not expect him.'

Peter asked, 'Lord, are you telling this parable to us, or to everyone?' The Lord answered, *'Who then is the faithful and wise manager, whom the master puts in charge of his servants to give them their food allowance at the proper time? It will be good for that servant whom the master finds doing so when he returns. I tell you the truth, he will put him in charge of all his possessions. But suppose the servant says to himself, "My master is taking a long time in coming," and he then begins to beat the menservants and maidservants and to eat and drink and get drunk. The master of that servant will come on a day when he does not expect him and at an hour he is not aware of. He will cut him to pieces and assign him a place with the unbelievers.*

'That servant who knows his master's will and does not get ready or does not do what his master wants will be beaten with many blows. But the one who does not know and does things deserving punishment will be beaten with few blows. From everyone who has been given much, much will be demanded and from the one who has been entrusted with much, much more will be asked.

'I have come to bring fire on the earth, and how I wish it were already kindled! But I have a baptism to undergo, and how distressed I am until it is completed! Do you think I came to bring peace on earth? No, I tell you, but division. From now on there will be five in one family divided against each other, three against two and two against three. They will be divided, father against son and son against father, mother against daughter and daughter against mother, mother-in-law against daughter-in-law and daughter-in-law against mother-in-law.'

He said to the crowd, *'When you see a cloud rising in the west, immediately you say, "It's going to rain," and it does. And when the south wind blows, you say, "It's going to be hot," and it is. Hypocrites! You know how to interpret the appearance of the earth and the sky. How is it that you don't know how to interpret this present time? Why don't you judge for yourselves what is right? As you are going with your adversary to the magistrate, try hard to be reconciled to him on the way, or he may drag you off to the judge,* and the judge turn you over to the officer, and the officer throw you into prison. I tell you, you will not get out until you have paid the last penny.'

A call to repentance

Now there were some present at that time who told Jesus about the Galileans whose blood Pilate had mixed with their sacrifices. Jesus answered, *'Do you think that these Galileans were worse sinners than all the other Galileans because they suffered this way? I tell you, no! But unless you repent, you too will all perish. Or those eighteen who died when the tower in Siloam fell on them do you think they were more guilty than all the others living in Jerusalem? I tell you, no! But unless you repent, you too will all perish.'*

Then he told this parable, *'A man had a fig tree planted in his vineyard, and he went to look for fruit on it, but did not find any. So he said to the man who took care of the vineyard, "For three years now I've been coming to look for fruit on this fig tree and haven't found any. Cut it down! Why should it use up the soil?" "Sir," the man replied, "leave it alone for one more year, and I'll dig around it and fertilise it. If it bears fruit next year, fine! If not, then cut it down."'*

On a Sabbath Jesus was teaching in one of the synagogues, and a woman was there who had been crippled by a spirit for eighteen years. She was bent over and could not straighten up at all. When Jesus saw her, he called her forward and said to her, *'Woman, you are set free from your infirmity.'* Then he put his hands on her, and immediately she straightened up and praised God. Indignant, because Jesus had healed on the Sabbath, the synagogue ruler said to the people, 'There are six days for work. So come and be healed on those days, not on the Sabbath.'

The Lord answered him, *'You hypocrites! Doesn't each of you on the Sabbath untie his ox or donkey from the stall and lead it out to give it water? Then should not this woman, a daughter of Abraham, whom Satan has kept bound for eighteen long years, be set free on the Sabbath day from what bound her?'*

When he said this, all his opponents were humiliated, but the people were delighted with all the wonderful things he was doing. Then Jesus asked, *'What is the kingdom of God like? What shall I compare it to? It is like a mustard seed, which a man took and planted in his garden. It grew and became a tree, and the birds of the air perched in its branches.'* Again he asked, *'What shall I compare the kingdom of God to? It is like yeast that a woman took and mixed into a large amount of flour until it worked all through the dough.'*

Then Jesus went through the towns and villages, teaching as he made his way to Jerusalem. Someone asked him, 'Lord, are only a few people going to be saved?' He said to them, *'Make every effort to enter through the narrow door, because many, I tell you, will try to enter and will not be able to. Once the owner of the house gets up and closes the door, you will stand outside knocking and pleading, "Sir, open the door for us." But he will answer, "I don't know you or where you come from." Then you will say, "We ate and drank with you, and you taught in our streets." But he will reply, "I don't know you or where you come from. Away from me, all you evildoers!"*

'There will be weeping there, and gnashing of teeth, when you see Abraham, Isaac and Jacob and all the prophets in the kingdom of God, but you yourselves will be thrown out. People will come from east and west and north and south, and will take their places at the feast in the kingdom of God. Indeed there are those who are last who will be first, and first who will be last.'

Chapter 17

Jesus Weeps Over Jerusalem

*'He who humbles himself will be exalted
and he who exalts himself
will be humbled.'*

At that time some Pharisees came to Jesus and said to him, 'Leave this place and go somewhere else. Herod wants to kill you.' He replied, *'Go tell that fox, "I will drive out demons and heal people today and tomorrow, and on the third day I will reach my goal." In any case, I must keep going today and tomorrow and the next day for surely no prophet can die outside Jerusalem!*

'O Jerusalem, Jerusalem, you who kill the prophets and stone those sent to you, how often I have longed to gather your children together, as a hen gathers her chicks under her wings, but you were not willing! Look, your house is left to you desolate. I tell you, you will not see me again until you say, "Blessed is he who comes in the name of the Lord."'

One Sabbath, when Jesus went to eat in the house of a prominent Pharisee, he was being carefully watched. There in front of him was a man suffering from dropsy. Jesus asked the Pharisees and experts in the law, *'Is it lawful to heal on the Sabbath or not?'* But they remained silent. So taking hold of the man, he healed him and sent him away. Then he asked them, *'If one of you has a son or an ox that falls into a well on the Sabbath day, will you not immediately pull him out?'* And they had nothing to say.

When he noticed how the guests picked the places of

honour at the table, he told them this parable, *'When some-one invites you to a wedding feast, do not take the place of honour, for a person more distinguished than you may have been invited. If so, the host who invited both of you will come and say to you, "Give this man your seat." Then, humiliated, you will have to take the least important place. But when you are invited, take the lowest place, so that when your host comes, he will say to you, "Friend, move up to a better place." Then you will be honoured in the presence of all your fellow guests. For everyone who exalts himself will be humbled, and he who humbles himself will be exalted.'*

Then Jesus said to his host, *'When you give a luncheon or dinner, do not invite your friends, your brothers or relatives, or your rich neighbours; if you do, they may invite you back and so you will be repaid. But when you give a banquet, invite the poor, the crippled, the lame, the blind, and you will be blessed. Although they cannot repay you, you will be repaid at the resurrection of the righteous.'*

When one of those at the table with him heard this, he said to Jesus, 'Blessed is the man who will eat at the feast in the kingdom of God.'

Jesus replied, *'A certain man was preparing a great banquet and invited many guests. At the time of the banquet he sent his servant to tell those who had been invited, "Come, for everything is now ready." But they all alike began to make excuses. The first said, "I have just bought a field, and I must go and see it. Please excuse me." Another said, "I have just bought five yoke of oxen, and I'm on my way to try them out. Please excuse me." Still another said, "I just got married, so I can't come." The servant came back and reported this to his master. Then the owner of the house became angry and ordered his servant, "Go out quickly into the streets and alleys of the town and bring in the poor, the crippled, the blind and the lame." "Sir," the servant said, "what you ordered has been done, but there is still room." Then the master told his servant, "Go out to the roads and country lanes and make them come in, so that my house will be full. I tell you, not one of those men who were invited will get a taste of my banquet."'*

The cost of being a disciple

Large crowds were travelling with Jesus, and turning to them he said, *'If anyone comes to me and does not hate his father and mother, his wife and children, his brothers and sisters yes, even his own life, he cannot be my disciple. And anyone who does not carry his cross and follow me cannot be my disciple.*

'Suppose one of you wants to build a tower. Will he not first sit down and estimate the cost to see if he has enough money to complete it? For if he lays the foundation and is not able to finish it, everyone who sees it will ridicule him, saying, "This fellow began to build and was not able to finish." Or suppose a king is about to go to war against another king. Will he not first sit down and consider whether he is able with ten thousand men to oppose the one coming against him with twenty thousand? If he is not able, he will send a delegation while the other is still a long way off and will ask for terms of peace. In the same way, any of you who does not give up everything he has cannot be my disciple.

'Salt is good, but if it loses its saltiness, how can it be made salty again? It is fit neither for the soil nor for the manure pile; it is thrown out. He who has ears to hear, let him hear.'

The lost coin, the lost sheep, the lost son

Now the tax collectors and 'sinners' were all gathering around to hear him. But the Pharisees and the teachers of the law muttered, 'This man welcomes sinners and eats with them.' Then Jesus told them this parable, *'Suppose one of you has a hundred sheep and loses one of them. Does he not leave the ninety-nine in the open country and go after the lost sheep until he finds it? And when he finds it, he joyfully puts it on his shoulders and goes home. Then he calls his friends and neighbours together and says, "Rejoice with me; I have found my lost sheep." I tell you that in the same way there will be more rejoicing in heaven over one sinner who repents than over ninety-nine righteous persons who do not need to repent.*

'Or suppose a woman has ten silver coins and loses one. Does she not light a lamp, sweep the house and search carefully until

she finds it? And when she finds it, she calls her friends and neighbours together and says, "Rejoice with me; I have found my lost coin." In the same way, I tell you, there is rejoicing in the presence of the angels of God over one sinner who repents.'

Jesus continued, *'There was a man who had two sons. The younger one said to his father, "Father, give me my share of the estate." So he divided his property between them.*

'Not long after that, the younger son got together all he had, set off for a distant country and there squandered his wealth in wild living. After he had spent everything, there was a severe famine in that whole country, and he began to be in need. So he went and hired himself out to a citizen of that country, who sent him to his fields to feed pigs. He longed to fill his stomach with the pods that the pigs were eating, but no one gave him anything. When he came to his senses, he said, "How many of my father's hired men have food to spare, and here I am starving to death! I will set out and go back to my father and say to him: Father, I have sinned against heaven and against you. I am no longer worthy to be called your son; make me like one of your hired men."

'So he got up and went to his father. But while he was still a long way off, his father saw him and was filled with compassion for him; he ran to his son, threw his arms around him and kissed him. The son said to him, "Father, I have sinned against heaven and against you. I am no longer worthy to be called your son." But the father said to his servants, "Quick! Bring the best robe and put it on him. Put a ring on his finger and sandals on his feet. Bring the fattened calf and kill it. Let's have a feast and celebrate. For this son of mine was dead and is alive again; he was lost and is found." So they began to celebrate.

'Meanwhile, the older son was in the field. When he came near the house, he heard music and dancing. So he called one of the servants and asked him what was going on. "Your brother has come," he replied, "And your father has killed the fattened calf because he has him back safe and sound." The older brother became angry and refused to go in. So his father went out and pleaded with him. But he answered his father, "Look! All these years I've been slaving for you and never disobeyed your orders. Yet you never gave me even a young goat so I could celebrate with my

friends. But when this son of yours who has squandered your property with prostitutes comes home, you kill the fattened calf for him!" "My son," the father said, "You are always with me, and everything I have is yours. But we had to celebrate and be glad, because this brother of yours was dead and is alive again; he was lost and is found." '

The shrewd manager

Jesus told his disciples, *'There was a rich man whose manager was accused of wasting his possessions. So he called him in and asked him, "What is this I hear about you? Give an account of your management, because you cannot be manager any longer." The manager said to himself, "What shall I do now? My master is taking away my job. I'm not strong enough to dig, and I'm ashamed to beg, I know what I'll do so that, when I lose my job here, people will welcome me into their houses." So he called in each one of his master's debtors. He asked the first, "How much do you owe my master?" "Eight hundred gallons of olive oil," he replied. The manager told him, "Take your bill, sit down quickly, and make it four hundred." Then he asked the second, "And how much do you owe?" "A thousand bushels of wheat," he replied. He told him, "Take your bill and make it eight hundred."*

'The master commended the dishonest manager because he had acted shrewdly. For the people of this world are more shrewd in dealing with their own kind than are the people of the light. I tell you, use worldly wealth to gain friends for yourselves, so that when it is gone, you will be welcomed into eternal dwellings.

'Whoever can be trusted with very little can also be trusted with much, and whoever is dishonest with very little will also be dishonest with much. So if you have not been trustworthy in handling worldly wealth, who will trust you with true riches? And if you have not been trustworthy with someone else's property, who will give you property of your own?

'No servant can serve two masters. Either he will hate the one and love the other, or he will be devoted to the one and despise the other. You cannot serve both God and Money.'

The Pharisees, who loved money, heard all this and were sneering at Jesus. He said to them, *'You are the ones who justify yourselves in the eyes of men, but God knows your hearts. What is highly valued among men is detestable in God's sight.*

'The Law and the Prophets were proclaimed until John. Since that time, the good news of the kingdom of God is being preached, and everyone is forcing his way into it. It is easier for heaven and earth to disappear than for the least stroke of a pen to drop out of the Law. Anyone who divorces his wife and marries another woman commits adultery, and the man who marries a divorced woman commits adultery.'

A poor rich man and a rich poor man

'There was a rich man who was dressed in purple and fine linen and lived in luxury every day. At his gate was laid a beggar named Lazarus, covered with sores and longing to eat what fell from the rich man's table. Even the dogs came and licked his sores. The time came when the beggar died and the angels carried him to Abraham's side. The rich man also died and was buried. In hell, where he was in torment, he looked up and saw Abraham far away, with Lazarus by his side. So he called to him, "Father Abraham, have pity on me and send Lazarus to dip the tip of his finger in water and cool my tongue, because I am in agony in this fire."

'But Abraham replied, "Son, remember that in your lifetime you received your good things, while Lazarus received bad things, but now he is comforted here and you are in agony. And besides all this, between us and you a great chasm has been fixed, so that those who want to go from here to you cannot, nor can anyone cross over from there to us." He answered, "Then I beg you, father, send Lazarus to my father's house, for I have five brothers. Let him warn them, so that they will not also come to this place of torment." Abraham replied, "They have Moses and the Prophets; let them listen to them." "No, father Abraham," he said, "But if someone from the dead goes to them, they will repent." He said to him, "If they do not listen to Moses and the Prophets, they will not be convinced even if someone rises from the dead."'

Forgiveness and faith

Jesus said to his disciples, *'Things that cause people to sin are bound to come, but woe to that person through whom they come. It would be better for him to be thrown into the sea with a millstone tied around his neck than for him to cause one of these little ones to sin. So watch yourselves.*

'If your brother sins, rebuke him, and if he repents, forgive him. If he sins against you seven times in a day, and seven times comes back to you and says, "I repent," forgive him.'

The apostles said to the Lord, 'Increase our faith!' He replied, *'If you have faith as small as a mustard seed, you can say to this mulberry tree, "Be uprooted and planted in the sea," and it will obey you.*

*'Suppose one of you had a servant ploughing or looking after the sheep. Would he say to the servant when he comes in from the field, "Come along now and sit down to eat"? Would he not rather say, "Prepare my supper, get yourself ready and wait on me while I eat and drink; after that you may eat and drink"? Would he thank the servant because he did what he was told to do? So you also, when you have done everything you were told to do, should say, "We are unworthy servants, we have only done our duty."' *

Chapter 18

The Last Months

'I am the resurrection and the life. He who believes in me will live and never die.'

Now a man named Lazarus was sick. He was from Bethany, the village of Mary and her sister Martha. This Mary, whose brother Lazarus now lay sick, was the same one who poured perfume on the Lord and wiped his feet with her hair. So the sisters sent word to Jesus, 'Lord, the one you love is sick.'

When he heard this, Jesus said, *'This sickness will not end in death. No, it is for God's glory so that God's Son may be glorified through it.'* Jesus loved Martha and her sister and Lazarus. Yet when he heard that Lazarus was sick, he stayed where he was two more days.

Then he said to his disciples, *'Let us go back to Judea.'* 'But Rabbi,' they said, 'A short while ago the Jews tried to stone you, and yet you are going back there?' Jesus answered, *'Are there not twelve hours of daylight? A man who walks by day will not stumble, for he sees by this world's light. It is when he walks by night that he stumbles, for he has no light.'* After he had said this, he went on to tell them, *'Our friend Lazarus has fallen asleep; but I am going there to wake him up.'* His disciples replied, 'Lord, if he sleeps, he will get better.' Jesus had been speaking of his death, but his disciples thought he meant natural sleep. So then he told them plainly, *'Lazarus is dead, and for your sake I am glad I was not there, so that you may believe. But let us go to him.'* Then Thomas (called Didymus) said to the rest of the disciples, 'Let us also go, that we may die with him.'

On his arrival, Jesus found that Lazarus had already been in the tomb for four days. Bethany was less than two miles from Jerusalem, and many Jews had come to Martha and Mary to comfort them in the loss of their brother. When Martha heard that Jesus was coming, she went out to meet him, but Mary stayed at home.

'Lord,' Martha said to Jesus, 'If you had been here, my brother would not have died. But I know that even now God will give you whatever you ask.' Jesus said to her, *'Your brother will rise again.'*

Martha answered, 'I know he will rise again in the resurrection at the last day.' Jesus said to her, *'I am the resurrection and the life. He who believes in me will live, even though he dies; and whoever lives and believes in me will never die. Do you believe this?'* 'Yes, Lord,' she told him, 'I believe that you are the Christ, the Son of God, who was to come into the world.' And after she had said this, she went back and called her sister Mary aside. 'The Teacher is here,' she said, 'And is asking for you.' When Mary heard this, she got up quickly and went to him. Now Jesus had not yet entered the village, but was still at the place where Martha had met him. When the Jews who had been with Mary in the house, comforting her, noticed how quickly she got up and went out, they followed her, supposing she was going to the tomb to mourn there.

When Mary reached the place where Jesus was and saw him, she fell at his feet and said, 'Lord, if you had been here, my brother would not have died.'

When Jesus saw her weeping, and the Jews who had come along with her also weeping, he was deeply moved in spirit and troubled. *'Where have you laid him?'* he asked. 'Come and see, Lord,' they replied. Jesus wept. Then the Jews said, 'See how he loved him!' But some of them said, 'Could not he who opened the eyes of the blind man have kept this man from dying?'

Jesus, once more deeply moved, came to the tomb. It was a cave with a stone laid across the entrance. *'Take away the stone,'* he said. 'But, Lord,' said Martha, the sister of the dead man, 'By this time there is a bad odour, for he has been there four days.' Then Jesus said, *'Did I not tell you that if you believed, you would see the glory of God?'* So they took away the stone. Then Jesus looked up and said, *'Father, I thank you that you have heard me. I knew that you always hear me, but I said this for the benefit of the people standing here, that they may believe that you sent me.'* When he had said this, Jesus called in a loud voice, *'Lazarus, come out!'* The dead man came out, his hands and feet wrapped with strips of linen, and a cloth around his face. Jesus said to them, *'Take off the grave clothes and let him go.'*

Therefore many of the Jews who had come to visit Mary, and had seen what Jesus did, put their faith in him. But some of them went to the Pharisees and told them what Jesus had done. Then the chief priests and the Pharisees called a meeting of the Sanhedrin. 'What are we accomplishing?' they asked. 'Here is this man performing many miraculous signs. If we let him go on like this, everyone will believe in him, and then the Romans will come and take away both our place and our nation.'

Then one of them, named Caiaphas, who was high priest that year, spoke up, 'You know nothing at all! You do not realise that it is better for you that one man die for the people than that the whole nation perish.'

He did not say this on his own, but as high priest that year, he prophesied that Jesus would die for the Jewish nation, and not only for that nation but also for the scattered children of God, to bring them together and make them one. So from that day on they plotted to take his life. Therefore Jesus no longer moved about publicly among the Jews. Instead he withdrew to a region near the desert, to a village called Ephraim, where he stayed with his disciples.

Ten lepers healed but only one gives thanks

Now on his way to Jerusalem, Jesus travelled along the border between Samaria and Galilee. As he was going into a village, ten men who had leprosy met him. They stood at a distance and called out in a loud voice, 'Jesus, Master, have pity on us!' When he saw them, he said, *'Go, show yourselves to the priests.'* And as they went, they were cleansed. One of them, when he saw he was healed, came back, praising God in a loud voice. He threw himself at Jesus' feet and thanked him, and he was a Samaritan. Jesus asked, *'Were not all ten cleansed? Where are the other nine? Was no one found to return and give praise to God except this foreigner?'* Then he said to him, *'Rise and go; your faith has made you well.'*

The coming of God's Kingdom

Once, having been asked by the Pharisees when the kingdom of God would come, Jesus replied, *'The kingdom of God does not come with your careful observation, nor will people say, "Here it is," or "There it is," because the kingdom of God is within you.'*

Then he said to his disciples, *'The time is coming when you will long to see one of the days of the Son of Man, but you will not see it. Men will tell you, "There he is!" or "Here he is!" Do not go running off after them. For the Son of Man in his day will be like the lightning, which flashes and lights up the sky from one end to the other. But first he must suffer many things and be rejected by this generation.*

'Just as it was in the days of Noah, so also will it be in the days of the Son of Man. People were eating, drinking, marrying and being given in marriage up to the day Noah entered the ark. Then the flood came and destroyed them all.

'It was the same in the days of Lot. People were eating and drinking, buying and selling, planting and building. But the day Lot left Sodom, fire and sulphur rained down from heaven and destroyed them all.

'It will be just like this on the day the Son of Man is revealed. On that day no one who is on the roof of his house, with his goods inside, should go down to get them. Likewise, no one in the field should go back for anything. Remember Lot's wife! Whoever tries to keep his life will lose it, and whoever loses his life will preserve it. I tell you, on that night two people will be in one bed; one will be

taken and the other left. Two women will be grinding grain together; one will be taken and the other left.'

'Where, Lord?' they asked. He replied, *'Where there is a dead body, there the vultures will gather.'*

Pray and keep praying

Then Jesus told his disciples a parable to show them that they should always pray and not give up. He said, *'In a certain town there was a judge who neither feared God nor cared about men. And there was a widow in that town who kept coming to him with the plea, "Grant me justice against my adversary." For some time he refused. But finally he said to himself, "Even though I don't fear God or care about men, yet because this widow keeps bothering me, I will see that she gets justice, so that she won't eventually wear me out with her coming!"'*

And the Lord said, *'Listen to what the unjust judge says. And will not God bring about justice for his chosen ones, who cry out to him day and night? Will he keep putting them off? I tell you, he will see that they get justice, and quickly. However, when the Son of Man comes, will he find faith on the earth?'*

To some who were confident of their own righteousness and looked down on everybody else, Jesus told this parable. *'Two men went up to the temple to pray, one a Pharisee and the other a tax collector. The Pharisee stood up and prayed about himself: "God, I thank you that I am not like other men, robbers, evildoers, adulterers or even like this tax collector. I fast twice a week and give a tenth of all I get." But the tax collector stood at a distance. He would not even look up to heaven, but beat his breast and said, "God, have mercy on me, a sinner." I tell you that this man, rather than the other, went home justified before God. For everyone who exalts himself will be humbled, and he who humbles himself will be exalted.'*

Marriage and divorce

When Jesus had finished saying these things, he left Galilee and went into the region of Judea to the other side of the Jordan. Again crowds of people came to him, and as was his custom, he taught them and healed them there.

Some Pharisees came and tested him by asking, 'Is it lawful for a man to divorce his wife for any and every reason?' *'What did Moses command you?'* he replied. They said, 'Moses permitted a man to write a certificate of divorce and send her away.' *'It was because your hearts were hard that Moses wrote you this law,'* Jesus replied. *'But at the beginning of creation God "made them male and female." "For this reason a man will leave his father and mother and be united to his wife, and the two will become one flesh." So they are no longer two, but one. Therefore what God has joined together, let man not separate.'*

When they were in the house again, the disciples asked Jesus about this. He answered, *'Anyone who divorces his wife, except for marital unfaithfulness, and marries another woman commits adultery against her. And if she divorces her husband and marries another man, she commits adultery.'*

The disciples said to him, 'If this is the situation between a husband and a wife, it is better not to marry.' Jesus replied, *'Not everyone can accept this word, but only those to whom it has been given. For some are eunuchs because they were born that way; others were made that way by men; and others have renounced marriage because of the kingdom of heaven. The one who can accept it should accept it.'*

Jesus blesses the little children

People were bringing little children to Jesus to have him put his hands on them and pray for them. But the disciples rebuked those who brought them. When Jesus saw this, he was indignant. He said to them, *'Let the little children come to me, and do not hinder them, for the kingdom of God belongs to such as these. I tell you the truth, anyone who will not receive the kingdom of God like a little child will never enter it.'* And he took the children in his arms, put his hands on them and blessed them.

A sad rich man

As Jesus started on his way, a certain ruler ran up to him and fell on his knees before him. 'Good teacher,' he asked, 'What good thing must I do to inherit eternal life?' *'Why do you call me good,'* Jesus answered. *'No one is good except God alone. If you want to enter eternal life obey the commandments.'* 'Which ones?' the man inquired. *'You know the commandments: "Do not murder, do not commit adultery, do not steal, do not give false testimony, do not defraud, honour your father and mother, and love your neighbour as yourself."'* 'Teacher,' he declared, 'All these I have kept since I was a boy, what do I still lack?' Jesus looked at him and loved him. *'One thing you lack,'* he said. *'If you want to be perfect go and sell everything you have and give to the poor, and you will have treasure in heaven. Then come, follow me.'* At this the man's face fell. He went away sad, because he had great wealth. Jesus looked around and said to his disciples, *'How hard it is for the rich to enter the kingdom of God!'*

The disciples were amazed at his words. But Jesus said again, *'Children, how hard it is to enter the kingdom of God! It is easier for a camel to go through the eye of a needle than for a rich man to enter the kingdom of God.'* The disciples were even more amazed, and said to each other, 'Who then can be saved?' Jesus looked at them and said, *'With man this is impossible, but not with God; all things are possible with God.'*

Peter said to him, 'We have left everything to follow you! What then will there be for us?' *'I tell you the truth,'* Jesus replied, *'At the renewal of all things, when the Son of Man sits on his glorious throne, you who have followed me will also sit on twelve thrones, judging the twelve tribes of Israel. And anyone who has left home or brothers or sisters or mother or father or children or fields for me and the gospel will receive a hundred times as much in this present age (homes, brothers, sisters, mothers, children and fields and with them, persecutions) and in the age to come, eternal life. But many who are first will be last, and many who are last will be first.*

'For the kingdom of heaven is like a landowner who went out early in the morning to hire men to work in his vineyard. He agreed

to pay them a denarius for the day and sent them into his vineyard. About the third hour he went out and saw others standing in the marketplace doing nothing. He told them, "You also go and work in my vineyard, and I will pay you whatever is right." So they went. He went out again about the sixth hour and the ninth hour and did the same thing. About the eleventh hour he went out and found still others standing around. He asked them, "Why have you been standing here all day long doing nothing?" "Because no one has hired us," they answered. He said to them, "You also go and work in my vineyard."

'When evening came, the owner of the vineyard said to his foreman, "Call the workers and pay them their wages, beginning with the last ones hired and going on to the first."

'The workers who were hired about the eleventh hour came and each received a denarius. So when those came who were hired first, they expected to receive more. But each one of them also received a denarius. When they received it, they began to grumble against the landowner. "These men who were hired last worked only one hour," they said, "and you have made them equal to us who have borne the burden of the work and the heat of the day." But he answered one of them, "Friend, I am not being unfair to you. Didn't you agree to work for a denarius? Take your pay and go. I want to give the man who was hired last the same as I gave you. Don't I have the right to do what I want with my own money? Or are you envious because I am generous?" So the last will be first, and the first will be last.'

They were on their way up to Jerusalem, with Jesus leading the way, and the disciples were astonished, while those who followed were afraid. Again he took the Twelve aside and told them what was going to happen to him, *'We are going up to Jerusalem, and everything written by the prophets about the Son of Man will be fulfilled. He will be betrayed to the chief priests and teachers of the law. They will condemn him to death and will hand him over to the Gentiles, who will mock him and spit on him, flog him and crucify him. Three days later he will rise.'* The disciples did not understand any of this. Its meaning was hidden from them, and they did not know what he was talking about.

To be a servant is the way to become a leader

Then the mother of Zebedee's sons, James and John came to Jesus with them, and kneeling down asked a favour of him. 'Teacher,' they said, 'We want you to do for us whatever we ask.' *'What do you want me to do for you?'* he asked. Their mother answered, 'Grant that one of these two sons of mine may sit at your right hand and the other at your left in your kingdom.' Her sons were fully agreeing, saying, 'Let one of us sit at your right and the other at your left in your glory.'

'You don't know what you are asking,' Jesus said. *'Can you drink the cup I am going to drink or be baptised with the baptism I am baptised with?'* 'We can,' they answered.

Jesus said to them, *'You will indeed drink the cup I drink and be baptised with the baptism I am baptised with, but to sit at my right or left is not for me to grant. These places belong to those for whom they have been prepared by my Father.'*

When the ten heard about this, they became indignant with James and John. Jesus called them together and said, *'You know that those who are regarded as rulers of the Gentiles lord it over them, and their high officials exercise authority over them. Not so with you. Instead, whoever wants to become great among you must be your servant, and whoever wants to be first must be slave of all. For even the Son of Man did not come to be served, but to serve, and to give his life as a ransom for many.'*

The blind are healed and the lost are saved

Then they came to Jericho and as they approached the city there were two blind men sitting by the roadside begging. When they heard the crowd going by they asked what was happening. They were told, 'Jesus of Nazareth is passing by.' When they heard this they shouted, 'Jesus, Son of David, have mercy on us!' Those who led the way in the crowd rebuked them and told them to be quiet, but they shouted all the louder, 'Lord, Son of David, have mercy on us!' Jesus stopped and called them, ordering that they be brought to him. *'What do you want me to do for you?'* he asked. 'Lord,' they answered, 'We want our sight.' Jesus had compassion on them and touched their eyes saying, *'Receive your sight, your faith has healed you.'* Immediately they received their sight.

One of those healed was Bartimaeus (that is, Son of Timaeus). When he heard that it was Jesus of Nazareth passing by, he began to shout, 'Jesus, Son of David, have mercy on me!' Many rebuked him and told him to be quiet, but he shouted all the more, 'Son of David, have mercy on me!' Jesus stopped and said, *'Call him.'* So they called him, saying, 'Cheer up! On your feet! He's calling you.' Throwing his cloak aside, he jumped to his feet and came to Jesus. *'What do you want me to do for you?'* Jesus asked him. 'Rabbi,' he said, 'I want to see.' *'Go,'* said Jesus, *'Your faith has healed you.'* Immediately he received his sight and followed Jesus along the road praising God. When all the people saw it they also praised God.

As Jesus entered Jericho and was passing through, a man was there by the name of Zacchaeus, he was a chief tax collector and very wealthy. He wanted to see who Jesus was but being a short man he could not, because of the crowd. So he ran ahead and climbed a sycamore-fig tree to see him, since Jesus was coming that way. When Jesus reached the spot, he looked up and said to him, *'Zacchaeus, come down immediately. I must stay at your house today.'* So he came down at once and welcomed him gladly.

All the people saw this and began to mutter, 'He has gone to be the guest of a "sinner."' But Zacchaeus stood up and said to the Lord, 'Look, Lord! Here and now I give half of my possessions to the poor, and if I have cheated anybody out of anything, I will pay back four times the amount.' Jesus said to him, *'Today salvation has come to this house, because this man, too, is a Son of Abraham. For the Son of Man came to seek and to save what was lost.'*

Use wisely what God gives you

While they were listening to this, he went on to tell them a parable, because he was near Jerusalem and the people thought that the kingdom of God was going to appear at once.

He said, '*A man of noble birth went to a distant country to have himself appointed king and then to return. So he called ten of his servants and gave them ten minas* (about three years wages). *"Put this money to work," he said, "until I come back." But his subjects hated him and sent a delegation after him to say, "We don't want this man to be our king." He was made king, however, and returned home. Then he sent for the servants to whom he had given the money, in order to find out what they had gained with it. The first one came and said, "Sir, your mina has earned ten more." "Well done, my good servant!" his master replied. "Because you have been trustworthy in a very small matter, take charge of ten cities." The second came and said, "Sir, your mina has earned five more." His master answered, "You take charge of five cities." Then another servant came and said, "Sir, here is your mina; I have kept it laid away in a piece of cloth. I was afraid of you, because you are a hard man. You take out what you did not put in and reap what you did not sow."*

'*His master replied, "I will judge you by your own words, you wicked servant! You knew, did you, that I am a hard man, taking out what I did not put in, and reaping what I did not sow? Why then didn't you put my money on deposit, so that when I came back, I could have collected it with interest?"*

'*Then he said to those standing by, "Take his mina away from him and give it to the one who has ten minas." "Sir," they said, "He already has ten!" He replied, "I tell you that to everyone who has, more will be given, but as for the one who has nothing, even what he has will be taken away. But those enemies of mine who did not want me to be king over them bring them here and kill them in front of me."*'

Jesus anointed at Bethany

After Jesus had said this, he went on ahead, going up to Jerusalem. When it was almost time for the Jewish Passover, many went up from the country to Jerusalem for their ceremonial cleansing before the Passover. They kept looking for Jesus, and as they stood in the temple area they asked one another, 'What do you think? Isn't he coming to the Feast at all?' But the chief priests and Pharisees had given orders that if anyone found out where Jesus was, he should report it so that they might arrest him.

Six days before the Passover Jesus arrived at Bethany, where Lazarus lived, whom Jesus had raised from the dead. Here a dinner was given in Jesus' honour in the home of a man known as Simon the Leper. Martha served, while Lazarus was among those reclining at the table with Jesus. Then Mary took about a pint of pure nard, an expensive perfume; she broke the jar and poured the perfume on Jesus' head and feet, wiping his feet with her hair. And the house was filled with the fragrance of the perfume.

Some of those present were saying indignantly to one another, 'Why this waste of perfume? It could have been sold for more than a year's wages and the money given to the poor.' And they rebuked her harshly.

One of his disciples, Judas Iscariot, who was later to betray him, also objected, with the same criticism. 'Why wasn't this perfume sold and the money given to the poor? It was worth a year's wages.' He did not say this because he cared about the poor but because he was a thief; as keeper of the money bag, he used to help himself to what was put into it.

'Leave her alone,' Jesus replied. *'Why are you bothering her? She has done a beautiful thing to me. The poor you will always have with you, and you can help them anytime you want. But you will not always have me. She did what she could. It was intended that she should save this perfume for the day of my burial and now she has poured it on my body beforehand to prepare for my burial. I tell you the truth, wherever the gospel is preached throughout the world, what she has done will also be told, in memory of her.'*

Meanwhile a large crowd of Jews, who had come for the Feast, found out that Jesus was there and came, not only because of him but also to see Lazarus, whom he had raised from the dead. So the chief priests made plans to kill Lazarus as well, for on account of him many of the Jews were going over to Jesus and putting their faith in him.

Chapter 19

The Last Week

*'Blessed is He
who comes in the name of the Lord.'*

Sunday

The triumphal entry – April AD 30

As they approached Jerusalem and came to Bethphage and
Bethany at the hill called the Mount of Olives, Jesus sent two
of his disciples, saying to them, *'Go to the village ahead of you,
and just as you enter it, you will find a donkey tied there, with her
colt tied by her, which no one has ever ridden. Untie them and
bring them to me. If anyone asks you, "Why are you doing this?"
tell him, "The Lord needs them," and he will send them right
away.'*

This took place to fulfil what was spoken through the
prophet:

'Do not be afraid, O Daughter of Zion,
　　See, your king comes to you,
gentle and riding on a donkey,
　　on a colt, the foal of a donkey.'

They went and did as Jesus had instructed, and found them
outside in the street, tied at a doorway. As they untied them,
some people standing there who were the owners asked,
'What are you doing, untying that colt?' They answered as
Jesus had told them to, saying, 'The Lord needs it,' and so
they let them go. Then they brought them to Jesus and threw

their cloaks on them. Jesus sat on the colt and as he went along, many people spread their cloaks on the road, while others spread branches they had cut in the fields.

When he came near the place where the road goes down the Mount of Olives, the whole crowd of disciples began joyfully to praise God in loud voices for all the miracles they had seen. Those who went ahead and those who followed shouted,

> 'Hosanna!'
> 'Blessed is he, the king who comes in the name of the Lord!'
> 'Blessed is the coming kingdom of our father David!'
> 'Peace in heaven and hosanna and glory in the highest!'

At first his disciples did not understand all this. Only after Jesus was glorified did they realise that these things had been written about.

Now the crowd that was with him when he called Lazarus from the tomb and raised him from the dead continued to spread the word. Many people, because they had heard that he had given this miraculous sign, went out to meet him. Some of the Pharisees in the crowd said to Jesus, 'Teacher, rebuke your disciples!' *'I tell you,'* he replied, *'If they keep quiet, the stones will cry out.'* So the Pharisees said to one another, 'See, this is getting us nowhere. Look how the whole world has gone after him!'

As Jesus approached Jerusalem and saw the city, he wept over it and said, *'If you, even you, had only known on this day what would bring you peace, but now it is hidden from your eyes. The days will come upon you when your enemies will build an embankment against you and encircle you and hem you in on every side. They will dash you to the ground, you and the children within your walls. They will not leave one stone on another, because you did not recognise the time of God's coming to you.'*

When Jesus entered Jerusalem, the whole city was stirred and asked, 'Who is this?' The crowds answered, 'This is Jesus, the prophet from Nazareth in Galilee.' Jesus went to the

Temple. He looked around at everything, but since it was already late, he went out to Bethany with the Twelve.

Monday

Jesus curses a fig tree and cleanses the Temple

The next day, early in the morning as they were leaving Bethany on the way back to the city, Jesus was hungry. Seeing in the distance a fig tree in leaf by the road, he went up to it to find out if it had any fruit. When he reached it, he found nothing but leaves, because it was not the season for figs. Then he said to the tree, *'May no one ever eat fruit from you again.'* And his disciples heard him say it.

On reaching Jerusalem, Jesus entered the Temple area and began driving out those who were buying and selling there. He overturned the tables of the money changers and the benches of those selling doves, and would not allow anyone to carry merchandise through the Temple courts. And as he taught them, he said, *'Is it not written:*

> *"My house will be called*
> *a house of prayer for all nations"?*
> *But you have made it "a den of robbers." '*

The blind and the lame came to him at the Temple, and he healed them. But when the chief priests and the teachers of the law saw the wonderful things he did and the children shouting in the Temple area, 'Hosanna to the Son of David,' they were indignant. 'Do you hear what these children are saying?' they asked him. *'Yes,'* replied Jesus, *'have you never read, "From the lips of children and infants you have ordained praise"?'*

The chief priests and the teachers of the law heard this and began looking for a way to kill him, for they feared him, because the whole crowd was amazed at his teaching. When evening came, Jesus left them and went out of the city to Bethany, where he spent the night.

Tuesday and Wednesday

Jesus teaches at the Temple

In the morning, as they went along, they saw the fig tree withered from the roots. Peter remembered and said to Jesus, 'Rabbi, look! The fig tree you cursed has withered!' The disciples were amazed. 'How did the fig tree wither so quickly?' they asked. *'Have faith in God,'* Jesus answered. *'I tell you the truth, if you have faith and do not doubt in your heart but believe that what you say will happen, not only can you do what was done to the fig tree, but also you can say to this mountain, "Go, throw yourself into the sea," and it will be done for you. Therefore I tell you, whatever you ask for in prayer, believe that you have received it, and it will be yours. And when you stand praying, if you hold anything against anyone, forgive him, so that your Father in heaven may forgive you your sins.'*

Every day he was teaching at the Temple. But the chief priests, the teachers of the law and the leaders among the people were trying to kill him. Yet they could not find any way to do it, because all the people hung on his words.

Now there were some Greeks among those who went up to worship at the Feast. They came to Philip, who was from Bethsaida in Galilee, with a request. 'Sir,' they said, 'We would like to see Jesus.' Philip went to tell Andrew; Andrew and Philip in turn told Jesus.

Jesus replied, *'The hour has come for the Son of Man to be glorified. I tell you the truth, unless a kernel of wheat falls to the ground and dies, it remains only a single seed. But if it dies, it produces many seeds. The man who loves his life will lose it, while the man who hates his life in this world will keep it for eternal life. Whoever serves me must follow me; and where I am, my servant also will be. My Father will honour the one who serves me. Now my heart is troubled, and what shall I say? "Father, save me from this hour"? No, it was for this very reason I came to this hour. Father, glorify your name!'*

Then a voice came from heaven, 'I have glorified it, and will glorify it again.' The crowd that was there and heard it said it had thundered; others said an angel had spoken to him.

Jesus said, *'This voice was for your benefit, not mine. Now is the time for judgement on this world; now the prince of this world will be driven out. But I, when I am lifted up from the earth, will draw all men to myself.'* He said this to show the kind of death he was going to die.

The crowd spoke up, 'We have heard from the Law that the Christ will remain forever, so how can you say, "The Son of Man must be lifted up"? Who is this "Son of Man"?'

Then Jesus told them, *'You are going to have the light just a little while longer. Walk while you have the light, before darkness overtakes you. The man who walks in the dark does not know where he is going. Put your trust in the light while you have it, so that you may become sons of light.'* When he had finished speaking, Jesus left and hid himself from them.

Even after Jesus had done all these miraculous signs in their presence, they still would not believe in him. This was to fulfil the word of Isaiah the prophet:

> 'Lord, who has believed our message
>> and to whom has the arm of the Lord been
>>> revealed?'

For this reason they could not believe, because, as Isaiah says elsewhere:

> 'He has blinded their eyes
>> and deadened their hearts,
> so they can neither see with their eyes,
>> nor understand with their hearts,
>> nor turn, and I would heal them.'

Isaiah said this because he saw Jesus' glory and spoke about him.

Yet at the same time many even among the leaders believed in him. But because of the Pharisees they would not confess their faith for fear they would be put out of the synagogue; for they loved praise from men more than praise from God.

Then Jesus cried out, *'When a man believes in me, he does not believe in me only, but in the one who sent me. When he looks at me, he sees the one who sent me. I have come into the world as a light, so that no one who believes in me should stay in darkness. As for the person who hears my words but does not keep them, I do not judge him. For I did not come to judge the world, but to save it. There is a judge for the one who rejects me and does not accept my words; that very word which I spoke will condemn him at the last day. For I did not speak of my own accord, but the Father who sent me commanded me what to say and how to say it. I know that his command leads to eternal life. So whatever I say is just what the Father has told me to say.'*

Jesus' authority is challenged

They arrived again in Jerusalem, and while Jesus was walking in the Temple courts and teaching, the chief priests and the elders and teachers of the law came to him. 'By what authority are you doing these things?' they asked. 'And who gave you this authority?' Jesus replied, *'I will also ask you one question. If you answer me, I will tell you by what authority I am doing these things. John's baptism, where did it come from? Was it from heaven, or from men?'*

They discussed it among themselves and said, 'If we say, "From heaven," he will ask, "Then why didn't you believe him?" But if we say, "From men" all the people will stone us, because they are persuaded that John was a prophet.' So they answered Jesus, 'We don't know where it was from.' Then he said, *'Neither will I tell you by what authority I am doing these things.'*

The story of the two sons

'What do you think? There was a man who had two sons. He went to the first and said, "Son, go and work today in the vineyard." "I will not," he answered, but later he changed his mind and went. Then the father went to the other son and said the same thing. He answered, "I will, sir," but he did not go. Which of the two did

what his father wanted?' 'The first,' they answered. Jesus said to them, *'I tell you the truth, the tax collectors and the prostitutes are entering the kingdom of God ahead of you. For John came to you to show you the way of righteousness, and you did not believe him, but the tax collectors and the prostitutes did. And even after you saw this, you did not repent and believe him.'*

The story of the evil farmers

'Listen to another parable. There was a landowner who planted a vineyard. He put a wall around it, dug a wine press in it and built a watchtower. Then he rented the vineyard to some farmers and went away on a journey. When the harvest time approached, he sent a servant to the tenants to collect some of the fruit of the vineyard.

'The tenants seized him, beat him and sent him away empty handed. He sent another servant, but that one they also beat and treated shamefully and sent away empty handed. He sent still a third, and they wounded him and threw him out. He sent many others, some they beat, others they killed. Then the owner of the vineyard said, "What shall I do? I will send my son, whom I love; perhaps they will respect him." But when the tenants saw him, they talked the matter over. "This is the heir," they said. "Let's kill him, and the inheritance will be ours." So they took him and threw him out of the vineyard and killed him. Therefore, when the owner of the vineyard comes, what will he do to those tenants?'

'He will bring those wretches to a wretched end,' they replied, 'and he will rent the vineyard to other tenants, who will give him his share of the crop at harvest time.' *'He will come and kill those tenants and give the vineyard to others,'* said Jesus. When the people heard this, they said, 'May this never be!' Jesus looked directly at them and asked, *'Then what is the meaning of that which is written, have you never read in the Scriptures:*

> *"The stone the builders rejected*
> *has become the capstone;*
> *the Lord has done this,*
> *and it is marvellous in our eyes"?*

'Therefore I tell you that the kingdom of God will be taken away from you and given to a people who will produce its fruit. He who falls on this stone will be broken to pieces, but he on whom it falls will be crushed.'

When the chief priests and the Pharisees heard Jesus' parables, they knew he was talking about them. They looked for a way to arrest him, but they were afraid of the crowd because the people held that he was a prophet.

The great wedding feast

Jesus spoke to them again in parables, saying, 'The kingdom of heaven is like a king who prepared a wedding banquet for his son. He sent his servants to those who had been invited to the banquet to tell them to come, but they refused to come. Then he sent some more servants and said, "Tell those who have been invited that I have prepared my dinner. My oxen and fattened cattle have been butchered, and everything is ready. Come to the wedding banquet." But they paid no attention and went off one to his field, another to his business. The rest seized his servants, mistreated them and killed them. The king was enraged. He sent his army and destroyed those murderers and burned their city.

'Then he said to his servants, "The wedding banquet is ready, but those I invited did not deserve to come. Go to the street corners and invite to the banquet anyone you find." So the servants went out into the streets and gathered all the people they could find, both good and bad, and the wedding hall was filled with guests. But when the king came in to see the guests, he noticed a man there who was not wearing wedding clothes. "Friend," he asked, "how did you get in here without wedding clothes?" The man was speechless. Then the king told the attendants, "Tie him hand and foot, and throw him outside, into the darkness, where there will be weeping and gnashing of teeth." For many are invited, but few are chosen.'

The religious leaders try to trap Jesus with questions

Then the Pharisees went out and laid plans to trap him in his words. Keeping a close eye on him they sent their disciples along with the Herodians to Jesus, to catch him. They were like spies hoping to catch him in something he said so that they might hand him over to the power and authority of the governor. 'Teacher,' they said, 'We know you are a man of integrity and that you teach the way of God in accordance with the truth. You aren't swayed by men, because you pay no attention to who they are. Tell us then, what is your opinion? Is it right to pay taxes to Caesar or not? Should we or shouldn't we pay?'

But Jesus, knowing their hypocrisy and seeing through their duplicity and evil intent, said, *'You hypocrites, why are you trying to trap me? Show me the coin, a denarius, used for paying the tax.'* They brought him a denarius, and he asked them, *'Whose portrait is this? And whose inscription?'* 'Caesar's,' they replied. Then he said to them, *'Give to Caesar what is Caesar's, and to God what is God's.'* When they heard this, they were amazed and astonished at his answer, and they became silent. So they left him and went away.

That same day the Sadducees, who say there is no resurrection, came to him with a question. 'Teacher,' they said, 'Moses told us that if a man dies without having children, his brother must marry the widow and have children for him. Now there were seven brothers among us. The first one married and died, and since he had no children, he left his wife to his brother. The same thing happened to the second and third brother, right on down to the seventh. Finally, the woman died. Now then, at the resurrection, whose wife will she be of the seven, since all of them were married to her?'

Jesus replied, *'You are in error because you do not know the Scriptures or the power of God. The people of this age marry and are given in marriage. But those who are considered worthy of taking part in that age and in the resurrection from the dead will neither marry nor be given in marriage, and they can no longer die for they are like the angels. They are God's children, since they are children of the resurrection. But about the resurrection of the dead have you not read in the book of Moses, in the account of the bush, what God said to him and you, "I am the God of Abraham, the*

God of Isaac, and the God of Jacob"? He is not the God of the dead but of the living, for to him all are alive. You are badly mistaken!'

When the crowds heard this, they were astonished at his teaching and some of the teachers of the law responded, 'Well said, teacher!'

The greatest commandment

Hearing that Jesus had silenced the Sadducees, the Pharisees got together. One of them, an expert in the law, tested him with this question, 'Teacher, which is the greatest commandment in the Law?' Jesus replied, *'The most important one is this, "Hear O Israel, the Lord our God, the Lord is one. Love the Lord your God with all your heart and with all your soul and with all your mind and with all your strength!" This is the first and greatest commandment. And the second is like it: "Love your neighbours as yourself." All the law and the prophets hang on these two commandments, for there is no commandment greater than these.'*

'Well said, teacher,' the man replied. 'You are right in saying that God is one and there is no other but him. To love him with all your heart, with all your understanding and with all your strength, and to love your neighbours as yourself is more important than all burnt offerings and sacrifices.' When Jesus saw that he had answered wisely, he said to him, *'You are not far from the kingdom of God.'* And from then on no one dared ask him any more questions.

While the Pharisees were gathered together to hear Jesus teaching in the Temple courts, he asked them, *'What do you think about the Christ? Whose son is he?'* 'The son of David,' they replied. He said to them, *'How is it then that David, speaking by the Spirit, calls him "Lord"? For he says,*

"The Lord said to my Lord:
  'Sit at my right hand
until I put your enemies
  under your feet.'"

'If then David calls him "Lord," how can he be his son?'

No one could say a word in reply, and from that day on no one dared to ask him any more questions and the large crowd listened to him with delight.

Jesus condemns the religious leaders

Then Jesus taught his disciples in the hearing of all the people, *'Beware and watch out for the teachers of the law and the Pharisees. They sit in Moses' seat so you must obey them and do everything they tell you. But do not do what they do, for they do not practise what they preach. They tie up heavy loads and put them on men's shoulders, but they themselves are not willing to lift a finger to move them.*

'Everything they do is done for men to see. They like to walk around in flowing robes making their phylacteries wide and the tassels on their prayer shawls long; they love the place of honour at banquets and the most important seats in the synagogues; they love to be greeted in the marketplaces and to have men call them "Rabbi." They devour widows' houses and for a show make lengthy prayers. Such men will be punished most severely. But you are not to be called "Rabbi," for you have only one Master and you are all brothers. And do not call anyone on earth "father," for you have one Father, and he is in heaven. Nor are you to be called "teacher," for you have one Teacher, the Christ. The greatest among you will be your servant. For whoever exalts himself will be humbled, and whoever humbles himself will be exalted.

'Woe to you, teachers of the law and Pharisees, you hypocrites! You shut the kingdom of heaven in men's faces. You yourselves do not enter, nor will you let those enter who are trying to.

'Woe to you, teachers of the law and Pharisees, you hypocrites! You travel over land and sea to win a single convert, and when he becomes one, you make him twice as much a son of hell as you are.

'Woe to you, blind guides! You say, "If anyone swears by the temple, it means nothing; but if anyone swears by the gold of the temple, he is bound by his oath." You blind fools! Which is greater: the gold, or the temple that makes the gold sacred? You also say, "If anyone swears by the altar, it means nothing; but if

anyone swears by the gift on it, he is bound by his oath.'' You blind men! Which is greater: the gift, or the altar that makes the gift sacred? Therefore, he who swears by the altar swears by it and by everything on it. And he who swears by the temple swears by it and by the one who dwells in it. And he who swears by heaven swears by God's throne and by the one who sits on it.

'Woe to you, teachers of the law and Pharisees, you hypocrites! You give a tenth of your spices, mint, dill and cummin. But you have neglected the more important matters of the law, justice, mercy and faithfulness. You should have practised the latter, without neglecting the former. You blind guides! You strain out a gnat but swallow a camel.

'Woe to you, teachers of the law and Pharisees, you hypocrites! You clean the outside of the cup and dish, but inside they are full of greed and self-indulgence. Blind Pharisee! First clean the inside of the cup and dish, and then the outside also will be clean.

'Woe to you, teachers of the law and Pharisees, you hypocrites! You are like whitewashed tombs, which look beautiful on the outside but on the inside are full of dead men's bones and everything unclean. In the same way, on the outside you appear to people as righteous but on the inside you are full of hypocrisy and wickedness.

'Woe to you, teachers of the law and Pharisees, you hypocrites! You build tombs for the prophets and decorate the graves of the righteous. And you say, ''If we had lived in the days of our forefathers, we would not have taken part with them in shedding the blood of the prophets.'' So you testify against yourselves that you are the descendants of those who murdered the prophets. Fill up, then, the measure of the sin of your forefathers!

'You snakes! You brood of vipers! How will you escape being condemned to hell? Therefore I am sending you prophets and wise men and teachers. Some of them you will kill and crucify; others you will flog in your synagogues and pursue from town to town. And so upon you will come all the righteous blood that has been shed on earth, from the blood of righteous Abel to the blood of Zechariah son of Berekiah, whom you murdered between the temple and the altar. I tell you the truth, all this will come upon this generation.

'O Jerusalem, Jerusalem, you who kill the prophets and stone those sent to you, how often I have longed to gather your children together, as a hen gathers her chicks under her wings, but you were not willing. Look, your house is left to you desolate. For I tell you, you will not see me again until you say, "Blessed is he who comes in the name of the Lord."'

The widow's offering

Jesus sat down opposite the place where the offerings were put and watched the crowd putting their money into the Temple treasury. As he looked up, he saw many rich people putting their gifts into the temple treasury. They were throwing in large amounts. He also saw a poor widow come along and put in two very small copper coins, worth only a fraction of a penny. Calling his disciples to him, Jesus said, *'I tell you the truth, this poor widow has put more into the treasury than all the others. They all gave their gifts out of their wealth; but she, out of her poverty, put in everything, all she had to live on.'*

As he was leaving the Temple, one of his disciples said to him, 'Look, Teacher! What massive stones! What magnificent buildings.' Others commented on how beautifully it was adorned with such gifts dedicated to God. *'Do you see all these great buildings?'* replied Jesus. *'I tell you the truth, the time will come when not one stone here will be left on another; every one of them will be thrown down.'*

The signs of Jesus' return

As Jesus was sitting on the Mount of Olives opposite the Temple, Peter, James, John and Andrew asked him privately, 'Tell us, when will this happen and what will be the sign of your coming and of the end of the age when all is about to be fulfilled?'

Jesus answered, *'Watch out that no one deceives you. For many will come in my name, claiming, "I am the Christ," and "The time is near." They will deceive many. Do not follow them. You will hear of wars, rumours of wars and revolutions, see to it that you are not alarmed and frightened. Such things must happen, but the end will not come right away. Nation will rise against nation, and kingdom against kingdom. There will be great earthquakes, famines and pestilences in various places, and fearful events and great signs from heaven. All these are the beginning of birth pains.*

'You must be on your guard. You will be handed over to the local councils, synagogues and prisons to be flogged, persecuted and put to death, and you will be hated by all nations and stand before governors and kings as witnesses to them because of me and on account of my name. Whenever you are arrested and brought to trial, do not worry beforehand about what to say. Just say whatever is given you at the time, for I will give you words and wisdom that none of your adversaries will be able to resist or contradict for it is not you speaking, but the Holy Spirit.

'At that time many will turn away from the faith and will betray and hate each other, brother will betray brother to death, and a father his child. You will be betrayed by friends and relatives and they will put some of you to death. Children will rebel against their parents and have them put to death, for all men will hate you because of me. But not a hair of your head will perish. Many false prophets will appear and deceive many people. Because of the increase of wickedness, the love of most will grow cold, but he who stands firm to the end will be saved and gain eternal life. And this gospel of the kingdom will be preached in the whole world as a testimony to all nations, and then the end will come.

'When you see Jerusalem being surrounded by armies, and you see standing in the holy place "The abomination that causes desolation," spoken of through the prophet Daniel (let the reader understand) you will know its desolation is near. Then let those who are in Judea flee to the mountains. Let those in the city get out, and let those in the country not enter the city. Let no one on the roof of his house go down to take anything out of the house. Let no one in the field go back to get his cloak. For this is the time of punishment in fulfilment of all that has been written. How dreadful it will be in those days for pregnant women and nursing mothers! Pray that your flight will not take place in winter or on the Sabbath. For those days will be days of great distress, unequalled from the beginning of the world until now, and never

to be equalled again. For there will be great distress in the land and wrath against this people. They will fall by the sword and will be taken as prisoners to all nations. Jerusalem will be trampled on by the Gentiles until the times of the Gentiles are fulfilled.

'If the Lord had not cut short those days, no one would survive, but for the sake of the elect, whom he has chosen, he has shortened them. At that time if anyone says to you, "Look, here is the Christ!" or, "Look there he is!" do not believe it. For false Christs and false prophets will appear and perform great signs and miracles to deceive even the elect if that were possible. Be on your guard; I have told you everything ahead of time.

'So if anyone tells you, "There he is, out in the desert," do not go out; or, "Here he is, in the inner rooms," do not believe it. For as lightning that comes from the east is visible even in the west, so will be the coming of the Son of Man. Wherever there is a carcass, there the vultures will gather.

'There will be signs in the sun, moon and stars.
'Immediately after the distress of those days

> *"the sun will be darkened,*
>   *and the moon will not give its light;*
> *the stars will fall from the sky,*
>   *and the heavenly bodies will be shaken."*

'On the earth, nations will be in anguish and perplexity at the roaring and tossing of the sea. Men will faint from terror, apprehensive of what is coming on the world, for the heavenly bodies will be shaken.

'At that time the sign of the Son of Man will appear in the sky, and all the nations of the earth will mourn. They will see the Son of Man coming on the clouds of the sky, with great power and great glory. And he will send his angels with a loud trumpet call, and they will gather his elect from the four winds, from the ends of the earth to the ends of the heavens. When these things begin to take place, stand up and lift up your heads, because your redemption is drawing near.

'Now learn this lesson from the fig tree: As soon as its twigs get tender and its leaves come out, you know that summer is near. Even so, when you see all these things happening, you know that

the kingdom of God is near, right at the door. I tell you the truth, this generation will certainly not pass away until all these things have happened. Heaven and earth will pass away, but my words will never pass away.

'Be careful, or your hearts will be weighed down with dissipation, drunkenness and all the anxieties of life, and that day will close on you unexpectedly like a trap. For it will come upon all those who live on the face of the earth. Be always on the watch and pray that you may be able to escape all that is about to happen, and that you may be able to stand before the Son of Man.

'No one knows about that day or hour, not even the angels in heaven, nor the Son, but only the Father. As it was in the days of Noah, so it will be at the coming of the Son of Man. For in the days before the flood, people were eating and drinking, marrying and giving in marriage, up to the day Noah entered the ark; and they knew nothing about what would happen until the flood came and took them away, destroying them all. That is how it will be at the coming of the Son of Man. Two men will be in the field; one will be taken and the other left. Two women will be grinding with a hand mill; one will be taken and the other left.

'Therefore keep watch, be on guard! Be alert because you do not know on what day your Lord will come. But understand this, if the owner of the house had known at what time of night the thief was coming, he would have kept watch and would not have let his house be broken into. So you also must be ready, because the Son of Man will come at an hour when you do not expect him.

'Who then is the faithful and wise servant, whom the master has put in charge of the servants in his household to give them their food at the proper time? Each servant has his assigned task, but the one at the door is told to keep watch. It will be good for that servant whose master finds him doing so when he returns. I tell you the truth, he will put him in charge of all his possessions. But suppose that servant is wicked and says to himself, ''My master is staying away a long time,'' and he then begins to beat his fellow servants and to eat and drink with drunkards. The master of that servant will come on a day when he does not expect him and at an hour he is not aware of. He will cut him to pieces and assign him a place with the hypocrites, where there will be weeping and *gnashing of teeth. Therefore keep watch because you do not know when the owner of the house will come back. Whether in the evening, or at midnight, or when the rooster crows, or at dawn. If he comes suddenly, do not let him find you sleeping. What I say to you, I say to everyone: "Watch!"'*

The parable of the wise and foolish virgins

'At that time the kingdom of heaven will be like ten virgins who took their lamps and went out to meet the bridegroom. Five of them were foolish and five were wise. The foolish ones took their lamps but did not take any oil with them. The wise, however, took oil in jars along with their lamps. The bridegroom was a long time in coming, and they all became drowsy and fell asleep. At midnight the cry rang out: "Here's the bridegroom! Come out to meet him!" Then all the virgins woke up and trimmed their lamps. The foolish ones said to the wise, "Give us some of your oil; our lamps are going out." "No," they replied, "There may not be enough for both us and you. Instead, go to those who sell oil and buy some for yourselves." But while they were on their way to buy the oil, the bridegroom arrived. The virgins who were ready went in with him to the wedding banquet. And the door was shut. Later the others also came. "Sir! Sir!" they said. "Open the door for us!" But he replied, "I tell you the truth, I don't know you." Therefore keep watch, because you do not know the day or the hour.'

The parable of the talents

'Again, it will be like a man going on a journey, who called his servants and entrusted his property to them. To one he gave five talents of money, to another two talents, and to another one talent, each according to his ability. Then he went on his journey. The man who had received the five talents went at once and put his money to work and gained five more. So also, the one with the two talents gained two more. But the man who had received the one talent went off, dug a hole in the ground and hid his master's money.

'After a long time the master of those servants returned and settled accounts with them. The man who had received the five talents brought the other five. "Master," he said, "you entrusted me with five talents. See, I have gained five more." His master replied, "Well done, good and faithful servant! You have been faithful with a few things; I will put you in charge of many things. Come and share your master's happiness!" The man with the two talents also came. "Master," he said, "You entrusted me with two talents; see, I have gained two more." His master replied, "Well done, good and faithful servant! You have been faithful with a few things; I will put you in charge of many things. Come and share your master's happiness!"

'Then the man who had received the one talent came. "Master," he said, "I knew that you are a hard man, harvesting where you have not sown and gathering where you have not scattered seed. So I was afraid and went out and hid your talent in the ground. See, here is what belongs to you." His master replied, "You wicked, lazy servant! So you knew that I harvest where I have not sown and gather where I have not scattered seed? Well then, you should have put my money on deposit with the bankers, so that when I returned I would have received it back with interest. Take the talent from him and give it to the one who has the ten talents. For everyone who has will be given more, and he will have an abundance. Whoever does not have, even what he has will be taken from him. And throw that worthless servant outside, into the darkness, where there will be weeping and gnashing of teeth."

'When the Son of Man comes in his glory, and all the angels with him, he will sit on his throne in heavenly glory. All the nations will be gathered before him, and he will separate the people one from another as a shepherd separates the sheep from the goats. He will put the sheep on his right and the goats on his left. Then the King will say to those on his right, "Come, you who are blessed by my Father; take your inheritance, the kingdom prepared for you since the creation of the world. For I was hungry and you gave me something to eat, I was thirsty and you gave me something to drink, I was a stranger and you invited me in, I needed clothes and you clothed me, I was sick and you looked after me, I was in prison and you came to visit me." Then the righteous *will answer him, "Lord, when did we see you hungry and feed you, or thirsty and give you something to drink? When did we see you a stranger and invite you in, or needing clothes and clothe you? When did we see you sick or in prison and go to visit you?" The King will reply, "I tell you the truth, whatever you did for one of the least of these brothers of mine, you did for me." Then he will say to those on his left, "Depart from me, you who are cursed, into the eternal fire prepared for the devil and his angels.*

'For I was hungry and you gave me nothing to eat, I was thirsty and you gave me nothing to drink, I was a stranger and you did not invite me in, I needed clothes and you did not clothe me, I was sick and in prison and you did not look after me." They also will answer, "Lord, when did we see you hungry or thirsty or a stranger or needing clothes or sick or in prison, and did not help you?" He will reply, "I tell you the truth, whatever you did not do for one of the least of these, you did not do for me." Then they will go away to eternal punishment, but the righteous to eternal life.'

Each day Jesus was teaching at the Temple, and each evening he went out to spend the night on the hill called the Mount of Olives, and all the people came early in the morning to hear him at the Temple.

Now the Passover, the Feast of Unleaven Bread, was approaching so when Jesus had finished saying all these things, he said to his disciples, *'As you know, the Passover is two days away, and the Son of Man will be handed over to be crucified.'*

Then the chief priests and the elders of the people assembled in the palace of the high priest, whose name was Caiaphas, and they plotted to arrest Jesus in some sly way and kill him. 'But not during the Feast,' they said, 'Or there may be a riot among the people.'

Then Satan entered Judas one of the Twelve, the one called Judas Iscariot, and he went to the chief priests and officers of the temple guard and discussed with them how he might betray Jesus asking, 'What are you willing to give me if I hand him over to you?' They were delighted to hear this and agreed to give him money counting out for him thirty silver coins.

He consented and from then on he watched for an opportunity to hand Jesus over to them when no crowd was present.

Thursday

On the first day of the Feast of Unleavened Bread, when it was customary to sacrifice the Passover Lamb, Jesus' disciples asked him, 'Where do you want us to go and make preparations for you to eat the Passover?'

He sent two of his disciples, Peter and John, saying, *'Go and make preparations for us to eat the Passover.'* 'Where do you want us to prepare it?' they asked. He replied, *'Go into the city, and as you enter it a man carrying a jar of water will meet you. Follow him. Say to the owner of the house he enters, "The Teacher says: My appointed time is near. I am going to celebrate the Passover with my disciples at your house, where is my guest room, where I may eat the Passover with my disciples?" He will show you a large upper room, furnished and ready. Make preparations for us there.'* The disciples left, went into the city and found things just as Jesus had told them. So they prepared the Passover.

When evening came, Jesus arrived with the Twelve. He knew that the time had come for him to leave this world and go to the Father. Having loved his own who were in the world, he now showed them the full extent of his love. The evening meal was being served, and the devil had already prompted Judas Iscariot, son of Simon, to betray Jesus.

And a dispute arose among them as to which of them was considered to be greatest. Jesus said to them, *'The kings of the Gentiles lord it over them; and those who exercise authority over them call themselves benefactors. But you are not to be like that. Instead, the greatest among you should be like the youngest, and the one who rules like the one who serves. For who is greater, the one who is at the table or the one who serves? Is it not the one who is at the table? But I am among you as one who serves. You are those who have stood by me in my trials. And I confer on you a kingdom, just as my Father conferred one on me, so that you may eat and drink at my table in my kingdom and sit on thrones, judging the twelve tribes of Israel.'*

Jesus washes the Disciples' feet

Jesus knew that the Father had put all things under his power, and that he had come from God and was returning to God; so he got up from the meal, took off his outer clothing, and wrapped a towel around his waist. After that, he poured water into a basin and began to wash his disciples' feet, drying them with the towel that was wrapped around him.

He came to Simon Peter, who said to him, 'Lord, are you going to wash my feet?' Jesus replied, *'You do not realise now what I am doing, but later you will understand.'* 'No,' said Peter, 'You shall never wash my feet.' Jesus answered, *'Unless I wash you, you have no part with me.'* 'Then, Lord,' Simon Peter replied, 'Not just my feet but my hands and my head as well!' Jesus answered, *'A person who has had a bath needs only to wash his feet; his whole body is clean. And you are clean, though not every one of you.'* For he knew who was going to betray him, and that was why he said not every one was clean.

When he had finished washing their feet, he put on his clothes and returned to his place. *'Do you understand what I have done for you?'* he asked them. *'You call me "Teacher" and "Lord," and rightly so, for that is what I am. Now that I, your Lord and Teacher, have washed your feet, you also should wash one another's feet. I have set you an example that you should do as I have done for you. I tell you the truth, no servant is greater than his master, nor is a messenger greater than the one who sent him. Now that you know these things, you will be blessed if you do them. I am not referring to all of you; I know those I have chosen. But this is to fulfil the scripture: "He who shares my bread has lifted up his heel against me." I am telling you now before it happens, so that when it does happen you will believe that I am He. I tell you the truth, whoever accepts anyone I send accepts me; and whoever accepts me accepts the one who sent me.'*

Chapter 20

The Last Supper

'I am the way, the truth and the life.'

When the hour came for them to eat the Passover meal, Jesus and his apostles reclined at the table. While they were eating Jesus said to them, *'I have eagerly desired to eat this Passover with you before I suffer. For I tell you, I will not eat it again until it finds fulfilment in the kingdom of God.'* After taking the cup, he gave thanks and said, *'Take this and divide it among you. For I tell you I will not drink again of the fruit of the vine until the kingdom of God comes.'* And he took bread, gave thanks and broke it, and gave it to them, saying, *'This is my body given for you; do this in remembrance of me.'*

In the same way, after the supper he took the cup saying, *'This cup is the new covenant in my blood, which is poured out for you.'* Then Jesus, troubled in spirit, said, *'One of you will betray me, one who is eating with me.'* They were very sad, and one by one they said to him, 'Surely not I, Lord?' *'I tell you the truth,'* he replied, *'The hand of him who is going to betray me is with mine on the table, one who dips bread into the bowl with me will betray me. The Son of Man will go as it has been decreed, but woe to that man who betrays him, it would be better for him if he had never been born.'*

His disciples stared at one another, at a loss to know which of them he meant. One of them, the disciple whom Jesus loved, was reclining next to him. Simon Peter motioned to this disciple and said, 'Ask him which one he means.' Leaning back against Jesus, he asked him, 'Lord, who is it?'

Jesus answered, *'It is the one to whom I will give this piece of bread when I have dipped it in the dish.'* Then, dipping the piece of bread, he gave it to Judas Iscariot, son of Simon. As soon as Judas took the bread, Satan entered into him.

Then Judas, the one who would betray him, said, 'Surely not I, Rabbi?' Jesus answered, *'Yes, it is you. What you are about to do, do quickly.'* But no one at the meal understood why Jesus said this to him. Since Judas had charge of the money, some thought Jesus was telling him to buy what was needed for the Feast, or to give something to the poor. As soon as Judas had taken the bread, he went out, and it was night.

When he was gone, Jesus said, *'Now is the Son of Man glorified and God is glorified in him. If God is glorified in him, God will glorify the Son in himself, and will glorify him at once.'* Then he took the cup, gave thanks and offered it to them, *'Drink from it, all of you. This is my blood of the covenant, which is poured out for many for the forgiveness of sins. I tell you the truth, I will not drink again of the fruit of the vine until that day when I drink it anew with you in my Father's kingdom.'*

Then Jesus told them, *'My children, I will be with you only a little longer. You will look for me, and just as I told the Jews, so I tell you now: Where I am going, you cannot come. A new command I give you: Love one another. As I have loved you, so you must love one another. By this all men will know that you are my disciples, if you love one another.'* Simon Peter asked him, 'Lord, where are you going?' Jesus replied, *'Where I am going, you cannot follow now, but you will follow later.'*

Peter asked, 'Lord, why can't I follow you now? I will lay down my life for you.' Jesus answered, *'Will you really lay down your life for me? Simon, Simon, Satan has asked permission to sift you as wheat. But I have prayed for you, Simon, that your faith may not fail. And when you have turned back, strengthen your brothers.'* But he replied, 'Lord, I am ready to go with you to prison and to death.' Jesus answered, *'I tell you, Peter, before the rooster crows today, you will disown me and deny three times that you know me.'*

Then Jesus asked them, *'When I sent you without purse, bag or sandals, did you lack anything?'* 'Nothing,' they answered. He said to them, *'But now if you have a purse, take it, and also a bag; and if you don't have a sword, sell your cloak and buy one. It is written: "And he was numbered with the transgressors"; and I tell you that this must be fulfilled in me. Yes, what is written about me is reaching its fulfilment.'*

The disciples said, 'See, Lord, here are two swords.' *'That is enough,'* he replied.

Jesus is the only way to God

'Do not let your hearts be troubled. Trust in God; trust also in me. In my Father's house are many rooms; if it were not so, I would have told you. I am going there to prepare a place for you. And if I go and prepare a place for you, I will come back and take you to be with me that you also may be where I am. You know the way to the place where I am going.'

Thomas said to him, 'Lord, we don't know where you are going, so how can we know the way?' Jesus answered, *'I am the way and the truth and the life. No one comes to the Father except through me. If you really knew me, you would know my Father as well. From now on, you do know him and have seen him.'*

Philip said, 'Lord, show us the Father and that will be enough for us.' Jesus answered, *'Don't you know me, Philip, even after I have been among you such a long time? Anyone who has seen me has seen the Father. How can you say, "Show us the Father"? Don't you believe that I am in the Father, and that the Father is in me? The words I say to you are not just my own. Rather, it is the Father, living in me, who is doing his work. Believe me when I say that I am in the Father and the Father is in me; or at least believe on the evidence of the miracles themselves. I tell you the truth, anyone who has faith in me will do what I have been doing. He will do even greater things than these, because I am going to the Father. And I will do whatever you ask in my name, so that the Son may bring glory to the Father. You may ask me for anything in my name, and I will do it.'*

The promise of the Holy Spirit

'If you love me, you will obey what I command. And I will ask the Father, and he will give you another Counsellor to be with you forever, the Spirit of truth. The world cannot accept him, because it neither sees him nor knows him. But you know him, for he lives with you and will be in you. I will not leave you as orphans; I will come to you. Before long, the world will not see me anymore, but you will see me. Because I live, you also will live. On that day you will realise that I am in my Father, and you are in me, and I am in you. Whoever has my commands and obeys them, he is the one who loves me. He who loves me will be loved by my Father, and I too will love him and show myself to him.'

Then Judas (not Judas Iscariot) said, 'But, Lord, why do you intend to show yourself to us and not to the world?' Jesus replied, *'If anyone loves me, he will obey my teaching. My Father will love him, and we will come to him and make our home with him. He who does not love me will not obey my teaching. These words you hear are not my own; they belong to the Father who sent me. All this I have spoken while still with you. But the Counsellor, the Holy Spirit, whom the Father will send in my name, will teach you all things and will remind you of everything I have said to you. Peace I leave with you; my peace I give you. I do not give to you as the world gives. Do not let your hearts be troubled and do not be afraid.*

'You heard me say, "I am going away and I am coming back to you." If you loved me, you would be glad that I am going to the Father, for the Father is greater than I. I have told you now before it happens, so that when it does happen you will believe. I will not speak with you much longer, for the prince of this world is coming. He has no hold on me, but the world must learn that I love the Father and that I do exactly what my Father has commanded me.

'Come now; let us leave.' And when they had sung a hymn Jesus, as was his custom, went out to the Mount of Olives and his disciples followed him.

Then Jesus told them, *'This very night you will all fall away on account of me, for it is written: "I will strike the shepherd, and the sheep of the flock will be scattered." But after I have risen, I will go ahead of you into Galilee.'* Peter replied, 'Even if all fall away on account of you, I never will.' *'I tell you the truth,'* Jesus answered, *'this very night, before the rooster crows twice you yourself will disown me three times.'* But Peter insisted emphatically, 'Even if I have to die with you, I will never disown you.' And all the other disciples said the same.

Jesus is the True Vine

Jesus said, *'I am the true vine, and my Father is the gardener. He cuts off every branch in me that bears no fruit, while every branch that does bear fruit he prunes so that it will be even more fruitful. You are already clean because of the word I have spoken to you. Remain in me, and I will remain in you. No branch can bear fruit by itself; it must remain in the vine. Neither can you bear fruit unless you remain in me.*

'I am the vine; you are the branches. If a man remains in me and I in him, he will bear much fruit; apart from me you can do nothing. If anyone does not remain in me, he is like a branch that is thrown away and withers; such branches are picked up, thrown into the fire and burned. If you remain in me and my words remain in you, ask whatever you wish, and it will be given you. This is to my Father's glory, that you bear much fruit, showing yourselves to be my disciples.

'As the Father has loved me, so have I loved you. Now remain in my love. If you obey my commands, you will remain in my love, just as I have obeyed my Father's commands and remain in his love. I have told you this so that my joy may be in you and that your joy may be complete. My command is this: Love each other as I have loved you. Greater love has no one than this, that he lay down his life for his friends. You are my friends if you do what I command. I no longer call you servants, because a servant does not know his master's business. Instead, I have called you friends, for everything that I learned from my Father I have made known to you. You did not choose me, but I chose you and appointed you to go and bear fruit, fruit that will last. Then the Father will give you whatever you ask in my name. This is my command: Love each other.

'If the world hates you, keep in mind that it hated me first. If you belonged to the world, it would love you as its own. As it is, you do not belong to the world, but I have chosen you out of the world. That is why the world hates you. Remember the words I spoke to you: "No servant is greater than his master." If they persecuted me, they will persecute you also. If they obeyed my teaching, they will obey yours also. They will treat you this way because of my name, for they do not know the One who sent me. If I had not come and spoken to them, they would not be guilty of sin. Now, however, they have no excuse for their sin. He who hates me hates my Father as well. If I had not done among them what no one else did, they would not be guilty of sin. But now they have seen these miracles, and yet they have hated both me and my Father. But this is to fulfil what is written in their Law: "They hated me without reason."

'When the Counsellor comes, whom I will send to you from the Father, the Spirit of truth who goes out from the Father, he will testify about me. And you also must testify, for you have been with me from the beginning.

'All this I have told you so that you will not go astray. They will put you out of the synagogue; in fact, a time is coming when anyone who kills you will think he is offering a service to God. They will do such things because they have not known the Father or me. I have told you this, so that when the time comes you will remember that I warned you. I did not tell you this at first because I was with you.

'Now I am going to him who sent me, yet none of you asks me, "Where are you going?" Because I have said these things, you are filled with grief. But I tell you the truth: It is for your good that I am going away. Unless I go away, the Counsellor will not come to you; but if I go, I will send him to you. When he comes, he will convict the world of guilt in regard to sin and righteousness and judgement: in regard to sin, because men do not believe in me; in regard to righteousness, because I am going to the Father, where you can see me no longer; and in regard to judgement, because the prince of this world now stands condemned.

'I have much more to say to you, more than you can now bear. But when he, the Spirit of truth, comes, he will guide you into all *truth. He will not speak on his own; he will speak only what he hears, and he will tell you what is yet to come. He will bring glory to me by taking from what is mine and making it known to you. All that belongs to the Father is mine. That is why I said the Spirit will take from what is mine and make it known to you. In a little while you will see me no more, and then after a little while you will see me.'*

Sadness will be turned to joy

Some of his disciples said to one another, 'What does he mean by saying, "In a little while you will see me no more, and then after a little while you will see me," and "Because I am going to the Father"?' They kept asking, 'What does he mean by "A little while"? We don't understand what he is saying.'

Jesus saw that they wanted to ask him about this, so he said to them, *'Are you asking one another what I meant when I said, "In a little while you will see me no more, and then after a little while you will see me"? I tell you the truth, you will weep and mourn while the world rejoices. You will grieve, but your grief will turn to joy. A woman giving birth to a child has pain because her time has come; but when her baby is born she forgets the anguish because of her joy that a child is born into the world. So with you: Now is your time of grief, but I will see you again and you will rejoice, and no one will take away your joy. In that day you will no longer ask me anything. I tell you the truth, my Father will give you whatever you ask in my name. Until now you have not asked for anything in my name. Ask and you will receive, and your joy will be complete.*

'Though I have been speaking figuratively, a time is coming when I will no longer use this kind of language but will tell you plainly about my Father. In that day you will ask in my name. I am not saying that I will ask the Father on your behalf. No, the Father himself loves you because you have loved me and have believed that I came from God. I came from the Father and entered the world; now I am leaving the world and going back to the Father.'

Then Jesus' disciples said, 'Now you are speaking clearly and without figures of speech. Now we can see that you know all things and that you do not even need to have anyone ask you questions. This makes us believe that you came from God.'

'You believe at last!' Jesus answered. *'But a time is coming, and has come, when you will be scattered, each to his own home. You will leave me all alone. Yet I am not alone, for my Father is with me. I have told you these things, so that in me you may have peace. In this world you will have trouble. But take heart! I have overcome the world.'*

Jesus prays to his Father

After Jesus said this, he looked toward heaven and prayed, *'Father, the time has come. Glorify your Son, that your Son may glorify you. For you granted him authority over all people that he might give eternal life to all those you have given him. Now this is eternal life: that they may know you, the only true God, and Jesus Christ, whom you have sent. I have brought you glory on earth by completing the work you gave me to do. And now, Father, glorify me in your presence with the glory I had with you before the world began.*

'I have revealed you to those whom you gave me out of the world. They were yours; you gave them to me and they have obeyed your word. Now they know that everything you have given me comes from you. For I gave them the words you gave me and they accepted them. They knew with certainty that I came from you, and they believed that you sent me. I pray for them. I am not praying for the world, but for those you have given me, for they are yours.

'All I have is yours, and all you have is mine. And glory has come to me through them. I will remain in the world no longer, but they are still in the world, and I am coming to you. Holy Father, protect them by the power of your name, the name you gave me, so that they may be one as we are one. While I was with them, I protected them and kept them safe by that name you gave me. None has been lost except the one doomed to destruction so that Scripture would be fulfilled.

'I am coming to you now, but I say these things while I am still in the world, so that they may have the full measure of my joy within them. I have given them your word and the world has hated them, for they are not of the world any more than I am of the world. My prayer is not that you take them out of the world but that you protect them from the evil one. They are not of the world, even as I am not of it. Sanctify them by the truth; your word is truth. As you sent me into the world, I have sent them into the world. For them I sanctify myself, that they too may be truly sanctified.

'My prayer is not for them alone. I pray also for those who will believe in me through their message, that all of them may be one, Father, just as you are in me and I am in you. May they also be in us so that the world may believe that you have sent me. I have given them the glory that you gave me, that they may be one as we are one: I in them and you in me. May they be brought to complete unity to let the world know that you sent me and have loved them even as you have loved me.

'Father, I want those you have given me to be with me where I am, and to see my glory, the glory you have given me because you loved me before the creation of the world.

'Righteous Father, though the world does not know you, I know you, and they know that you have sent me. I have made you known to them, and will continue to make you known in order that the love you have for me may be in them and that I myself may be in them.'

Jesus prays in Gethsemane

When he had finished praying, Jesus left with his disciples and crossed the Kidron Valley. On the other side there was an olive grove, a place called Gethsemane and he and his disciples went into it. Jesus said to them, *'Sit here while I go over there and pray.'* He took Peter and the two sons of Zebedee along with him, and he began to be deeply distressed and troubled. Then he said to them, *'My soul is overwhelmed with sorrow to the point of death. Stay here and keep watch with me.'*

Going a little farther, he withdrew a stone's throw beyond them, fell with his face to the ground and prayed, *'My Father, if it is possible, may this cup be taken from me. Yet not as I will, but as you will.'* An angel from heaven appeared to him and strengthened him. And being in anguish, he prayed more earnestly, and his sweat was like drops of blood falling to the ground.

Then he returned to his disciples and found them sleeping, exhausted from sorrow. *'Simon,'* he said to Peter, *'Are you asleep? Could you men not keep watch with me for one hour? Watch and pray so that you will not fall into temptation. The spirit is willing, but the body is weak.'*

He went away a second time and prayed, *'My Father, if it is not possible for this cup to be taken away unless I drink it, may your will be done.'*

When he came back, he again found them sleeping, because their eyes were heavy. They did not know what to say to him. So he left them and went away once more and prayed the third time, saying the same thing.

Jesus is arrested

Then he returned to the disciples and said to them, *'Are you still sleeping and resting? Enough, look, the hour has come, and the Son of Man is betrayed into the hands of sinners. Rise, let us go! Here comes my betrayer!'*

While he was still speaking, Judas, one of the Twelve, arrived. He knew the place well, because Jesus had often met there with his disciples. With him was a large crowd, which included a detachment of soldiers and some officials, sent from the chief priests, the teachers of the law and the elders of the people. They were carrying torches and lanterns and were armed with swords and clubs. Now the betrayer had arranged a signal with them: 'The one I kiss is the man; arrest him and lead him away under guard.' Jesus, knowing all that was going to happen to him, went out and asked them, *'Who is it you want?'* 'Jesus of Nazareth,' they replied. Going at once to Jesus, Judas said, 'Greetings, Rabbi!' and kissed him. Jesus replied, *'Judas, are you betraying the Son of Man with a kiss? Friend, do what you came for. I am he.'* (And Judas the traitor was standing there with them.) When Jesus said, *'I am he,'* they drew back and fell to the ground.

Again he asked them, *'Who is it you want?'* And they said, 'Jesus of Nazareth.' *'I told you I am he,'* Jesus answered. *'If you are looking for me, then let these men go.'* This happened so that the words he had spoken would be fulfilled: *'I have not lost one of those you gave me.'* Then the men stepped forward, seized Jesus and arrested him. When Jesus' followers saw what was going to happen, they said, 'Lord, should we strike with our swords?' And with that, Simon Peter, reached for his sword, drew it out and struck the servant of the high priest, cutting off his right ear. (The servant's name was Malchus.)

Jesus commanded Peter, *'Put your sword away! Shall I not drink the cup the Father has given me?'* And he touched the man's ear and healed him. Jesus said, *'All who draw the sword will die by the sword. Do you think I cannot call on my Father, and he will at once put at my disposal more than twelve legions of angels? But how then would the Scriptures be fulfilled that say it must happen in this way?'*

At that time Jesus said to the crowd, *'Am I leading a rebellion, that you have come out with swords and clubs to capture me? Every day I sat in the temple courts teaching, and you did not lay a hand on me to arrest me. This is your hour when darkness reigns. But this has all taken place that the writings of the prophets might be fulfilled.'* Then all the disciples deserted him and fled. A young man, wearing nothing but a linen garment, was following Jesus. When they seized him, he fled naked, leaving his garment behind.

Chapter 21

Jesus' Trials and the Crucifixion

'For this I came into the world.'

The Jewish Part of the Trial

Then the detachment of soldiers with its commander and the Jewish officials arrested Jesus. They bound him and brought him first to Annas, who was the father-in-law of Caiaphas, the high priest that year. Caiaphas was the one who had advised the Jews that it would be good if one man died for the people.

The high priest questioned Jesus about his disciples and his teaching. *'I have spoken openly to the world,'* Jesus replied. *'I always taught in synagogues or at the Temple, where all the Jews come together. I said nothing in secret. Why question me? Ask those who heard me. Surely they know what I said.'*

When Jesus said this, one of the officials nearby struck him in the face. 'Is this the way you answer the high priest?' he demanded. *'If I said something wrong,'* Jesus replied, *'Testify as to what is wrong. But if I spoke the truth, why did you strike me?'* Then Annas sent him, still bound, to Caiaphas the high priest.

They took Jesus to Caiaphas, and all the chief priests, elders and teachers of the law came and assembled together. The chief priests and the whole Sanhedrin were looking for false evidence against Jesus so that they could put him to death, but they did not find any, though many testified falsely against him, their statements did not agree.

Finally two stood up and came forward and gave this false testimony against him, 'We heard this fellow say, *"I will destroy this man-made Temple of God and in three days will build another, not made by man."'* Yet even then their testimony did not agree.

Then the high priest stood up before them and asked Jesus, 'Are you not going to answer? What is this testimony that these men are bringing against you?' But Jesus remained silent and gave no answer. Again the high priest said to him, 'I charge you under oath by the living God: Tell us if you are the Christ, the Son of the Blessed One?'

'Yes, it is as you say. I am,' said Jesus. *'But I say to all of you: In the future you will see the Son of Man sitting at the right hand of the Mighty One and coming on the clouds of heaven.'*

Then the high priest tore his clothes. 'Why do we need any more witnesses?' he asked. 'You have heard, he has spoken blasphemy. What do you think?' They all condemned him and said, 'He is worthy of death.' Then some began to spit at him; they blindfolded him and struck him with their fists. Others slapped him and said, 'Prophesy to us, Christ. Who hit you?' They said many other insulting things and the guards took him and beat him.

Peter denies Jesus

Simon Peter and another disciple were following Jesus at a distance. Because this disciple was known to the high priest, he went with Jesus into the high priest's courtyard, but Peter had to wait outside at the door. This other disciple, came back, spoke to the girl on duty there and brought Peter into the courtyard. There he sat with the guards and warmed himself at the fire they had kindled in the middle of the courtyard, for it was a cold night. He was waiting to see the outcome.

While Peter was sitting below in the courtyard, one of the servant girls of the high priest came by. It was the girl on duty at the door who had let him in. When she saw Peter warming himself, she looked closely at him. 'You also were with Jesus of Galilee,' she said. But he denied it before them all. 'I don't know or understand what you're talking about,' he said, and went out into the entryway. When another servant girl saw him there, she said again to those standing around, 'This fellow is one of them, he was with Jesus of Nazareth.' Again he denied it with an oath: 'I don't know the man!'

After a little while, about an hour later, those standing near said to Peter, 'Surely you are one of them, for you are a Galilean as your accent gives you away.' One of the high priest's servants, a relative of the man whose ear Peter had cut off, challenged him, 'Didn't I see you with him in the olive grove?'

Then he began to call down curses on himself, and he swore to them, 'I don't know this man you're talking about.' Just as he was speaking, the rooster crowed the second time. The Lord turned and looked straight at Peter. Then Peter remembered the word Jesus had spoken to him, *'Before the rooster crows twice you will disown me three times.'* And he went outside, broke down and wept bitterly.

At daybreak the council of the elders of the people, both the chief priests and teachers of the law, met together, and Jesus was led before them. 'If you are the Christ,' they said, 'Tell us.' Jesus answered, *'If I tell you, you will not believe me, and if I asked you, you would not answer. But from now on, the Son of Man will be seated at the right hand of the mighty God.'* They all asked, 'Are you then the Son of God?' He replied, *'You are right in saying I am.'* Then they said, 'Why do we need any more testimony? We have heard it from his own lips.'

When Judas, who had betrayed him, saw that Jesus was condemned, he was seized with remorse and returned the thirty silver coins to the chief priests and the elders. 'I have sinned,' he said, 'For I have betrayed innocent blood.' 'What is that to us?' they replied. 'That's your responsibility.' So Judas threw the money into the Temple and left. Then he went away and hanged himself.

The chief priests picked up the coins and said, 'It is against the law to put this into the treasury, since it is blood money.'

So they decided to use the money to buy the potter's field as a burial place for foreigners. That is why it has been called the Field of Blood to this day. Then what was spoken by Jeremiah the prophet was fulfilled: 'They took the thirty silver coins, the price set on him by the people of Israel, and they used them to buy the potter's field, as the Lord commanded me.' (With the reward he got for his wickedness, Judas bought a field; there he fell headlong, his body burst open and all his intestines spilled out. Everyone in Jerusalem heard about this, so they called that field in their language Akeldama, that is, Field of Blood.)

The Roman Part of the Trial

Very early in the morning, the chief priests, with the elders, the teachers of the law and the whole Sanhedrin, came to the decision to put Jesus to death. They bound and led him away and handed him over to Pilate, the Roman governor. To avoid ceremonial uncleanness the Jews did not enter the palace; they wanted to be able to eat the Passover. So Pilate came out to them and asked, 'What charges are you bringing against this man?'

'If he were not a criminal,' they replied, 'We would not have handed him over to you.' Pilate said, 'Take him yourselves and judge him by your own law.' 'But we have no right to execute anyone,' the Jews objected. This happened so that the words Jesus had spoken indicating the kind of death he was going to die would be fulfilled.

And they began to accuse him, saying, 'We have found this man subverting our nation. He opposes payment of taxes to Caesar and claims to be Christ, a king.'

So Pilate asked Jesus, 'Are you the king of the Jews?' *'Yes, it is as you say,'* Jesus replied. *'Is that your own idea or did others talk to you about me?'* 'Am I a Jew?' Pilate replied. 'It was your people and your chief priests who handed you over to me. What is it you have done?' Jesus said, *'My kingdom is not of this world. If it were, my servants would fight to prevent my arrest by the Jews. But now my kingdom is from another place.'* 'You are a king, then!' said Pilate.

Jesus answered, *'You are right in saying I am a king. In fact, for this reason I was born, and for this I came into the world, to testify to the truth. Everyone on the side of truth listens to me.'* 'What is truth?' Pilate asked. With this he went out again to the Jews and said, 'I find no basis for a charge against him.' The chief priests accused him of many things, but Jesus gave no answer. Then Pilate asked him, 'Aren't you going to answer? Don't you hear the testimony they are bringing against you and the many things they are accusing you of?' But Jesus still made no reply, not even to a single charge, to the great amazement of the governor. But they insisted, 'He stirs up the people all over Judea by his teaching. He started in Galilee and has come all the way here.'

On hearing this, Pilate asked if the man was a Galilean. When he learned that Jesus was under Herod's jurisdiction, he sent him to Herod, who was also in Jerusalem at that time.

When Herod saw Jesus, he was greatly pleased, because for a long time he had wanted to see him. From what he had heard about him, he hoped to see him perform some miracle. He plied him with many questions, but Jesus gave him no answer. The chief priests and the teachers of the law were standing there, vehemently accusing him. Then Herod and his soldiers ridiculed and mocked him. Dressing him in an elegant robe, they sent him back to Pilate. That day Herod and Pilate became friends, before this they had been enemies.

Now it was the custom at the Feast of Passover for the governor to release a prisoner chosen by the crowd. At that time they had a notorious prisoner, called Barabbas. He was a murderer who had taken part in a rebellion and uprising. Pilate called together the chief priests, the rulers and the people, and said to them, 'You brought me this man as one who was inciting the people to rebellion. I have examined him in your presence and have found no basis for your charges against him. Neither has Herod, for he sent him back to us; as you can see, he has done nothing to deserve death.

Therefore, I will punish him and then release him. It is your custom for me to release to you one prisoner at the time of the Passover. Do you want me to release "The king of the Jews"?' asked Pilate, knowing it was out of envy that the chief priests had handed him over to him.

While Pilate was sitting on the judge's seat, his wife sent him this message, 'Don't have anything to do with that innocent man, for I have suffered a great deal today in a dream because of him.' But the chief priests stirred up the crowd to have Barabbas released instead. They shouted back and cried out with one voice, 'Away with this man! Release Barabbas to us!'

Wanting to release Jesus, Pilate appealed to them again saying, 'What then shall I do with the one you call the king of the Jews, with Jesus who is called the Christ?' 'Crucify him! Crucify him!' they shouted. 'Why? What crime has he committed? I have found in him no grounds for the death penalty, therefore I will have him punished and then release him.' But they shouted all the louder demanding, 'Crucify him! Crucify him!' And their shouts prevailed.

When Pilate saw he was getting nowhere, but instead an uproar was starting, he took water and washed his hands in front of the crowd. 'I am innocent of this man's blood,' he said. 'It is your responsibility.' All the people answered, 'Let his blood be on us and on our children!' And so wanting to satisfy the crowd, Pilate surrendered to their will releasing Barabbas to them, the man who had been thrown into prison for rebellion and murder, and he handed Jesus over to be flogged.

Then the governor's soldiers took Jesus into the Praetorium, and gathered the whole company of soldiers around him. They stripped him and put a purple robe on him, and then twisted together a crown of thorns and set it on his head. They put a staff in his right hand and knelt in front of him and mocked him by going up to him again and again, saying, 'Hail, king of the Jews!' And they struck him in the face. They spat on him, and took the staff and struck him on the head again and again.

Once more Pilate came out and said to the Jews, 'Look, I am bringing him out to you to let you know that I find no basis for a charge against him.' When Jesus came out wearing the crown of thorns and the purple robe, Pilate said to them, 'Here is the man!'

As soon as the chief priests and their officials saw him, they shouted, 'Crucify! Crucify!' But Pilate answered, 'You take him and crucify him. As for me, I find no basis for a charge against him.' The Jews insisted, 'We have a law, and according to that law he must die, because he claimed to be the Son of God.'

When Pilate heard this, he was even more afraid, and he went back inside the palace. 'Where do you come from?' he asked Jesus, but Jesus gave him no answer. 'Do you refuse to speak to me?' Pilate said. 'Don't you realise I have power either to free you or to crucify you?'

Jesus answered, *'You would have no power over me if it were not given to you from above. Therefore the one who handed me over to you is guilty of a greater sin.'*

From then on, Pilate tried to set Jesus free, but the Jews kept shouting, 'If you let this man go, you are no friend of Caesar. Anyone who claims to be a king opposes Caesar.'

When Pilate heard this, he brought Jesus out and sat down on the judge's seat at a place known as the Stone Pavement (which in Aramaic is Gabbatha). It was the day of Preparation of Passover Week, about the sixth hour.

'Here is your king,' Pilate said to the Jews.

But they shouted, 'Take him away! Take him away! Crucify him!'

'Shall I crucify your king?' Pilate asked.

'We have no king but Caesar,' the chief priests answered.

Finally Pilate handed him over to them to be crucified.

Jesus' Death and Crucifixion

So the soldiers took charge of Jesus. They took off the robe and put his own clothes on him and led him away to crucify him having him carry his own cross. As they were going out, they met a man from Cyrene, named Simon, the father of Alexander and Rufus, he was passing by on his way in from the country, and they forced him to carry the cross walking behind Jesus. A large number of people followed him, including women who mourned and wailed for him. Jesus turned and said to them, *'Daughters of Jerusalem, do not weep for me; weep for yourselves and for your children. For the time will come when you will say, "Blessed are the barren women, the wombs that never bore and the breasts that never nursed!" Then they will say to the mountains, "Fall on us!" and to the hills, "Cover us!" for if men do these things when the tree is green, what will happen when it is dry?'*

Two other men, both criminals, were also led out with him to be executed. They came to a place which is called in Hebrew Golgotha (it means 'The Place of the Skull'). They offered Jesus wine to drink mixed with myrrh, but after tasting it he refused it. It was now about the third hour when along with the two criminals, one on his right and the other on his left they crucified him. Jesus said, *'Father, forgive them, for they do not know what they are doing.'*

Above his head they had set up the written charge against him, for Pilate had a notice prepared which read, 'JESUS OF NAZARETH, THE KING OF THE JEWS.' Many of the Jews read this sign, for the place where Jesus was crucified was near the city, and the sign was written in Aramaic, Latin and Greek. The chief priests of the Jews protested to Pilate, 'Do not write "The King of the Jews," but that this man claimed to be the king of the Jews.' Pilate answered, 'What I have written, I have written.'

When the soldiers crucified Jesus, they took his clothes, dividing them into four shares one for each of them, with the undergarment remaining. This garment was seamless, woven in one piece from top to bottom. 'Let's not tear it,' they said to one another. 'Let's decide by lot who will get it.' This happened that the scripture might be fulfilled which said, 'They divided my garments among them and cast lots for my clothing.' So this is what the soldiers did as they sat down and watched him there.

Those who stood watching and those who passed by hurled insults at him, shaking their heads and saying, 'So you who are going to destroy the temple and build it in three days, save yourself! Come down from the cross, if you are the Son of God!' In the same way the chief priests, the teachers of the law and the elders mocked and sneered at him. 'He saved others,' they said, 'But he can't save himself! Let this Christ, this King of Israel come down now from the cross, and we will believe in him. He trusts in God let God rescue him now if he wants him, for he said, "I am the Son of God." '

The soldiers also came up and mocked him. They offered him wine vinegar and said, 'If you are the king of the Jews, save yourself.' The two thieves who were crucified with him also heaped insults on him. As time passed, one of them became quiet while the other continued his insults, saying, 'Aren't you the Christ? Save yourself and us!' But the other criminal rebuked him. 'Don't you fear God,' he said, 'Since you are under the same sentence? We are punished justly, for we are getting what our deeds deserve. But this man has done nothing wrong.' Then he said, 'Jesus, remember me when you come into your kingdom.' Jesus answered him, *'I tell you the truth, today you will be with me in paradise.'*

Near the cross of Jesus stood his mother, his mother's sister, Mary, the wife of Clopas, and Mary Magdalene. When Jesus saw his mother there, and the disciple whom he loved standing nearby, he said to his mother, *'Dear woman, here is your son,'* and to the disciple, *'Here is your mother.'* From that time on, this disciple took her into his home. It was now about the sixth hour and darkness came over the whole land until the ninth hour, for the sun stopped shining. About the ninth hour Jesus cried out in a loud voice, *'Eloi, Eloi, lama sabachthani?'* which means, *'My God, my God, why have you forsaken me?'* When some of those standing there heard this, they said, 'He's calling Elijah.'

Knowing that all was now completed, and so that the scripture would be fulfilled, Jesus said, *'I am thirsty.'* Immediately one of them ran and got a sponge. He filled it with wine vinegar, from a jar that was there, he put the sponge on a stalk of the hyssop plant, and lifted it to Jesus' lips. The rest said, 'Now leave him alone. Let's see if Elijah comes to save him and take him down. When he had received the drink, Jesus cried out in a loud voice, *'It is finished. Father, into your hands I commit my spirit.'* With that he bowed his head, breathed his last and gave up his spirit. At that moment the curtain of the Temple was torn in two from top to bottom. The earth shook and the rocks split. The tombs broke open and the bodies of many holy people who had died were raised to life. They came out of the tombs, and after Jesus' resurrection they went into the holy city and appeared to many people.

When those who were guarding Jesus saw the earthquake and all that had happened, they were terrified and the centurion praised God and exclaimed, 'Surely this was a righteous man, he was the Son of God!' When all the people who had gathered to witness this saw what took place, they beat their breasts and went away. But all those who knew him, including all the women who had followed him from Galilee who had cared for his needs, stood at a distance watching these things. Among them were Mary Magdalene, Mary the mother of James the younger and of Joses, and Salome. There were also many other women there who had come up with him to Jerusalem.

Now it was the day of Preparation, and the next day was to be a special Sabbath. Because the Jews did not want the bodies left on the crosses during the Sabbath, they asked Pilate to have the legs broken and the bodies taken down. The soldiers therefore came and broke the legs of the first man who had been crucified with Jesus, and then those of the other. But when they came to Jesus and found that he was already dead, they did not break his legs. Instead, one of the soldiers pierced Jesus' side with a spear, bringing a sudden flow of blood and water. The man who saw it has given testimony, and his testimony is true. He knows that he tells the truth, and he testifies so that you also may believe. These things happened so that the scripture would be fulfilled: 'Not one of his bones will be broken,' and, as another scripture says: 'They will look on the one they have pierced.'

As evening approached, there came a rich man named Joseph, who was a prominent member of the council, a good and upright man, who had not consented to their decision and action. He had secretly become a disciple of Jesus, his secrecy was because he feared the Jews. He came from the Judean town of Arimathea and he was waiting for the kingdom of God. Going boldly to Pilate, he asked for Jesus' body. Pilate was surprised to hear that Jesus was already dead, and he summoned the centurion and asked him if Jesus had already died. When he learned that this was so, he ordered that the body be given to Joseph. So Joseph went and took the body down wrapping it in a clean linen cloth. He was helped and accompanied by Nicodemus, the man who had earlier visited Jesus at night, and together they took the body away. Nicodemus brought a mixture of myrrh and aloes, about seventy five pounds in weight. Taking Jesus' body, the two of them wrapped it, with the spices, in strips of clean linen in accordance with Jewish burial customs.

At the place where Jesus was crucified, there was a garden, with a new tomb which belonged to Joseph that he had cut out of the rock and no one had ever been buried in it. Because it was the Jewish day of Preparation and the Sabbath was about to begin and the tomb was nearby, they laid Jesus there, rolled a big stone in front of the entrance and went away. Mary Magdalene and Mary the mother of Joses were sitting there opposite the tomb and saw how the body was laid. They went home and prepared spices and perfumes. But they rested on the Sabbath in obedience to the commandment.

The next day, the one after Preparation Day, the chief priests and the Pharisees went to Pilate. 'Sir,' they said, 'We remember that while he was still alive that deceiver said, "After three days I will rise again." So give the order for the tomb to be made secure until the third day. Otherwise, his disciples may come and steal the body and tell the people that he has been raised from the dead. This last deception will be worse than the first.' 'Take a guard,' Pilate answered. 'Go, make the tomb as secure as you know how.' So they went and made the tomb secure by putting a seal on the stone and posting the guard.

Chapter 22

The Resurrection

'He is Risen!'

When the Sabbath was over, Mary Magdalene, Mary the mother of James and Salome bought spices so that they might go to anoint Jesus' body. It was very early on the first day of the week, and along with Joanna and some other women, they set out for the tomb while it was still dark. Just after sunrise, as they neared the tomb they were asking each other, 'Who will roll the stone away from the entrance of the tomb?'

Before dawn there had been a violent earthquake, for an angel of the Lord came down from heaven and, going to the tomb, rolled back the stone and sat on it. His appearance was like lightening, and his clothes were white as snow. The guards were so afraid of him that they shook with fear and became like dead men.

When the women came to the tomb and looked up, they saw that the stone, which was very large, had been rolled away, but when they entered, they did not find the body of the Lord Jesus. While they were wondering about this they saw a young man dressed in a white robe sitting on the right side, and they were alarmed. Then another angel suddenly appeared and their clothes were gleaming like lightening. They came near to the women and stood beside them. In their fright the women bowed down with their faces to the ground, 'Don't be alarmed,' one said. 'Why do you look for the living among the dead? You are looking for Jesus the Nazarene, who was crucified. He is not here. He has risen!

Come and see the place where they laid him. Remember how he told you, while he was still with you in Galilee: *"The Son of Man must be delivered into the hands of sinful men, be crucified and on the third day be raised again."* But now go quickly, tell his disciples and Peter, "He has risen from the dead and is going ahead of you into Galilee. There you will see him, just as he told you!"' Then they remembered his words. Trembling and bewildered, the women went out and fled from the tomb. They hurried away, afraid yet filled with joy and ran to tell his disciples, who were mourning and weeping, they said nothing to anyone as they went because they were afraid.

When Mary Magdalene had seen the stone removed from the tomb and Jesus' body not there she had left straightaway and came running to Simon Peter and the other disciple, the one Jesus loved, and said, 'They have taken the Lord out of the tomb, and we don't know where they have put him!'

So Peter and the other disciple started for the tomb. Both were running, but the other disciple outran Peter and reached the tomb first. He bent over and looked in at the strips of linen lying there but did not go in. Then Simon Peter, who was behind him, arrived and went into the tomb. Bending over, he saw the strips of linen lying by themselves as well as the burial cloth that had been around Jesus' head. The cloth was folded up by itself, separate from the linen. Finally the other disciple, who had reached the tomb first, also went inside. He saw and believed. (They still did not understand from Scripture that Jesus had to rise from the dead.) Peter went away, wondering to himself what had happened.

Then the disciples went back to their homes, but Mary stood outside the tomb crying. As she wept, she bent over to look into the tomb and saw two angels in white, seated where Jesus' body had been, one at the head and the other at the foot. They asked her, 'Woman, why are you crying?' 'They have taken my Lord away,' she said, 'And I don't know where they have put him.' At this, she turned around and saw Jesus standing there, but she did not realise that it was

Jesus. *'Woman,'* he said, *'Why are you crying? Who is it you are looking for?'* Thinking he was the gardener, she said, 'Sir, if you have carried him away, tell me where you have put him, and I will get him.' Jesus said to her, *'Mary.'* She turned toward him and cried out in Aramaic, 'Rabboni!' (which means Teacher).

Jesus said, *'Do not hold on to me, for I have not yet returned to the Father. Go instead to my brothers and tell them, "I am returning to my Father and your Father, to my God and your God." '*

While the other women were on their way, suddenly Jesus met them. *'Greetings,'* he said. They came to him, clasped his feet and worshipped him. Then Jesus said to them, *'Do not be afraid. Go and tell my brothers to go to Galilee; there they will see me.'* They went and told all these things to the Eleven and to all the others.

It was Mary Magdalene, Joanna, Mary the mother of James, and the others with them who told this to the apostles. Mary Magdalene said to them, 'I have seen the Lord!' and told them the things he had said to her. But they did not believe the women, because their words seemed to them like nonsense.

Some of the guards had gone into the city and reported to the chief priests everything that had happened. The chief priests met with the elders and devised a plan, they gave the soldiers a large sum of money, telling them, 'You are to say, "His disciples came during the night and stole him away while we were asleep." If this report gets to the governor, we will satisfy him and keep you out of trouble.' So the soldiers took the money and did as they were instructed. And this story has been widely circulated among the Jews to this very day.

The Emmaus Road

Now that same day two of Jesus' followers were going to a village called Emmaus, about seven miles from Jerusalem. They were talking with each other about everything that had happened. As they talked and discussed these things with each other, Jesus himself came up and walked along with them, but they were kept from recognising him.

He asked them, *'What are you discussing together as you walk along?'* They stood still, their faces downcast. One of them, named Cleopas, asked him, 'Are you the only one living in Jerusalem who doesn't know the things that have happened there in these days?' *'What things?'* he asked. 'About Jesus of Nazareth,' they replied. 'He was a prophet, powerful in word and deed before God and all the people. The chief priests and our rulers handed him over to be sentenced to death, and they crucified him; but we had hoped that he was the one who was going to redeem Israel. And what is more, it is the third day since all this took place. In addition, some of our women amazed us. They went to the tomb early this morning but didn't find his body. They came and told us that they had seen a vision of angels, who said he was alive. Then some of our companions went to the tomb and found it just as the women had said, but him they did not see.'

He said to them, *'How foolish you are, and how slow of heart to believe all that the prophets have spoken! Did not the Christ have to suffer these things and then enter his glory?'* And beginning with Moses and all the Prophets, he explained to them what was said in all the Scriptures concerning himself.

As they approached the village to which they were going, Jesus acted as if he were going further. But they urged him strongly, 'Stay with us, for it is nearly evening; the day is almost over.' So he went in to stay with them.

When he was at the table with them, he took bread, gave thanks, broke it and began to give it to them. Then their eyes were opened and they recognised him, and he disappeared from their sight. They asked each other, 'Were not our hearts burning within us while he talked with us on the road and opened the Scriptures to us?'

They got up and returned at once to Jerusalem. By now it was evening and they found the disciples and those with them assembled together eating a meal, hiding behind locked doors for fear of the Jews. They said, 'It is true! The Lord has risen and has appeared to Simon.' Then the two told what had happened on the way, and how Jesus was recognised by them when he broke the bread.

Jesus appears to his Disciples

While they were still talking about this, Jesus came and stood among them and said to them, *'Peace be with you.'* They were startled and frightened, thinking they saw a ghost. He rebuked them for their lack of faith and their stubborn refusal to believe those who had seen him after he had risen. He said to them, *'Why are you troubled, and why do doubts rise in your minds? Look at my hands and my feet. It is I myself! Touch me and see; a ghost does not have flesh and bones, as you see I have.'*

When he had said this, he showed them his hands and feet. And while they still did not believe it because of joy and amazement, he asked them, *'Do you have anything here to eat?'* They gave him a piece of broiled fish, and he took it and ate it in their presence. The disciples were overjoyed when they saw the Lord. Again Jesus said, *'Peace be with you! As the Father has sent me, I am sending you.'* And with that he breathed on them and said, *'Receive the Holy Spirit. If you forgive anyone his sins, they are forgiven; if you do not forgive them, they are not forgiven.'*

Now Thomas (called Didymus), one of the Twelve, was not with the disciples when Jesus came. So the other disciples told him, 'We have seen the Lord!' But he said to them, 'Unless I see the nail marks in his hands and put my finger where the nails were, and put my hand into his side, I will not believe it.'

A week later his disciples were in the house again, and Thomas was with them. Though the doors were locked, Jesus came and stood among them and said, *'Peace be with you!'* Then he said to Thomas, *'Put your finger here; see my hands. Reach out your hand and put it into my side. Stop doubting and believe.'* Thomas said to him, 'My Lord and my God!'

Then Jesus told him, *'Because you have seen me, you have believed; blessed are those who have not seen and yet have believed.'*

Jesus did many other miraculous signs in the presence of his disciples, which are not recorded in this book. But these are written that you may believe that Jesus is the Christ, the Son of God, and that by believing you may have life in his name.

Jesus appears to seven disciples and restores Peter

Afterward Jesus appeared again to his disciples, by the Sea of Tiberius. It happened this way: Simon Peter, Thomas (called Didymus), Nathanael from Cana in Galilee, the sons of Zebedee, and two other disciples were together. 'I'm going out to fish,' Simon Peter told them, and they said, 'We'll go with you.' So they went out and got into the boat, but that night they caught nothing.

Early in the morning, Jesus stood on the shore, but the disciples did not realise that it was Jesus. He called out to them, *'Friends, haven't you any fish?'* 'No,' they answered.

He said, *'Throw your net on the right side of the boat and you will find some.'* When they did, they were unable to haul the net in because of the large number of fish.

Then the disciple whom Jesus loved said to Peter, 'It is the Lord!' As soon as Simon Peter heard him say, 'It is the Lord,' he wrapped his outer garment around him (for he had taken it off) and jumped into the water. The other disciples followed in the boat, towing the net full of fish, for they were not far from shore, about a hundred yards. When they landed, they saw a fire of burning coals there with fish on it, and some bread.

Jesus said to them, *'Bring some of the fish you have just caught.'*

Simon Peter climbed aboard and dragged the net ashore. It was full of large fish, 153, but even with so many the net was not torn. Jesus said to them, *'Come and have breakfast.'*

None of the disciples dared ask him, 'Who are you?' They

knew it was the Lord. Jesus came, took the bread and gave it to them, and did the same with the fish. This was now the third time Jesus appeared to his disciples after he was raised from the dead.

When they had finished eating, Jesus said to Simon Peter, *'Simon, son of John, do you truly love me more than these?'* 'Yes, Lord,' he said, 'You know that I love you.' Jesus said, *'Feed my lambs.'*

Again Jesus said, *'Simon, son of John, do you truly love me?'* He answered, 'Yes, Lord, you know that I love you.' Jesus said, *'Take care of my sheep.'*

The third time he said to him, *'Simon, son of John, do you love me?'* Peter was hurt because Jesus asked him the third time, 'Do you love me?' He said, 'Lord, you know all things; you know that I love you.' Jesus said, *'Feed my sheep. I tell you the truth, when you were younger you dressed yourself and went where you wanted; but when you are old you will stretch out your hands, and someone else will dress you and lead you where you do not want to go.'* Jesus said this to indicate the kind of death by which Peter would glorify God. Then he said to him, *'Follow me!'*

Peter turned and saw that the disciple whom Jesus loved was following them. (This was the one who had leaned back against Jesus at the supper and had said, 'Lord, who is going to betray you?') When Peter saw him, he asked, 'Lord, what about him?'

Jesus answered, *'If I want him to remain alive until I return, what is that to you? You must follow me.'* Because of this, the rumour spread among the brothers that this disciple would not die. But Jesus did not say that he would not die; he only said, *'If I want him to remain alive until I return, what is that to you?'*

This is the disciple who testifies to these things and who wrote them down. We know that his testimony is true.

Jesus did many other things as well. If every one of them were written down, I suppose that even the whole world would not have room for the books that would be written.

The Great Commission and Jesus' Ascension

Then the eleven disciples, accompanied by more than five hundred of the brothers and James went to Galilee, to the mountain where Jesus had told them to go. When they saw him, they worshipped him; but some doubted. Then Jesus came to them and said, *'All authority in heaven and on earth has been given to me. Therefore go and make disciples of all nations, baptising them in the name of the Father and of the Son and of the Holy Spirit, and teaching them to obey everything I have commanded you. And surely I am with you always, to the very end of the age.'*

Jesus had now showed himself to his disciples and gave many convincing proofs that he was alive. He had appeared to them over a period of forty days and spoke about the kingdom of God. On one occasion while he was eating with them, he gave them this command, *'Do not leave Jerusalem but wait for the gift my Father promised, which you have heard me speak about.'* He said to them, *'This is what I told you while I was still with you: Everything must be fulfilled that is written about me in the Law of Moses, the Prophets and the Psalms.'* Then he opened their minds so they could understand the Scriptures. He told them, *'This is what is written: "The Christ will suffer and rise from the dead on the third day, and repentance and forgiveness of sins will be preached in his name to all nations, beginning at Jerusalem." You are witnesses of these things. I am going to send you what my Father has promised; but stay in the city until you have been clothed with power from on high. For John baptised with water, but in a few days you will be baptised with the Holy Spirit.'*

Then he led them out to the vicinity of Bethany. They asked him, 'Lord are you at this time going to restore the kingdom to Israel?' He said to them, *'It is not for you to know the times or dates the Father has set by his own authority. But you will receive power when the Holy Spirit comes on you, and you will be my witnesses in Jerusalem, and in all Judea and Samaria, and to the ends of the earth. Go into all the world and preach the good news to all creation. Whoever believes and is baptised will be saved, but whoever does not believe will be condemned. And these signs will accompany those who believe: In my name they will drive out demons, they will speak in new tongues, they will pick up snakes with their hands and when they drink deadly poison, it will not hurt them at all. They will place their hands on sick people, and they will get well.'*

After he said this he lifted up his hands and blessed them and while he was blessing them, he was taken up before their very eyes into heaven, and a cloud hid him from their sight. They were looking intently up into the sky as he was going, when suddenly two men dressed in white stood beside them. 'Men of Galilee,' they said, 'Why do you stand here looking into the sky? This same Jesus, who has been taken from you into heaven, will come back in the same way you have seen him go into heaven.'

So after the Lord Jesus had spoken to them, he was taken up into heaven and he sat down at the right hand of God. Then the disciples worshipped him and with great joy returned to Jerusalem from the hill called the Mount of Olives, a Sabbath day's walk from the city. When they arrived, they went upstairs to the room where they were staying. Those present were Peter, John, James and Andrew, Philip and Thomas, Batholomew and Matthew, James son of Alphaeus and Simon the Zealot, and Judas son of James. They all joined together constantly in prayer, along with the women and Mary, the mother of Jesus, and with his brothers. And they stayed continually at the Temple praising God.

When the day of Pentecost came, they were all together in one place. Suddenly a sound like the blowing of a violent wind came from heaven and filled the whole house where they were sitting. They saw what seemed to be tongues of fire that separated and came to rest on each of them. All of them were filled with the Holy Spirit and began to speak in other tongues as the Spirit enabled them. Then the disciples went out and preached everywhere, and the Lord worked with them and confirmed his word by the signs that accompanied it.

He Changed My Life

*'All my discoveries have been made
in answer to prayer.'*
(*Sir Isaac Newton*)

When the distinguished Scottish scientist Sir James Simpson, the discoverer of chloroform, was asked at a large public meeting what his greatest discovery had been, he replied without hesitation, 'That I have a saviour.' This is the greatest discovery that anyone can ever make and recorded below are just three testimonies that bear witness to this fact.

C.S. Lewis   He was one of this century's greatest writers and a professor at Oxford and, later, Cambridge University. He was born in Belfast, Northern Ireland, and raised in a nominal Protestant family. While still a child his mother died and this loss, combined with a sceptical tutor who taught him to think critically, led C.S. Lewis to become an atheist. He joined the army during World War I and was wounded which led him to conclude, 'There was nothing worth pursuing besides things of the mind and the pleasures of the flesh.'

Two of his favourite writers however, were Christians, G.K. Chesterton and George MacDonald. Their writings and some Christian friends played an important part in Lewis's reluctant conversion which took place when he was in his early thirties.

He told of his conversion experience in his book, *Surprised by Joy*. He describes how God closed in on him, 'For the first time I examined myself with a seriously practical purpose. And there I found what appalled me, a zoo of lusts, a bedlam of ambitions, a nursery of fears, a harem of fondled hatreds. My name was legion.' He went on, 'You must picture me alone in that room in Magdalene, night after night, feeling, whenever my mind lifted even for a second from my work, the steady, unrelenting approach of Him whom I so earnestly desired not to meet. In the Trinity term of 1929 I gave in, and admitted that God was God, and knelt and prayed.'

Later he told of how he came to know of a certainty that Jesus Christ was the Son of God. 'I was driven to Whipsnade Zoo one Sunday morning. When we set out I did not believe that Jesus Christ was the Son of God, and when we reached the zoo I did. Yet I had not exactly spent the journey in thought. Nor in great emotion. It was more like when a man, after a long sleep, still lying motionless in bed, becomes aware that he is now awake.'

Lewis was one of the greatest intellects and literary scholars this century and wrote many great classics, one of which is *Mere Christianity*, a book that was to be instrumental in the conversion of the person we consider next.

Chuck Colson He was known as President Nixon's 'hatchet man', a high powered attorney who joined the Nixon team as special counsel to the president and ended up a leading figure in the Watergate scandal. He was an active participant in the many dirty tricks of the disgraced US president forced to resign from office. He was rightly described by a former colleague, Jeb Stuart Magruder, 'as an evil genius, whose brilliance was undeniable, but it was too often applied to encouraging Richard Nixon's darker side.'

His life changed dramatically when due to the influence of a friend he agreed to read C.S. Lewis's apologetic for the Christian faith, *Mere Christianity*. He later surrendered his life to Jesus Christ and describes the change and the joy it brought in his book, *Born Again*.

Today he heads up a ministry he started that reaches hundreds of thousands of prison inmates. Prison Fellowship, which grew out of Colson's own jail house experience following Watergate, is now a worldwide outreach. It ministers to those in prison and helps them to readjust to life outside prison on their release.

Vycheslav Borisov   'Who?' I hear you ask. He is a Russian general with an amazing testimony. General Borisov's code name was 'General War'! He was the deputy commander of the Soviet Union's 100,000 combat troops in Afghanistan during the USSR's conflict with the country. He was considered the architect of Russia's strategy for Armageddon. While in Afghanistan, however, his helicopter was hit by enemy fire, it was going to crash! For the first time in his life General Borisov prayed. For many years he had been an atheist, communist and a persecutor of Christians, but that day he cried out to God for mercy, 'Dear God, if you really do exist, have mercy on me and save me. Then I will use my life for you!' The helicopter exploded as it hit the ground. Only one of the twelve men on board survived, General Borisov.

Today, he is using his high position of authority within the Russian army to bring the Gospel of Jesus Christ to millions of military personnel. Recently, more than 200 of America's top military leaders in the Pentagon heard him ask for their prayers, beg for more Bibles and for missionaries to come to his homeland with the Gospel. This is the first time a Russian general has spoken at the Pentagon. Through his influence the first Christian chapel has been built on a Russian military base and a military chaplaincy training programme has been started. He wants every soldier in Russia's Red Army to have a Bible.

He can change your life

You are only a prayer away:

> Lord Jesus Christ,
> I know that I have sinned in my thoughts, words and
> actions.
> There are many good things I have not done and many
> sinful things I have done.
> I am sorry for my sins and now turn from everything I
> know to be wrong.
> I put my trust in You and ask You to forgive me
> because You gave Your life for me upon the cross.
> Gratefully I give my life back to You and ask You to
> come into my life.
> Come in as my Saviour to cleanse and forgive me.
> Come in as my Lord to control me.
> Come in as my Friend to be with me.
> And I will serve you all the remaining years of my life.
> Amen.

SECTION 3

Appendices

Appendix 1

The Resurrection Accounts

'What death did to Jesus is nothing compared to what Jesus did to death.'

An agnostic professor ridiculed a little girl's faith for believing in the Lord Jesus. He said, 'There have been many who have claimed to be Christ, so how can you be so sure which one told the truth?' Without hesitation and with a big smile on her face she replied, 'I believe in the one who rose again from the dead.'

The sequence of events on that first Easter Sunday morning is not easy to give a chronology and harmony for. No individual Gospel gives all the exact times and details of what took place. This can be both assuring and disconcerting as we seek the complete picture of what actually happened. It is assuring because there is obviously no collusion between the writers. What we have here is independent testimony all pointing to the most amazing fact in history, Jesus rose from the dead. If all four accounts gave exactly the same story, in exactly the same order, with exactly the same details, we would immediately become suspicious. We would also wonder why there was need for four different accounts if they all merely repeated each other word for word.

Such testimony can however appear to be disconcerting, however, because at first sight when the four records are compared several difficulties and apparent discrepancies seem to appear. Such as:

1. Was it dark or dawn when the women set out and arrived at the tomb?

2.   How many angels were there and were they standing or sitting?

3.   Who did Jesus appear to first, Mary Magdalene or the other women?

4.   Why did the women take spices to a tomb they knew was being guarded, to anoint a body that we are told had already been anointed by Nicodemus and Joseph of Arimathea?

5.   When did Jesus appear to more than five hundred?

Before we seek to answer such questions, we need to remember two very important facts.

(a)   On that first Easter morning the garden tomb was the centre of a great deal of activity, with different groups of men and women coming and going. There were earthquakes and angels. There were terrified guards and confused disciples. There was the Risen Jesus, who Himself was mistaken for the gardener. All sorts of rumours and stories quickly began to circulate and far from the Gospel accounts being contradictory, they actually present a unified whole and bear the stamp of authenticity as each writer focuses on different aspects of what took place.

(b)   The individual Gospels did not intend to give us a complete record of all that happened. Even when seen together there are events we would love to know more about but the Holy Spirit saw fit to give us only the briefest of details. One is Jesus' appearance to Peter mentioned in 1 Corinthians 15:5 and Luke 24:34. Something amazing happened to James the brother of Jesus, which was probably the occasion of his conversion, because before the crucifixion and resurrection he had been antagonistic toward Jesus, but afterwards he became a leader in the church at Jerusalem. Paul tells us in 1 Corinthians 15:6, 7 that Jesus appeared to James and also on another occasion to five hundred people at one time, many of whom were still living to testify to their experience.

George Eldan Ladd in his book *I Believe in the Resurrection of Jesus*, sums this up when he says,

> 'The account in Luke's Gospel seems to have been compressed into a single day, but in opening the second volume of Luke – Acts, the author tells us that Jesus appeared to His disciples during a forty day period (Acts 1:3). John informs us that his Gospel consists of only a selection of the many things Jesus did (John 20:30–31). It is clear that the evangelists have no intention of giving us a complete history of the resurrection appearances. They select incidents from the tradition known to them for one purpose, to establish the fact that Jesus, the crucified, was alive again.'

1. Was it dark or dawn when the women set out and arrived at the tomb?

Robert H. Gundry in his book, *A Survey of the New Testament*, answers the question as to why Mark says that the women came to the tomb just after the sun had risen, while John says that Mary Magdalene came while it was still dark. He says,

> 'This is exactly what one would expect from independent accounts of the same event and proves that the story of Jesus' resurrection is not the result of collusion. It may be resolved by supposing that Mary came a little in advance of the other women, or that in John the women began their journey while it was still dark, whereas in Mark and Luke they arrived at the tomb just as the sun rose.'

Josh McDowell and Don Stewart in their book, *Answers to Tough Questions*, comment,

> 'The difficulty is solved when it is realised that the women had to walk quite some distance to reach the grave since they stayed in Jerusalem or Bethany. It was dark when they left the place in which they were staying, but when they arrived at the tomb the sun was beginning to shine. Therefore, Mark is speaking of their arrival, while John refers to their departure.'

2. How many angels were there and were they standing or sitting?

- Matthew and Mark mention one angel.
- Luke mentions two angels standing.
- John mentions two angels sitting.

They are all agreed to angelic activity being very prominent in what took place. When you read the accounts it is clear that such encounters took place at different times and to different people. The positions assumed by the angels also varied at different times. It has been pointed out that the Greek word in Luke, rendered 'stood by,' also means to come near, to appear to, often implying suddenness. It appears that as the women entered the tomb, they saw that the body of Jesus was gone (Luke 24:2, 3), and as they looked around wondering about this they saw an angel seated on the right side of them (Mark 16:5). They naturally were not only confused but now became alarmed. Suddenly another angel appeared and both of them came near to the women and stood by them (Luke 24:4). The angels' clothes gleamed like lightening and the women fell down with their faces to the ground. Later on when Mary came to the tomb after the others had left, she saw two angels in white, seated where Jesus' body had been, one at the head and the other at the foot (John 20:12).

Matthew and Mark do not say that there was only one angel at the tomb, but that one angel spoke. This does not contradict Luke and John, for Matthew and Mark specify that an angel spoke, but they do not say there was only one angel present. Quite possibly one of the angels was the spokesman for the two.

3. Who did Jesus appear to first, Mary Magdalene or the other women?

Seeking to answer this question raises several other questions as to the authenticity of the ending of Mark's Gospel and to the sequence of events on that first Easter Sunday.

Mark 16:9 says that Jesus appeared first to Mary Magdalene. Reading John's account of that meeting (John 20:11–18), we are given the definite impression that Mary was alone. When you read Matthew 28:9, we are told that Jesus suddenly appeared to a number of the women together as they made their way from the tomb.

Some harmonisation attempts (see Eldan Ladd, *I Believe in the Resurrection of Jesus*, page 92) suggest that since there is reason to regard Mark's ending (Mark 16:9–20), as not being authentic, the sequence of events, with Jesus having appeared to Mary Magdalene first does not have to be followed.

Note on Mark 16:9–20   Some manuscripts end at verse 8 with the phrase, 'or they were afraid.' There are a few manuscripts that contain two different short endings which are not considered by any textual scholar to be in the original manuscript. One manuscript brings the book to a close by adding after verse 8, 'But they reported briefly to Peter and those with him all that they had been told. And after this, Jesus himself sent out by means of them, from east to west, the sacred and imperishable proclamation of eternal salvation!'

Josh McDowell and Don Stewart state the arguments against accepting verses 9–20 as original and the arguments for accepting them as authentic. Briefly summarised they are:

Against
1. *External evidence.* In the two oldest manuscripts that contain the Gospel of Mark (Codex Siniaticus and Codex Vaticanus), the last 12 verses are omitted. Some of the early church fathers also spoke out against these verses being in the original.
2. *Internal evidence.* The vocabulary and style of Mark 16:9–20 is not consistent with the rest of the book and the connection between these verses and verse 8 is very awkward.
3. *Theological evidence.* Such fanciful ideas about drinking poison and handling snakes are contrary to the rest of Scripture.

For
1. *External evidence*. While it is true that the two oldest manuscripts which contain Mark 16 do not have the last 12 verses, there is an enormous amount of external evidence that supports it as being original, these verses are found in virtually all the remaining Greek manuscripts that contain the end of Mark. There are many early church fathers who quote from these verses.
2. *Internal evidence*. It is a well known fact that vocabulary and style change with subject matter and the argument that the connection is awkward does not help in the case for omitting it. If these verses were added by someone later, rather than by Mark, why did they not try to smooth out the discontinuity?
3. *Theological evidence*. The verses on drinking poison and snake handling do not deny their authenticity. In Acts 28:3–6 Paul is bitten by a deadly snake, yet survived. It is much easier to explain why the passage could have been omitted in some manuscripts rather than to try and explain how it received such a wide acceptance.

The reason for such detail is that one's view of Mark 16:9 in particular can have a great bearing on the sequence of events regarding the resurrection appearances of Jesus. Those who do not accept Mark 16:9–20 simply overcome the difficulty of who Jesus appeared to first. I believe that it is perfectly possible to retain Mark 16:9 as authentic, with Jesus appearing to the other women later on in the day after His first appearance to Mary Magdalene.

It seems that as the women came to the tomb Mary Magdalene, either with or before the others, drew near but when she saw the tomb empty and the body gone, she immediately feared the worst and overcome with anger and sorrow, leaves to find Peter and John, with the message that Jesus' body has been taken away and she doesn't know where they have taken Him. The other women have ventured into the tomb, wondering what was going on. The first angel they saw was sitting on the right side, so Mary Magdalene would not have seen him before she left. The women are told what has happened by the angels as another one suddenly appears and are told to tell the news to the disciples. By this time Mary Magdalene has found Peter and John, quite naturally the two to go and tell what has happened.

It seems likely that the eleven disciples had not all been together, but were probably scattered around the city staying with family and friends, or had left the city and made their way back to Bethany where they would have felt safer. They were frightened men keeping well out of sight (Matthew 26:56). Quite likely Peter and John had stayed together, as they were together when they followed Jesus at His trials, and were also close friends.

When they hear the news they leave Mary behind making her own way back to the tomb. She is tired, exhausted both physically and emotionally. John, being the younger of the two, outruns Peter and gets to the tomb first. By this time the other women have left, both joyful and fearful, wondering what to do about the things they have seen and heard. Peter runs to the tomb and finds John outside standing and staring in. Being the more impulsive of the two he goes straight in and John follows. They are amazed, and faith begins to rise amidst the confusion.

They leave the tomb and walk away from the garden as Mary Magdalene arrives. They don't know what to make of it all. She stands outside the tomb weeping, and through the tears bends over to look inside and sees two angels. They ask why she is crying and she says that someone had taken her Lord away and she didn't know where. Then Jesus comes and meets with her. Mary mistakes Him for the gardener. She is emotionally spent with the effects of the past few days, and with tears streaming down her face, Jesus standing in the garden was not who she was expecting to see. She was looking for a body. The last time she had seen Him He was bloodied, bruised and battered by the crucifixion, now He had risen in splendour. The Gospel record has all the hallmarks of authenticity and truth about it.

Jesus mentions Mary's name and she cries out, 'Teacher.'

She reaches out and takes hold of Him, but Jesus says, *'Do not hold on to me, for I have not yet returned to my Father.'* Later on Jesus allowed the other women to clasp His feet and worship Him, so why not now with Mary? Naturally she never wanted to let Him go again. Jesus is not forbidding her to touch Him, but is giving her a gentle reassurance that she need not fear to leave Him and for her to tell her good news to the others, for His ascension to the Father is not just yet. Mary then left full of joy and excitement to tell the disciples that she had seen the Lord.

Meanwhile the other women are on their way trying to locate the scattered disciples. Mark comments that they at first kept silent because they were afraid (Mark 16:8). Suddenly Jesus appears to them, (Matthew 28:9 does not say that this meeting occurred in the garden.) They had run away from the tomb but Jesus confirms the word that the angels had given them. Strengthened and excited they now go and find the disciples to tell them the news.

The disciples find it hard to believe such news. Mary confirms the other women's testimony and as they are discussing these things, Jesus appears to two others on the Emmaus road. Some time that afternoon Jesus also appeared to Peter (Luke 24:34). In the evening when all the disciples are together having heard the testimony of the two who had been on their way to Emmaus, Jesus appears in the midst of them. Sadly Thomas is absent but a week later Jesus appears to them again and this time Thomas is present and has a dramatic encounter with His risen Lord.

Jesus meets with them often during the next few weeks in Galilee and by Tiberius. He appears to five hundred at one time. Finally they return to Jerusalem and He makes His final appearance to them before His ascension.

Having said all this we must allow some overlap to the precise timing of each incident and flexibility. This is often the case when one testimony focuses on a particular detail while another is describing the same event but is speaking in more general terms.

4. Why did the women go to anoint Jesus' body with spices when we are told in John 19:39–43 that the body had already been anointed by Nicodemus and Joseph of Arimathea?

Joseph of Arimathea is described as a rich man, a respected member of the Sanhedrin, who had not consented to the decision and action against Jesus. He was also a good man who was looking for the kingdom of God. Along with Jesus' followers he must have realised that the body of Jesus would shortly be pulled down and thrown into the common criminals' grave along with the corpses of the other two thieves. Joseph resolves the dilemma by allowing the use of his own, newly cut tomb nearby. Plucking up courage he goes along with Nicodemus to see Pilate and asks for permission to be given the body of Jesus. This must have been late afternoon about the time of the waving of the first fruits, an important ceremony in the Passover season at which the chief priests would probably have been present. This would account for the fact that Joseph met with no opposition from them when he made his request.

Joseph and Nicodemus return with the body and probably take counsel with the women about what to do in such a short period of time before nightfall and the onset of the Sabbath. Normally the body would have been washed and anointed with perfumed oils before being dressed in a clean outer garment. But there was clearly insufficient time to do all this. So it seems likely that Joseph agreed to get a large linen cloth from the market to wrap the body in and for Nicodemus to get a liberal supply of dry spices to pack around the body to act as a partial anti-putrifacient as a temporary measure. The women would then return to the tomb at the first possible moment after the Sabbath was over to anoint the body properly.

5. What about Jesus appearing to more than five hundred at one time?

Paul tells us in 1 Corinthians 15:6 that Jesus appeared to more than five hundred people on one occasion. It is likely that this is the occasion referred to in Matthew 28:17. Although he only mentions the eleven disciples, he also says, 'some doubted,' which surely cannot mean them after meeting Him already on several earlier occasions.

It is also implied that there was a large number present. Therefore such a location would be necessary for such a large company. Luke 10:1 mentions seventy two others whom Jesus commissioned for ministry. It seems that as Jesus approached the crowd gathered on the mountainside, the eleven recognise Him and fall down in worship. Some of the others, though fully aware that Jesus had risen, were slower to let themselves believe that the approaching figure was really Him.

A Final Note

It is clear from reading the accounts that it was not only the empty tomb that caused belief in the resurrection, rather it was a personal encounter with the risen Jesus. However, the grave clothes were left in such a manner that John tells us that when he saw them left in two distinct and orderly piles, it caused him to believe (John 20:8). Luke tells us that when Peter saw them lying neatly by themselves it caused him to leave the tomb wondering what had taken place (Luke 23:12).

How much and what John believed we do not know, how far his faith went at that moment is unclear. We are told later that the disciples did not and would not believe the report of the other women. Maybe this refers to the other nine, or it meant them all, as John could not fully comprehend at that moment what had taken place. The grave clothes had been left in such a way that divine intervention was the only way it could have happened. Jesus' body dematerialised and the grave clothes had simply collapsed and were still in their place, but now with nothing inside them. Jesus had risen with a new resurrected body. We are told that He could instantly appear and disappear and then suddenly be present with the disciples even when they were hiding behind locked doors. The stone then was rolled away not to let Jesus out but to let the others in.

An empty tomb theology and apologetic can be helpful for showing the historical evidence on which the resurrection is based, but empty tombs do not change lives, an encounter with the risen Jesus does today, just as much as it did on that first Easter morning.

One final thought, Jesus' resurrection eternalised forever His humanity. He arose not a spirit but in human form.

> *'There is one mediator between man and God, the man Christ Jesus.'*   (2 Timothy 2:5)

Appendix 2

Notes on Chronologising and Harmonising Some Difficult Passages

'No one ever graduates from Bible study until they have met the author face to face.'

The Temptations of Jesus (Matthew 4:1–12; Mark 1:12, 13; Luke 4:1–12)

Matthew and Luke reverse the order of the last two temptations, but this would only be a contradiction if both claimed to present the correct order. In fact each one closes with the temptation most suited to his theme. Matthew presents Jesus as king, while Luke presents Him as a man.

Probably Matthew has the original order since he introduces his second temptation with 'then', while Luke connects the second and third merely with the word 'and'. Matthew's account also finishes with Jesus telling satan, 'Away from me.'

The Sermon on the Mount (Matthew 5–7; Luke 6)

Are the accounts referring to the same incident or to a different one?

It is possible that the accounts refer to two different occasions. This possibility is indicated by the fact that whereas Matthew is clear that Christ preached on a mountainside (Matthew 5:1), Luke speaks of Him standing on a level place (Luke 6:17). This is not conclusive, however, as it is possible to find a level place on a mountainside. As Jesus may have preached the sermon on different occasions, it is equally possible that during the same sermon He repeated the same teaching in different ways.

It also needs to be noted that the healing of the Centurion's servant follows both accounts in Matthew and Luke. This points to the two accounts referring to the same sermon, but again it is not absolutely conclusive as Luke implies that the event followed on immediately, while Matthew makes a more definite break between chapter 7:29 and 8:5.

The Centurion's Servant (Matthew 8:5–10; Luke 7:1–10)

- In Matthew the Centurion appears to come to Jesus himself.
- In Luke he first sends Jewish elders and then friends.

Some think that Matthew's record is a condensed version of what happened while Luke gives the fuller detail. Matthew therefore speaks of the Centurion as himself doing something which is really accomplished by proxy. In sending the elders and his friends he was coming himself. The words 'Came to him' in Matthew may be literally translated 'approached.' Compare Matthew 11:2–3 where John sent two disciples to Jesus and the words literally read, 'And he said to him.'

It is also possible that as Jesus came closer to his home, driven by the anxiety and urgency of the situation, the Centurion came to Jesus after the elders and friends to repeat his request.

The calling of James, John, Peter and Andrew (Matthew 4:18–22; Mark 2:16–20; Luke 5:1–11; John 1:35–42)

John describes the first encounter that these disciples had with Jesus. They stayed with Him for a short time, attended the wedding in Cana, but afterward returned for a while to their ordinary employment as fishermen. They accompanied Jesus down to Capernaum and then to Jerusalem for the Passover. During this time He went into the temple and turned over the tables and drove the animals and money-changers out. This must have caused them to wonder who was this man and what were they getting themselves into. They also went with Him through Samaria and again would have been amazed at His loving and gracious attitude towards the Samaritans, as Jews had no dealings with Samaritans. Peter also had a family to take care of and James and John were working for their father, Zebedee.

Some time later there is the account given by Matthew and Mark and then the event referred to by Luke. These appear to speak of two separate occasions. Therefore the process of the call of these disciples could have had as many as three stages.

The Gerasene Demoniacs (Matthew 8:28–34; Mark 5:1–20; Luke 8:26–39)

- In Matthew the place is called, 'The country of the Gadarenes.'
- In Mark and Luke the place is called, 'The country of the Gerasenes.'

Gadara is some six miles south east of Galilee, while Gerasa is almost forty miles south west of Galilee. Mark 5:20 refers to the Decapolis. Both Gadara and Gerasa were towns of this district. Therefore all three writers were speaking of the general geographical designation applying to the territory in which Gadara and Gerasa were situated. It could be that while the miracle took place on the lakeside near Gadara, the man was originally a resident of Gerasa. Matthew describes two men, while Mark and Luke refer to only one. There were obviously two delivered but one seems to have become more prominent and well known.

The Healing of the Blind Men at Jericho (Matthew 20:29–34; Mark 10:46–52; Luke 18:35–43)

- Matthew records two blind men healed as Jesus left Jericho.
- Mark records one blind man, Bartimaeus, healed as Jesus left Jericho.

– Luke records one blind man healed as Jesus arrived at Jericho.

Commentators and chronologies are not all agreed as to how exactly these passages should be harmonised. Some commentators think that there were three blind men healed, one when Jesus entered the city, the other two when He left it. Others, like Leon Morris in his commentary on Luke, believe that there were only two saying, 'There is little doubt that all three passages refer to the same incident, but with our present information it may be impossible to give a satisfactory explanation of these differences.'

Many solutions have been suggested to resolve the problems, but two of the most reasonable are as follows:

1. Jesus entered Jericho and, although it was late, no one offered Him hospitality for the night and He was therefore 'passing through' (Luke 19:1) on His way out of the city. As He was leaving He met Zacchaeus, called him down from the tree and invited Himself to stay at his home (Luke 19:5). It was as the party now turned to re-enter Jericho that Bartimaeus and his companion were healed of their blindness. If this was what took place then why did Luke place the account of Zacchaeus after that of Bartimaeus when it came first? It is clear that the teaching given in Luke 19:11–27 is directly connected, not with the healing of Bartimaeus, but with the conversion of Zacchaeus. Luke therefore placed the story of Bartimaeus outside its correct order in the events of that evening so that it would not separate the story of Zacchaeus and the instruction that followed. Neither Matthew nor Mark refers to Zacchaeus and therefore they do not face the same problem of separating the two stories.

2. Alternatively, the blind men were sitting in the entrance of the city and began calling to Jesus as He passed. He took no notice and the crowd ordered them to be silent. Such a refusal to immediately stop and listen was not unusual in Christ's ministry when He wanted to draw

out a stronger appeal to Himself (Matthew 15:21–28). Jesus entered the city, met Zacchaeus and stayed with him for the night. During the evening or early morning the blind men crossed the city to renew their appeal as Jesus left in the morning. It was on this occasion that Jesus stopped and healed them. This reconstruction assumes that the Gospel writers decided not to break up the story before and after Jesus' night at Jericho but to complete it as one event. It is most natural that Matthew and Mark should deal with it on the departure, since that is when the appeal was answered and that Luke should deal with it on the entry, since that is when the appeal began and he wanted to keep it separate from the story of Zacchaeus and the instructions that followed.

Some possible explanations help to resolve the difficulty:

1. It has also been pointed out that there were two Jerichos. Old and New Jericho were two distinct towns. The old one, famous in the Old Testament, and the new one established nearby, south of the Old Jericho, by Herod the Great. Therefore, some hold that the healing took place as Jesus was leaving one city and entering the other. Matthew and Mark record the healing as Jesus left one Jericho, while Luke locates the miracle as Jesus entered the other Jericho.

2. There are those who emphasise that the Greek verb in Luke translated 'approached' or 'drew near to' can also be understood in the sense, 'to be nigh or near' and take the passage as meaning simply that Jesus was still near the city when the miracle happened. In this case all three writers could well have been speaking of the same Jericho.

3. Mark in particular and Luke in general highlight the better known of the two men healed. Bartimaeus probably became the more prominent in later Christian history. This is implied by Mark's reference to his father (Mark 10:46). In the same way Matthew refers to two demoniacs while Mark and Luke mention only one, compare Matthew 8:28 with Mark 5:2.

I have followed the most common belief that there were only two blind men healed. You will also notice that in the account I repeated a little of what took place to give due emphasis and significance to the only blind man who is named, Bartimaeus.

The Cursing of the Fig Tree and the Cleansing of the Temple (Matthew 21:12–22; Mark 11:12–25; Luke 19:45)

Matthew and Luke seem to imply that Jesus cleansed the Temple on the Sunday, the day of His triumphant entry. Mark states that after His triumphant entry into Jerusalem, Jesus went into the Temple and saw all that was taking place, but because it was already late He returned with His disciples to Bethany.

It is important to note that nowhere do Matthew or Luke actually state that Jesus cleansed the Temple on the day of His triumphant entry. The correct sequence of events is to insert Mark 11:11 between Matthew 21:11 and 12.

The reference to the fig tree in Matthew 21:18 refers to what took place on the Monday morning, the day He cleansed the Temple. Matthew does not say, 'next morning' but 'early in the morning.' It seems that Matthew records the events of that amazing day, with the focus on Jesus cleansing the Temple, and then records what was a less significant event of the fig tree that happened earlier in the morning. The word 'immediately' that he uses is to be understood in the context of Mark's account, as 'the following day.' This again is not only possible but also the most likely sequence of events and there is no contradiction between the accounts.

The Parable of the Tenants (Matthew 21:33–41; Mark 12:1–9; Luke 20:9–16)

Matthew records the priests and Pharisees as answering Jesus' question of what will the owner of the vineyard do to them. Mark and Luke have Jesus answer His own question at the conclusion of the parable. Which is correct?

Both are. It is quite reasonable to assume that Jesus drew the answer from His hearers because such a conclusion was inevitable and He was inviting a response. However, after having drawn their response He then repeats their answer for emphasis.

Peter's Denials of Jesus (Matthew 26:34; Mark 14:30)

Jesus tells Peter in Matthew, Luke and John that before the rooster crows, Peter would deny Him three times. In Mark's Gospel Jesus says to Peter that before the rooster crowed twice Peter would deny Him three times.

It is perfectly reasonable to assume that Jesus made both statements. He told Peter that He would deny Him before the crowing of the rooster, and before it crowed twice He would deny Him three times. What we have is Mark relating the account in more detail. This would seem natural since it was Peter who influenced the writing of this Gospel and so he adds further personal detail to what took place. Thus all four of the Gospel writers predicted Peter's denial of Jesus, with Mark adding further details.

Who is the Greatest? (Luke 22:24–30; John 13:1–17)

The final Passover meal (the Last Supper) which Jesus shared with His disciples is recorded in all four Gospels. Luke's account refers to a dispute that arose regarding which of the disciples was the greatest and John's account records far more detailed teaching by Jesus preceded by the washing of the disciples' feet. It seems incredible that after three years such squabbles and jealousy are arising among the disciples. Satan had already put it into Judas' heart to betray Jesus and now as the cross was drawing near, it seems that all the powers of evil were gathering and seeking to make this meal one shrouded in pain and anguish for Jesus. It's also ridiculous when you think of it, how they could argue which of them was the greatest, when clearly Jesus was, but when we take our eyes off Him we start focusing on one another.

There was much tension and apprehension at the start of the Passover meal. This needs to be taken into account when giving a chronology and harmonisation for what took place that night. Luke records the dispute about who was the greatest, but where does this fit in to the sequence of events that night? Does it come before Jesus washed the disciples' feet or after He had done so? There are some commentaries and chronologies that state it was before, others it was after. I have followed the sequence of it happening before the washing of the disciples' feet for the following reasons.

1. It was customary for large water pots to be near the door of such rooms where the meal was to be celebrated. These were used for washing and cleansing guests' feet before they sat down to eat. The sandals of the guests were no protection for all the sand and dirt picked up walking the streets of Palestine, so foot washing was both customary and courteous. This task was undertaken by a servant, but there were no household servants this night, only Jesus and His disciples. It appears that not one of the twelve made any move to perform such a lowly task. This is quite understandable if there was jealousy and debate about which of them was the greatest.

2. Jesus took a towel and bowl and began to wash their feet, and by so doing spoke powerfully into their proud arguments. He explains there is no place for their competitive spirit in the Kingdom of God. It must have been a humbling and awesome lesson for them to learn.

3. It seems hard to imagine therefore that their dispute about who was the greatest came after this act of humility and love, for Jesus goes on to teach them about the greater things they would do in His name. If the argument came after the foot washing, He would have taught them about the destructiveness of pride not the powerful ministry that God had prepared for those who were willing to serve.

Peter's Denials and Confrontations (Matthew 26:69–75; Mark 14:66–72; Luke 22:54–62; John 18:15–27)

The accounts of Matthew and Mark correspond exactly provided we do not assume that 'the servant girl' in Mark 14:69 is the same one as in verse 66, since Matthew refers to her as 'another girl' (Matthew 26:71). We may harmonise

Luke's account (Luke 22:54–62) in the following way. The second maid identified Peter to the bystanders (Matthew 26:73 and Mark 14:69), and it was one of the men who confronted Peter (Luke 22:58). After a while, Luke says about one hour, the crowd challenged him again and all three Gospels agree in this detail. There is nothing in John's account that conflicts with the others. He merely adds other details that came to him from his better acquaintance with the people involved.

The Death of Judas (Matthew 27:5; Acts 1:18–19)

Matthew records the end of Judas with the simple statement that, 'He went away and hanged himself.' Luke adds to Matthew's account by stating that Judas 'Bought a field' with his betrayal money. Judas did buy the field but it was never his intention, the priests made the purchase for him with the betrayal money he threw back at them. It was the very field in which he committed suicide. Judas went and hanged himself (Matthew 27:5), his body fell to the ground and broke open (Acts 1:18).

The Time of Jesus' Crucifixion (Mark 15:2; John 19:14)

The time given by Mark for the beginning of Jesus' crucifixion is the third hour. The night was divided into four watches, each consisting of three hours, and the day was to some extent likewise divided into four periods. The third hour would be around 9 am. Mark, Matthew and Luke tell us that on the sixth hour darkness covered the whole land and at the ninth hour Jesus cried out, *'My God, my God, why have you forsaken me?'* It was at this precise moment all over Jerusalem that the Passover lambs were being sacrificed for the Jewish festival.

John tells us that Jesus was handed over to be crucified by Pilate about the sixth hour. According to Jewish time this would be about noon and so this appears to be at variance with Mark's account and the others.

A number of solutions have been proposed, but the most obvious one is that John is using a different method from

Mark for reckoning time. He is well aware of Mark's Gospel and if he wanted to point out any discrepancy he could have easily said so, but he doesn't. Whereas the Mark, Matthew and Luke accounts were written first, John's record is the last and his audience is now the whole world. Christianity had spread across the continents, therefore he does not use the Jewish method of calculating time. Romans calculated the day from midnight to midnight, just as we do today, therefore John's 'sixth hour' would be 6 am in the morning and Jesus was crucified at 9 am. This harmonises with the other Gospels. There is very good evidence that John used this method of computing time. In John 20:19, the evening of the day Jesus rose from the dead is considered part of the same day. If John was using the Jewish method of reckoning time that evening would have been considered to be part of Monday, since the Jewish day began at sunset.

Appendix 3

Dates and Seasons

'The simple message of Easter is that Jesus will always have the last word.'

No one is able to give an absolute and definite time sequence to all that took place in Jesus' life, but it is possible to give at least an approximate dating such as Dr Henry Halley gives in his book, *Halley's Bible Handbook*.

Early Judean Ministry

Between Matthew 4:11, *'Then the devil left him and angels came and attended to him,'* and verse 12, *'When Jesus heard that John had been put in prison, he returned to Galilee,'* almost one year elapses. This includes Jesus' early Judean Ministry, covering the events of John 1:19–4:54.

Duration and Chronology of the Galilean Ministry

The Galilean Ministry started 'four months before harvest,' in December (John 4:35, 43). It closed just before the Feast of Tabernacles, October, or just before the Feast of Dedication, December (Luke 9:51; John 7:2; 10:22). It covered a Passover mentioned in John 6:4, and another Passover, if, as is generally thought, the Feast spoken of in John 5 was also a Passover.

Therefore starting in December, and extending past the second Passover to the following October or December, it lasted about two years, or only one year, if the feast of John 5:1 was not a Passover.

Duration and Chronology of Jesus' Public Life

Jesus was still a young child at the death of Herod (Matthew 2:19–20). He was about 30 years old in the fifteenth year of Tiberius Caesar (Luke 3:1, 23).

Mark and John say nothing about the birth and childhood of Jesus, while Matthew and Luke record different incidents. To harmonise these into exact chronological sequence is not easy and straight forward. Here are approximate probable dates.

5 BC	Announcement to Zechariah (Luke 1:5–25)
6 months later	Announcement to Mary (Luke 1:26–38) Mary's visit to Elizabeth (Luke 1:39–56)
3 months later	Mary's return to Nazareth (Luke 1:56) Birth of John the Baptist (Luke 1:57–80) Announcement to Joseph (Matthew 1:18–24)
4 BC	Birth of Jesus (Matthew 1:25; Luke 2:1–7) Announcement to shepherds (Luke 2:8–20)
8 days later	Jesus' circumcision (Luke 2:21)
32 days later	Jesus' presentation (Luke 2:22–38)
3 BC	Visit of the Wise Men (Matthew 2:1–12) Flight to Egypt (Matthew 2:13–15) Slaughter of children (Matthew 2:16–18)
2 BC	Return to Nazareth (Matthew 2:19–23; Luke 2:39)

Why Was Christ Born Four Years 'Before Christ'?

When Christ was born time was reckoned in the Roman Empire from the founding of the city of Rome. When Christianity became the universal religion over what was the Roman world, a monk named Dionysius Exiguus, at the request of the Emperor Justinian, made a calendar, AD 526, reckoning time from the birth of Christ, to supersede the Roman calendar. Long after this Christian calendar had replaced the Roman one it was found that Dionysius had made a mistake in placing the birth of Christ in 753 from the founding of Rome, when it should have been 749 or possibly a year or two earlier.

Outline of Jesus' Public Life

Autumn or winter AD 26	Baptism. Temptation. First disciples. First miracle.
AD 27	Cleanses Temple in Jerusalem.
Passover	Early Judean ministry in Lower Jordan. This is told only in John's Gospel. It lasted eight months, beginning at Passover time (John 2:13), April, and ending 'four months' before harvest (John 4:3, 35), December. It includes the cleansing of the Temple, the visit of Nicodemus, and the ministry by the Jordan. The return through Samaria.
December	Begins the Galilean ministry. From Cana heals nobleman's son at Capernaum. Visits Nazareth and is rejected. Makes Capernaum His headquarters. Calls Simon, Andrew, James and John. Heals demoniac, Peter's mother-in-law, many others. Journeys about, heals a leper and a paralytic. Calls Matthew Questions about fasting and the Sabbath.
AD 28 Passover?	Visits Jerusalem. Heals on the Sabbath, arouses opposition of rulers, asserts His deity, returns to Galilee.
Midsummer	Journeys, multitudes, miracles, fame, the twelve disciples chosen. Sermon on the Mount. Journeys about. Speaks many parables. Stills the tempest. Heals Gadarene Demoniacs. Raises Jairus' daughter from the dead. Is accused of being in league with the devil. Raises the widow of Nain's son from the dead. Receives messengers from John the Baptist. Visits Nazareth again. Heals centurion's servant, forgives sinful woman.
AD 29 February	The Twelve sent out. The Twelve return. John the Baptist beheaded.
April	The 5,000 fed, Jesus walks on water.

Passover	Discourse on bread of life.
	Refuses popular demand to be made king.
	Heals many. Discourses on defilement.
	Rebukes cities. Says, 'Come unto me.'
	Retires to the north. Syro-Phoenician woman.
	Returns to Galilee. Deaf mute healed.
	4,000 fed. Sign of Jonah. Blind man healed.
October?	Visits Jerusalem. Discourses. Woman taken in adultery.
	Blind man healed. Open conflict with rulers.
November	Returns to Galilee.
	Retires to Caesarea Philippi, Peter's confession.
	The Transfiguration, demonised boy.
	Passion foretold three times.
	In Galilee again. Tax money.
	Disciples argue over 'Who is the greatest'?
	Children. 'Unknown wonder worker.'
December?	Final departure from Galilee.
(Or October)	Again in Jerusalem (John 10:22).
	Later Judean and Perean Ministry (about 4 months).
AD 30 Passover	Crucifixion and Resurrection.
May (Nisan)	Ascension.

Appendix 4

The Life of Jesus – Scripture References

'It may be stated categorically that no archaeological discovery has ever controverted a biblical reference.'

(Nelson Glueck, famous Jewish archaeologist)

Chapter 8 – Announcing the Birth of Jesus
John 1:1–18; Luke 1:1–80; Matthew 1:18–25.

Chapter 9 – The Early Years
Luke 2:1–38; Matthew 2:1–23; Luke 2:39–52; Mark 1:1–8;
Matthew 3:1–12; Luke 3:1–18; Mark 1:9–11; Matthew
3:13–17; Luke 3:21–23; Mark 1:12–13; Matthew 4:1–11;
Luke 4:1–13.

The First Year

Chapter 10 – Jesus' Early Ministry
John 1:19–51; John 2:1–22; John 2:23–3:21; John 3:22–36;
John 4:1–3; Matthew 4:12; Luke 3:19–20; John 4:4–42.

The Second Year

Chapter 11 – The Great Galilean Ministry
Luke 4:14–15; John 4:43–54; Luke 4:16–30; Matthew
4:13–17; Mark 1:14–20; Matthew 4:18–25; Luke 5:1–11;
Mark 1:21–39; Luke 4:31–44; Matthew 8:14–17; Mark
1:40–45; Matthew 8:2–4; Luke 5:12–16; Mark 2:1–12;

Matthew 9:1–8; Luke 5:17–26; Mark 2:13–17; Matthew 9:9–13; Luke 5:27–32; Mark 2:18–22; Matthew 9:14–17; Luke 5:33–39; John 5:1–47; Mark 2:23–28; Matthew 12:1–8; Luke 6:1–5; Mark 3:1–6; Matthew 12:9–14; Luke 6:6–11; Mark 3:7–12; Matthew 12:15–21.

Chapter 12 – The Sermon on the Mount
Mark 3:13–19; Luke 6:12–16; Matthew 10:1–4; Matthew 5:1–8:1; Luke 6:17–49.

Chapter 13 – Jesus Comes Down the Mountain
Matthew 8:5–13; Luke 7:1–35; Matthew 11:2–30; Luke 7:36–50; Luke 8:1–3; Mark 3:20–35; Matthew 12:22–50; Luke 8:19–21; Mark 4:1–34; Matthew 13:1–53; Luke 8:4–18; Mark 4:35–5:43; Matthew 8:18–34; Matthew 9:18–26; Luke 8:22–56; Matthew 9:27–34.

The Third Year
Chapter 14 – The Year of Opposition
Mark 6:1–56; Matthew 13:44–48; Matthew 9:35–11:1; Luke 9:1–17; Matthew 14:1–36; John 6:1–7:1; Mark 7:1–30; Matthew 15:1–28; Mark 7:31– 8:26; Matthew 15:29–16:12.

Chapter 15 – Who Do You Say That I Am?
Mark 8:27–9:1; Matthew 16:13–26; Luke 9:18–27; Mark 9:2–50; Matthew 17:1–18:14; Luke 9:28–50; Matthew 18:15–35; Luke 9:51–6 Luke 9:51–62; John 7:2–10:21.

Chapter 16 – Jesus, the Light of the World
Luke 10:1–13:21; John 10:22–42.

Chapter 17 – Jesus Weeps Over Jerusalem
Luke 13:22–17:10.

Chapter 18– The Last Months
John 11:1–54; Luke 17:11–18:14; Mark 10:1–52; Matthew 19:1–20:34; Luke 18:15–19:27; John 11:55–12:11; Mark 14:3–9; Matthew 26:6–13.

Chapter 19 – The Last Week

Mark 11:1–11; Matthew 21:1–11; Luke 19:29–44; John 12:12–19; Mark 11:12–26; Matthew 21:12–22; Luke 19:45–48; John 12:20–50; Mark 11:27–12:12; Matthew 21:23–46; Luke 20:1–19; Mark 12:13–44; Matthew 22:1–23:39; Luke 20:20–21:4; Mark 13:1–37; Matthew 24:1–25:46; Luke 21:5–38; Mark 14:1–2, 10–11; Matthew 26:1–5, 14–16; Luke 22:1–6.

Chapter 20 – The Last Supper

Mark 14:12–52; Matthew 26:17–56; Luke 22:7–53; John 13:1–18:11.

Chapter 21 – Jesus' Trials and the Crucifixion

John 18:12–14, 19–23; Mark 14:53, 55–65; Matthew 26:57, 59–68; Luke 22:54a, 63–65; Mark 14:54, 66–72; Matthew 26:58, 69–75; Luke 22:54b-62; John 18:15–18, 25–27; Mark 15:1–5 Matthew 27:1–2, 11–14; Luke 22:66–71; Matthew 27:3–10; Acts 1:18–19; Luke 23:1–5; John 18:28–38; Luke 23:6–12; Mark 15:6–19; Matthew 27:15–30; Luke 23:13–25; John 18:39–19:16; Mark 15:20–47; Matthew 27:31–66; Luke 23:26–56; John 19:16–42.

Chapter 22 – The Resurrection and Ascension

Matthew 28:1–8; Mark 16:1–8; Luke 24:1–12; John 20:1–18; Matthew 28:9–15; Luke 23:13–43; John 20:19–25; John 20:26–31; 1 Corinthians 15:3–7; Matthew 28:16–20; Mark 16:9–19; Luke 24:44–53; Acts 1:3–14, Acts 2:1–4; Mark 16:20.

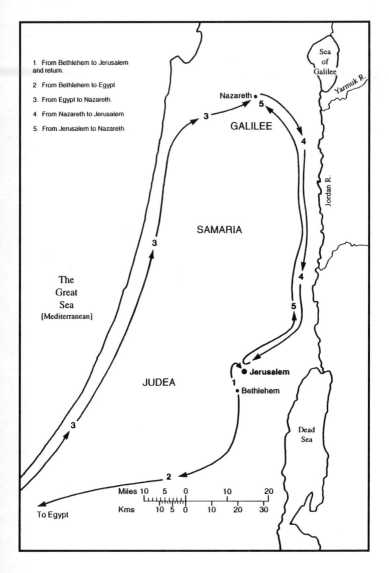

Map 1 Journeys of Jesus in His Early Life.

284

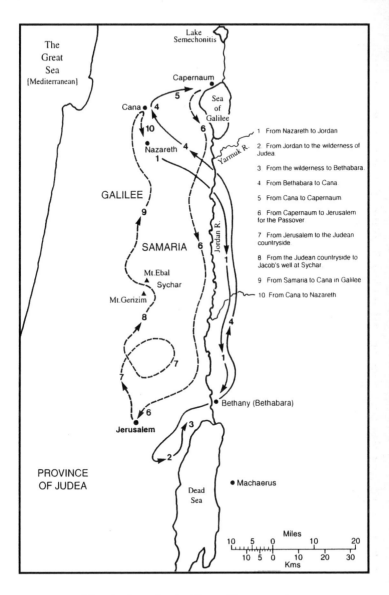

The Great Sea [Mediterranean]

Lake Semechonitis

Capernaum

5

Cana ● 4

Sea of Galilee

10

6

Nazareth

4

1

Yarmuk R.

GALILEE

9

SAMARIA

6

Jordan R.

1

Mt.Ebal ▲

Sychar

Mt.Gerizim ▲

8

7

7

6

Jerusalem

3

2

PROVINCE OF JUDEA

Dead Sea

● Machaerus

4

1

Bethany (Bethabara)

1 From Nazareth to Jordan

2 From Jordan to the wilderness of Judea

3 From the wilderness to Bethabara

4 From Bethabara to Cana

5 From Cana to Capernaum

6 From Capernaum to Jerusalem for the Passover

7 From Jerusalem to the Judean countryside

8 From the Judean countryside to Jacob's well at Sychar

9 From Samaria to Cana in Galilee

10 From Cana to Nazareth

Miles
10 5 0   10   20
10 5 0   10   20   30
Kms

Map 2   Jesus in the Year of Inauguration.

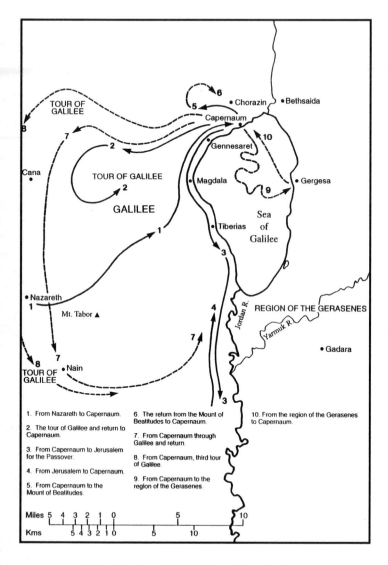

Map 3 Jesus in His Year of Popularity.

1. From Nazareth through the Galilean towns and villages to Capernaum.
2. From Capernaum to the desert near Bethsaida.
3. From the desert near Bethsaida to Gennesaret.
4. From Gennesaret to Capernaum.
5. From Capernaum to Phoenicia.
6. From Phoenicia through Decapolis.
7. From Decapolis by boat to Dalmanutha.
8. From Dalmanutha by boat to Bethsaida.
9. From Bethsaida to Caesarea Philippi.
10. From Caesarea Philippi to the Mount of Transfiguration.
11. From the Mount of Transfiguration to Capernaum.
12. From Capernaum through Samaria.
13. From Samaria to Jerusalem.
14. From Jerusalem to Bethany.
ABILENE
Mt. Hermon
The Great Sea (Mediterranean)
Tyre
ITURAEA
Caesarea Philippi (Panias)
TRACHONITIS
GAULANTIS
Lake Semechonitis
BATANEA
PHOENICIA
GALILEE
Capernaum
Bethsaida
Gennesaret
Cana
Dalmanutha
Sea of Galilee
Mt. Carmel
GALILEE
REGION OF THE GERASENES
Yarmuk R.
Nazareth
Mt. Tabor
Nain
SAMARIA
DECAPOLIS
DECAPOLIS
Caesarea
Synthopolis
Pella
SAMARIA
Samaria
Mt. Ebal
Mt. Gerizim
Jordan R.
Jabbok R.
PEREA
Joppa
Arimathea
JUDEA
JUDEA
Ephraim
Jabneh
Jericho
Bethany (Bethabara)
Jerusalem
Bethany
Mt. Nebo
Azotus
Bethlehem
Ascalon
Herodium
Miles 10 5 0 10 20
Kms 10 5 0 10 20 30
Dead Sea
Machaerus
Hebron
Gaza
IDUMEA

Map 4 Jesus in the Year of Opposition.

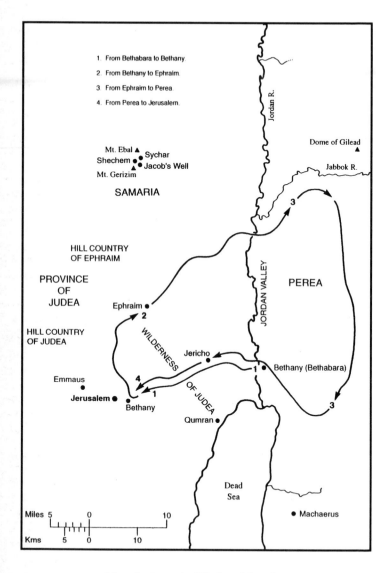

Map 5   Jesus in His Last Months.